The New Testament & The Latter-day Saints

JOHN K. CARMACK

SUSAN EASTON-BLACK

ALAN K. PARRISH

CLARK V. JOHNSON

DENNIS LARGEY

VICTOR L. LUDLOW

ROBERT J. MATTHEWS

JOSEPH FIELDING MCCONKIE

KEITH H. MESERVY

T. JOHN NIELSEN II

WALTER A. NORTON

MONTE S. NYMAN

CHAUNCEY C. RIDDLE

JOSEPH BARNARD ROMNEY

RODNEY TURNER

CLYDE J. WILLIAMS

RICHARD P. ANDERSON

CFI

SPRINGVILLE, UTAH

© 2010 John K. Carmack, Susan Easton-Black, Alan K. Parrish, Clark V. Johnson, Dennis Largey, Victor L. Ludlow, Robert J. Matthews, Joseph Fielding McConkie, Keith H. Meservy, T. John Nielsen II, Walter A. Norton, Monte S. Nyman, Chauncey C. Riddle, Rodney Turner, Clyde J. Williams, and Richard P. Anderson

ISBN 13: 978-1-59955-486-0

Published by CFI, an imprint of Cedar Fort, Inc.
2373 W. 700 S., Springville, UT 84663
Distributed by Cedar Fort, Inc., www.cedarfort.com

Cover design by Angela D. Olsen
Cover design © 2010 by Lyle Mortimer

Printed in the United States of America

10 9 8 7 6 5 4 3 2 1

Printed on acid-free paper

CONTENTS

CHAPTER ONE

e⁀ᴐ ᴄᴀᴐ

The New Testament and the Latter-day Saints

ᴄᴀᴐ ᴄᴀᴐ

John K. Carmack

Have you ever had the experience of reading something you or someone close to you prepared decades ago and being struck by the feeling that it is still sound and useful? Perhaps you have had the opposite and more common experience of reading something you or someone else wrote which excited and moved you but now you find that the impact you originally felt is no longer there and, in fact, it needs revision or is no longer relevant.

Do some things you read seem sound and fundamentally true? Do other writings strike you as cynical, shallow, or otherwise lacking in basic soundness? How long has it been since you picked up the United States Constitution and read it? If you do this, you may experience, as I did recently, a vague and uneasy feeling that it would be a miracle if fifty-five men and women representing our states today could produce a new document to govern this nation, equal to the Constitution in brevity and good sense, and solidly rooted in timeless principles as did those who gathered in Philadelphia that hot summer of 1787.

In your opinion, could any small group of men today write a series of letters and religious documents equal in wisdom and inspiration to those comprising the New Testament canon? If they tried, do you think it would end up being used and revered by millions of people for thousands of years?

Are some ideas more important than others? Is there a center of things? Are some principles, doctrines, and ideas of infinitely greater value and more basic than others? Is that written today by our best minds likely to be of greater value to people who are continually evolving upward in knowledge, wisdom, and understanding than that written many years ago by the best available authors? If modern man is thousands of years along in the evolutionary process, then would his thoughts not be of infinitely more value than those of his ancestors in Palestine who wrote the documents comprising the New Testament? And if that is true, does the New Testament have *any* relevance today?

In this paper, I shall try to address a few of these questions.

Is the New Testament Authoritative or Relevant Today?

One addressing a Church group will often ask, "Did you bring your scriptures?" To the world this means generally, "Did you bring your Holy Bible?" To the Latter-day Saint it means, "Did you bring your triple combination, containing the Book of Mormon, the Doctrine and Covenants, and the Pearl of Great Price, as well as your Bible?" One of the most revered books of scripture is the New Testament. It is not only that these "holy men of God spake as they were moved upon by the Holy Ghost,"[1] (2 Peter 1:21) but that these New Testament authors wrote their messages. Then what they wrote became, in process of time, accepted by the Church as especially authoritative, binding, and inspired as well as useful for doctrine and instruction in the Church generally. On the other hand, much, even most, of what was spoken and written, though useful and instructive, does not quite have that authoritative status in Church literature. For example, there is available to the student a large amount of ancient literature dating to biblical days, in biblical-sounding language, including the writings of the apostolic fathers and those included in the pseudepigrapha which are not accepted generally as scripture, although useful to scholars.

We accept the New Testament as scripture,[2] that is, as authoritative and inspired. We use it constantly; we cite it as authority; and we read and study it at home and in our church instructional sessions. We clearly prefer the King James Version of the New Testament,[2] but we are not adamant about that. Any responsibly prepared version could be used and might be helpful to us. It is the doctrine and the teachings in their historical setting which are useful and authoritative to Latter-day Saints.

Unlike some students of ancient history and scripture who reject any suggestion of influence from a divine source in the writing of scripture, following as they do the notions of science that nothing is worth much if it cannot be established by analytical and scientific means, believing Latter-day Saints accept without such qualification the influence of the Holy Spirit and heavenly messengers in the lives of men, including those who wrote the scriptures. We believe that Matthew did write what is known as The Gospel According to St. Matthew and that indeed all of the books of the New Testament are inspired. For thousands of years people have felt something basic, special, and authoritative in the New Testament. We have that same feeling today as Latter-day Saints. I will try to identify a few reasons for our feeling.

A Rational Approach to the New Testament

It would not shake our faith if it were proven that someone other than the ascribed author penned one or more of the books of the New Testament. We doubt that evidence will ever be found of this, but Latter-day Saints are realists who believe that "truth is knowledge of things as they are, and as they were, and as they are to come" (D&C 93:24). We do not reject truth in favor of fairy tales.

The essence of our practical approach to truth can be gathered from this brief and earthy statement by Brigham Young:

> Were you to ask me how it was I embraced "Mormonism," I should answer, for the simple reason that it embraces all truth in heaven and on earth, in the earth, under the earth, and in hell, if there be any truth there. There is no truth outside of it; there is no good outside of it; there is nothing holy and honorable outside of it; for, wherever these principles are found among all the creations of God, the Gospel of Jesus Christ, and his order and Priesthood embraces them.[3]

Whatever is found to be true of the New Testament, therefore, becomes *ipso facto*, a part of the religion and belief of the Latter-day Saint.

It is interesting and useful to read the conclusions of a noted scholar, Paul Johnson, concerning the authenticity of the books of the New Testament. He concluded:

> The earliest Christian document is Paul's first epistle to the Thessalonians, which can plausibly be dated to about AD 51. Paul was

3

writing in his fifties and early sixties; his authentic epistles (Romans, 1 and 2 Corinthians, Galatians, Philippians, 1 Thessalonians and Philemon) are in an evidential sense straightforward written documents; there is no oral tradition behind them and the editing process is minimal. Indeed some of them may have been circulated or "published" in edited form even during Paul's lifetime.[4]

If such an assertion of fact concerning the authenticity of books of the New Testament as that made by Johnson should prove to be correct, which is possible, it would not change the faith of the Latter-day Saint at all, although it would add to his factual knowledge of how the New Testament came into being as a book. The Latter-day Saint would be quick to recognize that if those few books which Johnson listed as surely authentic were the only authentic books of the New Testament, they would be sufficient to clearly establish early Christian teachings on such crucial doctrines as the fatherhood of God; the divine mission of his Son Jesus Christ; his identity as a separate and distinct, though closely related personage; the principles of love, patience, and faith in the Lord Jesus Christ as basic doctrines; the important role of the Holy Ghost; the crucifixion, death, and resurrection of Christ; and the salvational aspects of the Atonement of Christ in the lives of those who believe and practice the principle of the gospel of Jesus Christ. Even the doctrine of the Second Coming of Christ is established in those epistles clearly labeled as authentic and historic by Johnson. The book of Romans would add the Christian assertion that Jesus is of the seed of David and would establish that the early Christian sequence and priority of teaching was that the gospel was to be taught first to the Jew and then to the Greek, meaning the Gentiles.

In summary, then, we believe in the historicity of the New Testament and in the divinely inspired nature of these writings. We rise above domatism, however, because we believe only what is ultimately true about these writings. The Book of Mormon adds emphasis to our rational viewpoint when it quotes Jacob as teaching that "the Spirit . . . speaketh of things as they really are, and of things as they really will be" (Jacob 4:13).

A Special Endorsement of the New Testament

We have a special endorsement of the New Testament from an unexpected source—section 20 of the Doctrine and Covenants. The endorsement began, oddly enough, by a special reference to the Book of Mormon and a statement that the book is true because it was confirmed to certain witnesses by the administration of angels who disclosed to the world that the Book of Mormon was true. Then, suddenly and in point for our discussion of the New Testament, it states that one of the key reasons for bringing forth another sacred and inspired book was to prove "to the world that the holy scriptures are true" (D&C 20:11).

It is obvious from the context of the section of the Doctrine and Covenants just quoted that the term *holy scriptures* used in the section means the Bible, including, of course, the New Testament. Latter-day Saints, therefore, have an unexpected ringing endorsement of the New Testament in the coming forth of the Book of Mormon and its clearly established authenticity by witnesses to whom angels appeared and who publicly endorse every published copy of the Book of Mormon by their printed testimony. Accepting the Book of Mormon as authentic, the member automatically accepts the divine authenticity of the New Testament. Indeed, one of the principle reasons for the necessity of another book of ancient scripture being found, translated, and published is to establish the divinity of the New Testament for a world largely turned to secular thinking, which was taken away from the lives of men and women what was formerly a central role for the New Testament among Christians. But more about that later. A reading of section 20 of the Doctrine and Covenants allows the careful reader to identify the things of enduring value in religion and life, but I shall also return to that topic later.

Religion and Real History

To Latter-day Saints, New Testament religious history is real, meaning that events written and described actually happened. We believe there was a man named Jesus who was hung on a cross on a hill called Calvary which actually existed, and in fact still does. Special and deeply spiritual experiences occurred in a garden called Gethsemane on the Mount of Olives. These were real events in real time. They are not stories or parables which form part of a doubtful and largely symbolic literature for the purpose of establishing a set of ideas making up a philosophy called "Christianity."

We believe firmly that real events on earth have been, are, and will be again directly connected with our Heavenly Father, his Son Jesus Christ, and by inspiration to man through the Holy Spirit. We also believe that there have been and are on earth virtuous and inspired men called prophets.

When we speak of religious history, we add to places familiar to Christians, like Galilee and the upper room, places in our age where special revelatory experiences with heavenly influences came to virtuous and inspired men such as Joseph Smith and Ezra Taft Benson, to name only two. Places such as Nauvoo, Liberty Jail, and the farm of Joseph Smith, Sr., are not only real places but sacred as Bethlehem is sacred. One can visit these places and learn more about man's relationship to God. We believe that God does influence man's course on earth by occasional and even continuous inspiration and revelation to those living virtuous lives who ask and seek.

Understanding this view of the New Testament helps one understand the religion espoused by the members of The Church of Jesus Christ of Latter-day Saints. It is a tangible and historical religion but not a superstitious or dogmatic one. These things either happened or they didn't happen. If they happened, as Church members believe, they indicate that God loves and interacts directly with men and women. The ultimate implication is, of course, that God informs man how he should live and act to receive salvation. And that gets us to the heart of things.

As Far as It Is Translated Correctly

An oft-quoted qualification to the belief of Church members in the Bible is the article of faith stating, "We believe the Bible to be the word of God as far as it is translated correctly."[5] This statement implies that errors were possible, even probable, in the Bible. To some Christians that is blasphemous. To imply that there could be errors in God's word! Yes, Latter-day Saints believe that errors are possible. This belief is consistent with what I have already said about the history of the New Testament. And even more to the point, the Book of Mormon contains language which indicates that "plain and precious things" have been removed from the Bible.[6]

Another way of stating this idea is that in the authors of the Bible, we are dealing with real people, often humble people of limited literary education, who were involved in and reported real events. In turn, other men copied these writings by hand. Reporting errors were inevitable in such circumstances, even when those men were inspired, virtuous, and operating with excellent intentions. A book made of such writings is more believable, tangible, and real to us than one created perfectly and delivered by deity to men who had no part in creating it. Working through humble, often less educated men seems to be God's *modus operandi*.

What Do We Believe About Christ?

Let us now turn to a crucial question—what do Latter-day Saints believe about Christ? Remember, as Paul Johnson confidently asserts, "Christianity is essentially a historical religion. It bases its claim on the historical facts it asserts."[7] And, examining the scanty, but firmly established evidence, he concludes that "there can, at least, be absolutely no doubt about his (Christ's) historical existence."[8] He then reminds us of the few, but sufficient, references to Christ in well-authenticated historical documents. He includes the references in *Antiquities* by Josephus (published about AD 93), another reference by Tacitus in his *Annals*, in which he wrote concerning the AD 64 fire in Rome, mentioning in passing, "Christus, the founder of this sect" (referring to Christ and Christianity) and another reference to *Christ* by Pliny the Younger, written in AD 112.

Thus, firm evidence clearly establishes that a person named Jesus Christ actually lived. We believe that.

As to the authenticity of the Gospels, though it may be true as many scholars of the New Testament assert, that these manuscripts are based originally on oral teachings which were not written until well after Paul's letters were written, I am confident that the four Gospels are based on actual writings by Matthew and John, who were Jesus' apostles, and by Mark and Luke, disciples and missionaries of Jesus. There may also have been early source documents by unknown authors and witnesses, such as the one called by modern scholars simply "Q," which may have been used by the authors of the Gospels as sources. These Gospels are not biographical manuscripts but rather a statement of the doctrine and teachings of Christ in the context of his life and brief ministry. But these authors were eyewitnesses of many of the events described, and their writings bear marks of authority and authenticity. Although we do not have originals of the books of the New Testament, one eminent scholar has concluded:

> It is reassuring at the end to find the general result of all these discoveries and all this study is to strengthen the proof of the authenticity of the scriptures, and our conviction that we have in our hands, in substantial integrity, the veritable Word of God.[9]

He adds in a later publication:

> The interval then between the dates of original composition and the earliest extant evidence becomes so small as to be in fact negligible, and the last foundation for any doubt that the scriptures have come down to us substantially as they were written has not been removed. Both the *authenticity* and the *general integrity* of the books of The New Testament may be regarded as finally established.[10]

We Latter-day Saints believe that Kenyon was essentially correct in those conclusions. Doubt cast on the New Testament by higher criticism and the fact of not having available originals of the books is almost completely overcome for us by the strong evidence that what we have was directly descended from authentic documents and that, although mistakes in copying and probably deletions and insertions occurred in the documents by those who reproduced them by hand, they are basically what they purport to be.

We also have another authenticating witness. The Book of Mormon account of Christ's visit to America and his teachings to those living there at Christ's crucifixion amounts to another gospel, without the same problem of establishing the provenance of these records that is faced by the New Testament scholar in dealing with the complex problem of provenance of the New Testament books. That the Book of Mormon account so closely confirms the substance of and parallels the New Testament account is evidence to those of us accepting the Book of Mormon, "that the holy scriptures [meaning the Bible] are true."[11]

Thus the Christ one meets in Matthew, Mark, Luke, John, Acts, and the epistles of the New Testament is basically the Christ in whom Latter-day Saints literally believe. His teachings, his divine sonship, his Atonement, and his Resurrection are for us an established historical fact. His doctrine and teachings are essentially true as presented in the New Testament, with a few interesting deviations or defects.

Joseph Smith did a thorough work, considering his limited tools, in revising the New Testament and restoring concepts lost in it so that the "key of knowledge, the fulness of the scriptures"[12] could be available to man.

One may ask, why has the so-called Inspired Version of the Bible not been made more generally available to Church members if meanings have been recaptured therein and errors corrected by Joseph Smith? One answer to that excellent question is that through extensive footnotes, cross-references, and excerpts in the appendix, many of the significant additions and corrections by Joseph Smith are now available to the student using the 1979 edition of the King James Version of the Holy Bible published by The Church of Jesus Christ of Latter-day Saints. With the cross-referencing, footnoting, and other integration of the Bible, the Book of Mormon, the Doctrine and Covenants, and the Pearl of Great Price, scriptural access has been integrated and has, therefore, made available a coherent fulness of the standard works to any careful student using those recently published editions of the four standard works of scripture.

Christ is revealed in those four books in great detail, especially his teachings and divine mission. What Latter-day Saints believe about Christ is found therein. More scriptural explanations and references are available to the careful student than have ever before been available to man. As an example of this enhanced availability, a quick look at the Topical Guide included in the Church's 1979 publication will reveal many pages of references to Christ from a number of different conceptual bases.

In addition to personal revelation through the Holy Ghost, the real key to understanding Christ is in studying him in the New Testament and then expanding that knowledge by adding what inspired men have known of him in the Old Testament, the Pearl of Great Price, the Book of Mormon, and the Doctrine and Covenants. Thus, for example, Jacob of the Book of Mormon, writing about 500 BC, explained that he wrote:

> For this intent . . . that they may know that we knew of Christ, and we had a hope of his glory many hundred years before his coming; and not only we ourselves had a hope of his glory, but also all the holy prophets which were before us. (Jacob 4:4)

This adds a breathtaking dimension to our knowledge of Christ totally unknown to those bereft of the additional books of scriptures available to us.

So not only do we have a strong belief in the Christ of the New Testament but a much expanded global and dispensational view of Christ through "the fulness of the scriptures." Our view is not that of the fundamentalist who sees the New Testament as the only source of knowledge of Christ as a perfect document from God. It does not bother us to find, for example, three varying accounts of Christ's visit to Paul on the road to Damascus.[13] We expect that there will be a need for further reconciliation, expansion, and even correction of these New Testament documents precisely because they are real and historical writings. This does not in any way diminish their inspired nature.

God continually reveals his will to man, and therefore we have an expanding, ever-increasing body of revealed will rather than a closed, sterile, perfect canon.

What Use Did Joseph Smith Make of the New Testament?

For his part, Joseph Smith made constant use of the New Testament. Inspired at an early age by the passage of the New Testament found in James 1:5–6 to seek inspiration from God, the role of the New Testament in Joseph's life continued and expanded. His two-hour sermons presented regularly to the Saints during the zenith of his prophetic career in Nauvoo were peppered with New Testament passages. His mastery of the scriptures was phenomenal.

Most of the time Joseph spoke extemporaneously, to our knowledge, writing only one talk for delivery to the Church. On that occasion he was working with his scribe, Robert B. Thompson, who read the talk Joseph dictated in general conference on October 5, 1840. The subject of that address was "Treatise on Priesthood." This description of the process of preparation by Howard Coray, one of his clerks, is interesting:

> One morning, I went as usual, into the Office to go to work: I found Joseph sitting on one side of a table and Robert B. Thompson on the opposite side, and the understanding I got was that they were examining or hunting in the manuscript of the new translation of the Bible for something on Priesthood, which Joseph wished to present, or have read to the people the next Conference: Well, they could not find what they wanted and Joseph said to Thompson "put the manuscript one side, and take some paper and I will tell you what to write." Brother Thompson took some foolscap paper that was at his elbow and made himself ready for the business. I was seated probably 6 or 8 feet on Joseph's left side, so that I could look almost squarely into Joseph's left eye—I mean the side of his eye. Well, the Spirit of God descended upon him, and a measure of it upon me, insomuch that I could fully realize that God, or the Holy Ghost, was talking through him. I never, neither before or since, have felt as I did on that occasion. I felt so small and humble I could have freely kissed his feet."[14]

On that occasion though he had no Bible at hand, Joseph accurately cited and dictated fourteen scriptural passages. Only twice did he not remember the chapter and verse of a passage, but quoted it accurately anyway.[15]

Joseph Smith summed up his own view of the Bible as follows:

> I believe the Bible as it read when it came from the pen of the original writers. Ignorant translators, careless transcribers or designing and corrupt priests have committed many errors.[16]

Central Ideas and Doctrines and the New Testament

As we implied in our introduction, some ideas are more important than others. Some are central to the guidance of man into a righteous life, and some are on the periphery. Christ's teachings are without any question central to the gospel in all ages, and that is true for the era of restoration commenced through Joseph Smith. Elder Bruce R. McConkie summarized his thoughts on the subject as follows:

> Nothing in the entire plan of salvation compares in any way in importance with that most transcendent of all events, the atoning sacrifice of our Lord. It is the most important single thing that has ever occurred in the entire history of created things; it is the rock foundation upon which the gospel and all other things rest. Indeed, all "things which pertain to our religion are only appendages to it."[17]

We do not subscribe to the notion, perhaps influenced and fed by Darwinism, that man is a purely physical animal, evolving slowly upward to higher form so that the latest generation of men and women is higher in ability and intelligence than were men living in earlier eras. Our view is dispensational. At times the truths of the gospel are more generally available with greater intensity among men than at other times. In other words, the availability of the gospel fades and flickers to dimmer brightness at times, then is reestablished and grows brighter again.

We believe that men, as Richard Weaver observed, need constantly to "return to center" and thus recapture days in which truth is held in high value and when men are driven more nearly by ideas which properly position them *vis-à-vis* God. Weaver sees that "there is a center of things, and . . . every feature of modern disintegration is a flight from this (center of things) toward periphery."[18] Of course, our notion and Weaver's is the ancient and much maligned one that there are eternal verities which can be lost by concentrating on less important peripheral things and by too much specialization and fragmentation.

For us, as found in the New Testament, there is then a center of things, and that center is Christ as revealed in the New Testament and discovered anew in the restoration of his gospel.

In my view, the reason President Ezra Taft Benson emphasized again and again a return to the Book of Mormon is that the book is the restorational vehicle for the return to center accomplished by reestablishing, in a document not ravaged by time and uninspired interpretation, the primacy of the New Testament Christ.

Thus, the Book of Mormon brings us back to the center of things once again. When we fly toward the periphery, we leave the center and are in danger of drifting outward from eternal and solid principles to wander in treacherous byways. How interesting it is that our venerable prophet saw that point so immediately and so clearly communicated it. He was determined to know only Christ and him crucified as taught in the New Testament and as established in our day by the Book of Mormon—Another Testament of Christ.

The prophet Mormon aptly taught in the Book of Mormon:

> This [meaning the Book of Mormon] is written for the intent that ye may believe that [meaning the Bible]; and if ye believe that ye will believe this also. (Mormon 7:9)

Had there been no drift from the central doctrines of the New Testament, there would have been no need for the Book of Mormon to bring us back to the basics. But there was clearly a fateful flight from the solid central doctrines needed by man.

The consequences of leaving the center is spiritual wandering. Man drifts easily from the central truth that he is a divine son of God into the variant view that man is just another beast wandering on earth in a society in which animal-like abuse of children by parents and grandparents, selfishness and war, unbridled sexual pleasure without family responsibility, homosexuality, egotism, lack of interest in one's daily work, and pride rule. The Book of Mormon teaches that if such a society is unchecked, civilization will eventually decline and be destroyed by hatred, bloodshed, and war. We seem to be teetering on the edge. Only a return to the center of things, as taught in the New Testament authenticated for our generation by the Book of Mormon, can save this generation.

As pessimistic as it may sound, that is our view of the state of civilization in an era in which men leave the New Testament Christ and drift aimlessly or fly swiftly from the eternal verities of the center to uninspired and vain philosophies of men who are hung up on peripheral and uninspired doctrines and ideas. Secularism, founded on the ideas of men who have scoffed at God and his teachings, has had its day and has lacked the ability to ennoble, inspire, and exalt men. When God and his dealings with man are thoroughly debunked, what takes the place of that core concept in men's lives? What inspires men to do well and serve each other?

A Word about the New Testament and the Constitution

Actually, the New Testament influence is more pervasive in our lives than we will ever know. The lives of countless great men and women have been deeply influenced by its teachings. Institutions have been shaped by its doctrines. As an example of this influence, although it is beyond the scope of these remarks to undertake a detailed analysis of the underlying concepts of the United States Constitution and trace some of them to the underlying concepts of the New Testament, I want to say a word or two about the Constitution. What I say should be looked at more as an intuition of a situation (to borrow a phrase from Weaver) than a careful analysis.

In general, those most responsible for drafting the Constitution were men schooled in theology and religion in the colleges and churches of their day. In both church and school, the New Testament was always a primary text. Thus, since the men who wrote the Constitution were schooled in the scriptures, the influence was undoubtedly there.

For example, James Madison of Virginia, often called the father of the Constitution, was a brilliant, well-educated man who began his schooling under a Christian minister and completed it with a college education, including graduate school at the College of New Jersey (now Princeton). Madison, together with James Wilson of Pennsylvania, was most responsible for the final form of our Constitution. The curriculum Madison followed seems to have revolved around religion and politics, the primary educational goals of most colleges in those days of colonial America.

My intuition of the situation is that New Testament principles were well known to all of the delegates of the Constitutional Convention and had a profound influence on what they thought and wrote, irrespective of their religious persuasion. In addition, of course, they had available almost all of the writings of the day on the theories of government and politics.

These men accomplished a miracle. In the concluding paragraph of *The Federalist,* a series of eighty-five essays defending the Constitution and published to assist the ratification of that document by authors Alexander Hamilton, James Madison, and John Jay, Hamilton wrote:

> The establishment of a Constitution, in time of profound peace, by the voluntary consent of a whole people, is a prodigy to the completion of which I look forward with trembling anxiety.[19]

These participants sensed the greatness of the achievement of which they were a part.

Washington wrote to Lafayette these words about the completion of the Constitution:

> It appears to me, then, little short of a miracle, that the Delegates from so many different states . . . in their manner, circumstances, and prejudices, should write in forming a system of national Government, so little liable to well-founded objections.[20]

As great as the underlying principles of the Constitution are, they are not the miracle. Those principles always existed and are eternal. The miracle is that these fifty-five men were able to come together that hot muggy summer and agree on a constitution establishing a form of government incorporating those principles and then persuade the states to adopt the Constitution. We haven't time to more than touch on an example or two illustrating the point we here make.[21]

The Lord made it clear by revelation to Joseph Smith that the Constitution was inspired of God (D&C 98:5–7; 101:77, 78; 109:54). What he meant was that it was based on principles which were not new but which had their source in God. Many of those principles can be found in the New Testament. I will now mention a few of those principles.

1. The New Testament teaches that men are children of God and thus heirs of his attributes and destiny.[22]

A natural tracing of that noble and far-reaching view of man to the Constitution is the foundational notion of the document that man clearly has the capacity and intelligence to participate in the process of governing himself. As either Hamilton or Madison (scholars aren't sure which one wrote it) observed in Essay No. 49 of *The Federalist*, "The people are the only legitimate fountain of power, and it is from them that the constitutional charter . . . is derived."[23]

2. The New Testament, however, also teaches the reality of evil and the temptations facing men of selfishness, power, and greed.[24]

In the Constitution, a system of checks and balances is imposed on those elected or appointed to positions of power in recognition of men's evil tendencies. Further, and also in point, the powers granted by the people to those governing were carefully limited in scope.

Again, as an illustration that this point had not escaped the founding fathers, we read the following in *The Federalist*:

> Men, upon too many occasions, do not give their own understandings fair play, but, yielding to some untoward bias, they entangle themselves in words and confound themselves in subtleties.[25]

3. In the New Testament, we find an account of men defying the corrupt and well-established order of religious things in Israel and seizing the inherent right to preach and proclaim the gospel, speak freely of their faith, and speak in favor of a despised and misunderstood new faith. The ideas of Gamaliel, Paul's teacher and a member of the Sanhedrin, are interesting and seem almost to be from the colonial America era. He advised his fellow council members in these words:

> Refrain from these men, and let them alone: for if this counsel or this work be of men it will come to nought: But if it be of God, ye cannot overthrow it; lest haply ye be found even to fight against God. (Acts 5:38–39)

This kind of thinking also found its way into the Constitution. The first ten amendments to the Constitution, adopted almost as a part of the original Constitution and called as a block "The Bill of Rights," begin with the well-known guarantees of freedom of speech, the right to a free press, and not only freedom of religion, but the guarantee against a state-established religion. The New Testament ideas in favor of religious freedom are therefore clearly incorporated in the Constitution.

I must refrain from further analysis. My intuition of the situation is that the New Testament had both a direct and indirect influence on the men who drafted the United States Constitution and that it influenced the form of government established by that document. The underlying principles of the Constitution were from a place near the center of things. That such basic principles were involved seemed to be recognized by Hamilton when he observed:

> In disquisitions of every kind there are certain primary truths, or first principles, upon which all subsequent reasonings must depend. These contain an internal evidence which, antecedent to all reflection or combination, commands the assent of the mind. Where it produces not this affect, it must proceed either from some defect or disorder in the organs of perception, or from the influence of some strong interest, or passion, or prejudice.[26]

Again, we find evidence that a clear thinker has noticed man's tendency to leave the center and move to the periphery unless brought back to basic ideas or truths. The New Testament, especially as restored to its center place through the Book of Mormon, brings us back home to that center. Perhaps, as Weaver observed:

> It has been well said the chief trouble with the contemporary generation is that it has not read the minutes of the last meeting.[27]

Maybe those minutes of the last meeting are in the New Testament.

It is not enough, however, to have a great Constitution. As a people drift into the periphery and lose sight of the center of things, we are in danger of losing the moral force and righteousness necessary to retain the benefits of our government created by that inspired and excellent document. The more we recede from the inspired precepts of the New Testament, the more danger there is that we shall lose what we have so long enjoyed.

As the New Testament teaches, we are children of a loving God and are capable of growth and development beyond our wildest imagination if we do not lose the way and drift away from our spiritual roots in Christ.

Our Acceptance of the Whole New Testament

As we come near the conclusion, it is important to add that our acceptance of the New Testament includes all parts of it, insofar as correctly translated. We accept and follow the principles of Christ found in the four Gospels, Acts, Paul's epistles, the epistles of Peter, James, John, Jude, the book of Hebrews, and the book of Revelation. We don't apologize for or ignore James's appeal for good works or Paul's emphasis on grace. There is a unity and a harmony in the view of the Latter-day Saints concerning the New Testament.

Our early history places us in a position to understand and empathize with the early Christian Saints. As they experienced, we believe that angels played a part in the nineteenth-century restoration, and we also had a seminal founding person who experienced extreme persecution and martyrdom. We have twelve apostles, missionaries who have experienced hardships in arduous journeys, and a form of Church government similar to that of the New Testament Church. The doctrine of the Church also conforms closely to that found in the earlier Church. Temple worship and ordinances have played a major role in both societies.

Summary

1. The New Testament is historical and real to The Church of Jesus Christ of Latter-day Saints.
2. We believe it to be basically accurate, fairly complete, and in the greater measure true.
3. We have extensively supplemented it and have reestablished its authority with Another Testament of Christ, The Book of Mormon.
4. With the help of that book, modern inspiration and revelation, and with careful scholarship, we have a fulness of the scriptures not known to others which sheds great light on the New Testament and illuminates its doctrines and teachings.
5. The New Testament was a central and guiding document in the ministry of Joseph Smith.
6. Leaving the central theme of Christ and his doctrine, including atonement, resurrection, baptism, and so forth, is a dangerous move to the periphery of ideas leaving society bankrupt of those special truths which can save and preserve mankind.
7. The influence of the New Testament has been more pervasive upon men and institutions than we can ever discover. One

example of an important document influenced by it is the United States Constitution.

8. We accept, use, and love all of the New Testament. It plays a central role in the gospel plan.

I have always loved the New Testament. It has the ring of truth, is not only profitable for instruction but binding as canonized scripture, and establishes the basic doctrines of the gospel of Jesus Christ in beauty and power. I add my special witness to its divinity. Through the inspiration of the Holy Ghost, I have had experiences which entitle and obligate me to bear that special witness, not only of the New Testament but of the Lord and Savior who is revealed in it. I do so with full understanding of the words I have chosen.

Notes

1. Peter's reference was to Old Testament scriptures, but the principle also applies equally to New Testament scriptures.
2. See J. Reuben Clark Jr., *Why the King James Version* (Salt Lake City: Deseret Book, 1952) for an interesting and scholarly exposition of how various versions of the New Testament came to be published and the author's opinion of their relative value.
3. *Journal of Discourses*, 11:213.
4. Paul Johnson, *A History of Christianity* (New York: Atheneum, 1980), 23.
5. Articles of Faith 1:8.
6. See 1 Nephi 13:40.
7. *A History of Christianity*, vii.
8. Ibid., 21.
9. Sir Frederic G. Kenyon, *The Story of the Bible* (1936), 144.
10. Kenyon, *The Bible and Archaeology* (1940), 228; italics added.
11. Doctrine and Covenants 20:11.
12. Luke 11:52, adding Joseph Smith's revision in footnote 52a of the 1979 LDS publication of the Bible in which he adds the phrase "the fulness of the scriptures" after the phrase "key of knowledge."
13. See accounts in Acts 9, 22, 26.
14. *The Words of Joseph Smith* (compiled and edited by Andrew F. Ehat and Lyndon W. Cook), 51.
15. Ibid.
16. Joseph Smith, *History of The Church of Jesus Christ of Latter-day Saints* (Salt Lake City: *Deseret News*, 1912), 6:57.
17. Bruce R. McConkie, *Mormon Doctrine* (Bookcraft, 1958), 57–58.

18. Richard Weaver, *Ideas Have Consequences* (Chicago: University of Chicago Press, paperback edition, 1984), 52–53.

19. Quoted from Robert Maynard Hutchins, ed. in chief, *Great Books of the Western World*, vol. 43, 259.

20. Letter dated February 7, 1788, quoted in Catherine Drinker Bowen, *Miracle at Philadelphia* (New York: Atlantic-Little, 1966), xvii.

21. For further thoughts on this subject, see Dean Mannion, "The Founding Fathers and the Natural Laws: A Study of the Source of Our Legal Institutions," *American Bar Assn. Journal*, vol. 35 (1949), 461.

22. See John 10:34–36; 1 John 3:1–3; and Revelation 3:21.

23. Quoted in *Great Books of the Western World*, vol. 43, 159.

24. See the account of the temptations of Jesus in Matthew 4:1–10.

25. Quoted in *Great Books of the Western World*, vol. 43, 104.

26. *Great Books of the Western World*, vol. 43, 103.

27. *Ideas Have Consequences*, 176.

Chapter Two

New Testament Women: The Exemplars

Susan Easton-Black
Alan K. Parrish

The women disciples in the New Testament Gospels are wonderful examples for women in our dispensation. Their example sets the pattern for young women, wives, mothers, and widows. Whether their circumstance indicated suffering or blessing, they are mighty portraits of true womanhood as they find Christ: the Way, the Truth, and the Life. The women of the Gospels knew Jesus. They sought for his blessing and were recipients of his divine favor. Having been highly favored of him, they lived faithfully and became influences for good in their dispensation and the exemplars for the latter days.

Their model of goodness is replicated in the lives of latter-day women. In our dispensation, women are admonished to become righteous and devoted wives, mother, sisters, and handmaidens to the Lord. They are to seek with full purpose of heart for blessings from the Lord in order to become a blessing in the lives of others.

The similarities between women disciples in the New Testament dispensation and our own strike harmonious chords. It is our purpose to highlight exemplary womanhood in both the early and the latter-day Church by acknowledging the often overlooked and unsung in expression of appreciation for the faithful devotion of both generations of women.

Women in the Gospel Record

Many women followed Jesus. Perhaps they were more numerous than the men. Aside from the twelve whom he called as apostles, and the Seventy, about whom little is known, few male disciples are mentioned in the Gospels. The infrequent accounts of women disciples are thinly scattered in the Gospels, probably because of cultural restraints. It is understood that "Jesus contradicted rabbinic tradition in associating with women socially."[1] It has been stated, "For a Jewish woman to leave home and travel with a rabbi was not only unheard of, it was scandalous."[2]

In light of these cultural restraints, the quantity of material about women in the Gospels is impressive.[3] For example, in the Gospels we find women identified by various titles. *Mother* is mentioned eighty-five times; *woman/women,* eighty-eight; *wife/wives,* fifty-five; *daughter,* thirty-nine; and *maid/maiden,* fourteen. Jesus used these terms with reverence and respect. He refrained from referring to any woman as an adulteress, a harlot,[4] a hypocrite, or any other degrading title (Luke 7:45, Matthew 9:22, Luke 13:12).

Often the Lord's respect for womanhood was illustrated in his stories and parables. He chose as exemplar of generosity and sacrifice a certain poor widow who threw two mites into the treasury. He said:

> Verily I say unto you, That this poor widow hath cast more in, than all they which have cast into the treasury:
> For all they did cast in of their abundance; but she of her want did cast in all that she had, even all her living. (Mark 12:43–44 [41–44])

Jesus likened the people of the last days, whose faith would have them waiting to enter the kingdom with the bridegroom, to ten virgins (maidens).

> Then shall the kingdom of heaven be likened unto ten virgins, which took their lamps, and went forth to meet the bridegroom.
> And five of them were wise. The wise took oil in their vessels with their lamps. (Matthew 25:1–2, 4 [1–13])

The Savior used one woman's joy at the recovery of a lost piece of silver to illustrate angelic joy over one soul that repents. Her diligent efforts to find the piece are symbolic of needed efforts to return lost souls to Christ:

> What woman having ten pieces of silver, if she lose one piece, doth not light a candle, and sweep the house, and seek diligently till she find it?

> And when she hath found it, she calleth her friends and her neighbours together, saying, Rejoice with me; for I have found the piece which I had lost. (Luke 15:8–10)

To teach his disciples the value of continual prayer, Jesus portrayed the persistence of a widow seeking redress from a judge, who said:[5]

> Yet because this widow troubleth me, I will avenge her, lest by her continual coming she weary me. And the Lord said, Hear what the unjust judge saith. And shall not God avenge his own elect, which cry day and night unto him, though he bear long with them? I tell you that he will avenge them speedily. (Luke 18:5–8 [1–8])

His Women Disciples

As the life of Jesus unfolded, women became witnesses of his divine sonship. Mary, the handmaiden of the Lord, a pattern of virtue, reverence, maidenhood, and motherhood, was told of the Lord's birth by an angel. Her witness of his divinity and mission is among the most beautiful of any found in the Gospels.

> Be it unto me according to thy word. . . . My soul doth magnify the Lord, And my spirit hath rejoiced in God my Savior. For he that is mighty hath done to me great things; and holy is his name. (Luke 1:38, 46–47, 49)

Elizabeth, the wife of the presiding priest, because of her personal righteousness late in her life, became the mother of an Elias. Her assignment included caring for Mary, the mother of the Son of God. She, who welcomed Mary to her home,

> was filled with the Holy Ghost: . . . and said, Blessed art thou among women, and blessed is the fruit of thy womb. And whence is this to me, that the mother of my Lord should come to me? (Luke 1:41–43)

These two righteous women received the earliest witness recorded in the gospels of the life and mission of Jesus Christ.

Waiting for the infant Messiah at the temple was the prophetess Anna, whose life is a pattern of temple service and spirituality. A widow of eighty-four years,

> which departed not from the temple, but served God with fastings and prayers night and day. And she coming in that instant gave

thanks likewise unto the Lord, and spake of him to all them that looked for redemption in Jerusalem. (Luke 2:37–38)

In the home of Jesus were several women (see Matthew 13:54–56). At the marriage feast in Cana surely as many women witnessed the miracle as did men. It was Mary who requested this first miracle in full assurance of his divine power (see John 2:1–11).

On his first Passover journey to Jerusalem, Jesus declared his true identity to Nicodemus and to the woman at the well in Samaria. Nicodemus was impressed but apparently did little. In contrast, to the woman this was a meeting of great consequence, for Jesus taught her perceptively and she responded with understanding and belief.[6] "I know that Messias cometh, which is called Christ," she declared. Jesus answered saying, "I that speak unto thee am he" (John 4:25–26). The woman went to her city and returned with what may be considered the first branch of the early church, for

many of the Samaritans of that city believed on him for the saying of the woman, which testified, He told me all that I ever did. . . . And said unto the woman, Now we believe, not because of thy saying: for we have heard him ourselves, and know that this is indeed the Christ, the Saviour of the world. (John 4:39, 42)

In Galilee, Jesus gathered his twelve disciples and also Mary Magdalene, Joanna, Suzanna, the other Mary's, the widow of Nain, the wife and daughter of Jairus, the woman with an issue of blood, and many others. These were stalwart women disciples. Many had been healed of evil spirits and infirmities through their faith in Jesus. For example, seven devils went out of Mary Magdalene. The seven devils are an indication of the seriousness of her disease, not of an evil life. Having been made whole by her faith, Mary devoted her strength, like the other women, to his service. She became the chief woman disciple.

Joanna, the wife of Chuza, a steward in the court of Herod Antipus, gave much support to the ministry of Jesus. It is believed that she had considerable wealth, prominence, and learning.[7]

Two miracles of women being healed deserve added comment because of their uniqueness. Jesus did not tell the woman with an issue of blood, "Arise, and take up thy bed" (Mark 2:11) or "Thy sins be forgiven thee" (Matthew 9:2) or "Go, wash in the pool" (John 9:7). After she was healed at the touch of his garment, he said,

24

> Who touched me? . . . Somebody hath touched me: for I per-
> ceive that virtue is gone out of me. And when the woman saw that
> she was not hid, she came trembling, and falling down before him,
> she declared unto him before all the people for what cause she had
> touched him, and how she was healed immediately. And he said unto
> her, Daughter, be of good comfort: thy faith hath made thee whole;
> go in peace. (Luke 8:45–48)

Another woman (Syrophenician) sought a blessing in behalf of her
daughter. Jesus, recognizing that she was not of Israel, did not say, "Fear
not: believe only, and she shall be made whole" (Luke 8:50). Instead he
proclaimed:

> Let the children first be filled: for it is not meet to take the chil-
> dren's bread, and to cast it unto the dogs. And she answered and said
> unto him, Yes, Lord: yet the dogs under the table eat of the children's
> crumbs. And he said unto her, *For this saying to thy way*; the devil is
> gone out of thy daughter. (Mark 7:27–29; italics added).

It was by these women's faith that they received the blessing of
healing.

In Bethany of Judea lived Mary and Martha, sisters of Lazarus.
They are a study in contrasts as to the nature of their faith. Three distinct
occasions deserve comment in the lives of these devoted women. The
first centered on Martha's request that Jesus influence Mary to assist
her. His reply:

> Martha, Martha, thou art careful and troubled about many
> things: But one thing is needful: and Mary hath chosen that good
> part, which shall not be taken away from her. (Luke 10:41–42)

Mary's desire to sit at the feet of Jesus cannot be faulted, but neither
can Martha's sacrifice of personal interests and comfort to better serve
him.

The second incident was at the death of Lazarus. To Martha his death
was impractical and unnecessary, and had Jesus been there it would not
have happened. She added, "I know, that even now, whatsoever thou
wilt ask of God, God will give it thee" (John 11:22). What a powerful
declaration of faith! To her the act of Jesus raising Lazarus was the
exercise of a skill or a duty incumbent in his nature just as maintaining
an orderly household or caring for her guests was incumbent in her.
Mary, weeping with the mourners, appeared to have accepted the loss.

Feeling her grief and that of their friends, "he groaned in the spirit and was troubled" (John 11:33). They are very different emotions, but can one clearly say which had the greater faith?

The third occasion was on the eve of his triumphal entry. With a pound of very costly ointment, Mary anointed the feet of Jesus and dried them with her hair. Judas was critical of the extravagance, but Jesus defended her, saying, "Let her alone: against the day of my burying hath she kept this" (John 12:7).

In the days of his deepest agony the women were notably true. John was the only male disciple mentioned between the trial and the death of Jesus (John 19:27). All the Gospel accounts indicate women disciples keeping watch through the trial, the crucifixion, the burial, and the resurrection. "There stood by the cross of Jesus his mother, and his mother's sister, Mary the wife of Cleophas, and Mary Magdalene" (John 19:25).[8]

They continued their vigil as Joseph of Arimathaea removed his body from the cross and, with Nicodemus, anointed and wrapped it in clean linen cloth, laid it in Joseph's own tomb, rolled the great stone to the door of the sepulcher, and departed. Yet, unwilling to leave, "There was Mary Magdalene, and the other Mary, sitting over against the sepulcher" (Matthew 27:61). It is not known how long they remained, but it is known "they returned, and prepared spices and ointments; and rested the Sabbath day according to the commandment" (Luke 23:56). "In the end of the Sabbath, as it began to dawn toward the first day of the week, came Mary Magdalene and the other Mary to see the sepulcher" (Matthew 28:1).[9]

In the presence of these women, an angel descended, rolled back the stone, and declared,

> Fear not ye: for I know that ye seek Jesus, which was crucified. He is not here: for he is risen, as he said. Come, see the place where the Lord lay. And go quickly, and tell his disciples that he is risen from the dead; and, behold, he goeth before you into Galilee; there shall ye see him: lo, I have told you. (Matthew 28:5–7)

Following the declaration of the angel, these women were privileged to behold the resurrected Lord. Their unswerving love, unsurpassed devotion, and abiding faith were recognized by Christ, heralded by gospel writers, and proclaimed by the righteous throughout the ages. In deep appreciation we join the chorus as we humbly give praise to these women who knew that true womanhood was to find Christ: the Way, the Truth, and the Life.

Ancient and Modern Seekers of a Blessing from the Lord

The Desire to Receive Heavenly Comfort

As Mary stood weeping at the sepulcher, the resurrected Lord inquired:

> Woman, why weepest thou? whom seekest though? She, supposing him to be the gardener, saith unto him, Sir, if thou have borne him hence, tell me where thou hast laid him, and I will take him away. Jesus saith unto her, Mary. (John 20:15–16)

Centuries later, Joseph Smith watched faithful sisters work on the veils for the Kirtland Temple. "Well, sisters," observed Joseph, "you are always on hand. Mary was first at the resurrection, and the sisters are the first to work on the inside of the temple."[10]

As we observed Mary waiting at the tomb of Jesus (Matthew 9:20), so centuries later we view Lydia Knight,[11] a recent widow of Newel Knight, contemplating the care of her seven children and the call of Brigham to move west. In her desperate loneliness she wondered:

> How could she . . . prepare herself and family to . . . take a journey a thousand miles into the Rocky Mountains? The burden weighed her spirit down until she cried out in pain, "Oh Newel, why hast thou left me!"
>
> As she spoke, he stood by her side . . . and said: "Be calm, let no sorrow overcome you. It was necessary that I should go. I was needed behind the veil. . . . You cannot fully comprehend it now; but the time will come when you shall know why I left you and our little ones. Therefore, dry up your tears. Be patient, I will go before you and protect you in your journeying. And you and your little ones shall never perish for lack of food!"[12]

The Desire to Be Healed

> Behold, there was a woman which had a spirit of infirmity eighteen years, and was bowed together, and could in no wise lift up herself. And when Jesus saw her, he called her to him, and said unto her, Woman, thou art loosed from thine infirmity. And he laid his hands on her: and immediately she was made straight, and glorified God. (Luke 13:11–13)

The healing of the sick by those with the authority to act in the name of God is a blessing sought by latter-day women. Isabella Park, a sixty-two-year-old member of Captain McArthur's second handcart company, was a recipient of the Lord's healing blessing by being loosed from her infirmity. Wilford Woodruff reported an accident that Isabella had on the journey west:

> Old Sister Isabella Park ran in before the wagon to see how her [sick] companion was. The driver, not seeing her, hallowed at his team and they being quick to mind, Sister Park could not get out of the way, and the fore wheel struck her and threw her down and passed over both hips. Brother Leonard grabbed hold of her to pull her out of the way before the hind wheel could catch her. He only got her part way and the hind wheels passed over her ankles. We all thought that she would be mashed to pieces, but to the joy of us all, there was not a bone broken, although the wagon had something like two tons burden on it, a load for four yoke of oxen. We went right to work [giving a priesthood blessing] and applying the same medicine to her we did to the sister who was bitten by the rattlesnake, and although quite sore for a few days, Sister Park got better, so that she was on the tramp before we got into the Valley.[13]

The Desire to Hear the Word of God

> Now it came to pass, as they went, that he entered into a certain village: and a certain woman named Martha received him into her house.
> And she had a sister called Mary, which also sat at Jesus' feet, and heard his word. (Luke 10:38–39)

To hear and learn the word of God is also a desire of latter-day women. Mary Elizabeth Rollins[14] saw her first Book of Mormon at Isaac Morley's home in Kirtland. She later wrote, "I felt such a desire to read it, that I could not refrain from asking him to let me take it home and read it, while he attended meeting."[15] Her desire was granted on the condition she would bring it back before breakfast.

> True to her promise, she returned it before Brother Morley's breakfast. He commented, "I guess you did not read much in it." She showed him how far, recited the first verse to him, and gave him an outline of the story of Nephi. Surprised, he capitulated: "Child, take

this book home and finish it, I can wait."

She was close to the last chapter when Joseph and Emma Smith moved to Kirtland. When the Prophet saw the Book of Mormon in the Rollins home, he identified it as the one he had sent to brother Morley and wanted to see the girl who had acquired it in such an impressive manner. "When he saw me," she remembers, "he looked at me so earnestly, I felt almost afraid. After a moment or two he came and put his hands on my head and gave me a great blessing, the first I ever received, and made me a present of the book, and said he would give Brother Morley another."[16]

The Desire to Give Their Best to Further the Work of the Lord

And, behold, a woman in the city, which was a sinner, when she knew that Jesus sat at meat in the Pharisee's house, brought an alabaster box of ointment,

And stood at his feet behind him weeping, and began to wash his feet with tears, and did wipe them with the hairs of her head, and kissed his feet, and anointed them with the ointment. (Luke 7:37–38)

Such desire to give the best we have to the Lord was shown by Lydia Goldthwaite. Lydia, recently separated from her husband, had just arrived in Kirtland when she was approached by Vincent Knight, who exclaimed:

"Sister, the Prophet is in bondage and has been brought into distress by the persecutions of the wicked, and if you have any means to give, it will be a benefit to him."

"Oh yes, sir," she replied, "here is all I have. I only wish it was more," emptying her purse, containing perhaps fifty dollars, in his hand as she spoke.

He looked at it and counted it and fervently exclaimed: "Thank God, this will release and set the Prophet free!"

The young girl was without means now, even to procure a meal or a night's lodging. Still that sweet spirit that rested upon her whispered "all will be well."

As evening drew on, Vincent Knight returned and brought the welcome news that Joseph was at liberty, and Lydia's joy to think that she had been the humble means of helping the Prophet was unbounded.[17]

The Desire to Overcome Even Death

And, behold, there came a man named Jairus, and he was a ruler of the synagogue: and he fell down at Jesus' feet, and besought him that he would come into his house:

For he had one only daughter, about twelve years of age, and she lay a dying. . . .

While he yet spake, there cometh one from the ruler of the synagogue's house, saying to him, Thy daughter is dead; trouble not the Master.

But when Jesus heard it, he answered him, saying, Fear not: believe only, and she shall be made whole. . . . He said, Weep not; she is not dead, but sleepeth.

And they laughed him to scorn, knowing that she was dead.

And he put them all out, and took her by the hand, and called, saying, Maid, arise. (Luke 8:41–42, 49–50, 52–54)

Thus overcoming even death was a privilege also extended to Ella Jensen, a resident of Brigham City. For many weeks she lingered between life and death suffering from scarlet fever.

As her death came, her father, Jacob Jensen, wanted Lorenzo Snow to speak at her funeral. Knowing that President Snow was at a meeting in the town, Brother Jensen hurried to the tabernacle.

I went into the vestry, behind the main hall, wrote a note [to Lorenzo]. When the note was placed on the pulpit, President Snow stopped his talking, read the note, and then explained to the saints that it was a call to visit some people who were in deep sorrow and asked to be excused.[18]

Rudger Clawson, president of the Box Elder Stake, was invited by President Snow to join him at the Jensen home. He wrote of the experience, saying:

As we entered the home we met Sister Jensen, who was very much agitated and alarmed. We came to Ella's bedside and were impressed by the thought that her spirit had passed out of the body and gone beyond.

Turning to me President Snow said: "Brother Clawson, will you anoint her?" Which I did. We then laid our hands upon her head and the anointing was confirmed by President Snow, who blessed her and among other things, used this very extraordinary expression, in a commanding tone of voice, "Come back, Ella, come back. Your work upon the earth is not yet completed, come back." Shortly afterward we left the home.[19]

Ella's father recorded what happened next:

Ella remained in this condition for more than an hour after President Snow administered to her, or more than three hours in all after she died. We were sitting there watching by the bedside, her mother and myself, when all at once she opened her eyes. She looked about the room, saw us sitting there, but still looked for someone else. And the first thing she said was: "Where is he? Where is he?" We asked, "Who? Where is who?" "Why, Brother Snow," she replied. "He called me back."[20]

The Desire to Be a Blessing to Others

In Proverbs we read, "Her children arise up, and call her blessed; her husband also, and he praiseth her" (31:28). Why? It is because such women desire to be a blessing and an influence for good in the lives of others. During the time of Christ, "Many women were there beholding afar off, which followed Jesus from Galilee, ministering unto him" (Matthew 27:55). This care and concern continued even after the death of Jesus as women diligently watched by the sepulcher (Matthew 27:61).

Women in the latter days who have had their heartfelt prayers answered desire to bless the lives of others.

The minutes of the Female Relief Society of Nauvoo, August 5, 1843, taken by Eliza R. Snow, record:

Sister Joshua Smith found many sick in the Fourth Ward and some destitute, in want of things to eat, and to use. Went and visited Sister McEwan and Sister Modley, found them and their families in suffering want—they need attendance every day. Sister Mecham visited Nehimiah Harmon's, found them poor, sick, and distressed, and no bedding—nothing comfortable, entirely destitute. Sister Mecham and Sister Billings solicited donations for the same. Sister Anderson gave one pair of stockings—$.25. Sister Farr a calico dress and cape. Sister B. Ames, a peck of onions, one pound of sugar. Sister Clayton gave fourteen pounds of flour—$.52; Lydia Moore one shirt—$.50; Margaret Moore one shawl. Eliza R. Snow, secretary.[21]

Elizabeth Ann Whitney[22] and her husband, Newel, provided a three-day feast in their home for the poor of the Church. Of this event, Joseph Smith's history states:

> Attended a sumptuous feast at Bishop Newel K. Whitney's. This feast was after the order of the Son of God—the lame, the halt, and the blind were invited, according to the instructions of the Savior.[23]

As with the early Relief Society members and the wife of a bishop, women in our era desire to help and be an influence for good. Whether it is the quiet visiting of the sick, the nurturing of the young, or the listening to a confused teenager, a righteous woman is there. May these noble women continue to be blessed as they give their lives to follow the great Exemplar, Jesus Christ.

Conclusion

One of the best ways to appreciate the women who had the privilege of knowing Jesus Christ in the meridian of time is to know the feeling of the Lord toward these women. In every recorded reference where Christ speaks of or to these women he does so with honor and respect. No wonder these righteous women humbly sought and received blessings from their Redeemer. Once blessed they then desired to be in his service. Whether it meant bathing his feet with tears or watching at the tomb, these women were moved by their devotion to serve him.

The example of these great women is mirrored by women in our dispensation. Even though many centuries apart in technology, educational opportunities, recreational activities, and clearly defined roles, the common denominators are the same: exemplary wife, mother, sister, and handmaiden to the Lord.

Gratefully, we review our sacred past as we learn to function in today's society. We look to the future as we seek blessings from the Lord, and at the same time seek to be a blessing to him and to all mankind. We hope for a glorious resurrection and a unity with Jesus Christ. We desire to be united with women of the New Testament who courageously set the pattern for all righteous women to follow.

Notes
1. Munro Winsome, "Women Disciples in Mark," *Catholic Biblical Quarterly*, vol. 44, no. 2 (see note 12, 232).

2. Ben Witherington III, *Women in the Ministry of Jesus* (Cambridge: Cambridge University Press, 1984), 117.

3. In an era of greater cultural equality, their lives and examples deserve ever greater attention.

4. In what may seem at first an exception, note that the term is general, not specific, and at the same time is a positive reference: "Whether of them twain did the will of his father? They say unto him, The first. Jesus saith unto them, Verily I say unto you, That the publicans and the harlots go into the kingdom before you" (Matthew 21:31).

5. See also Doctrine and Covenants 101:81–90.

6. It is interesting that John devoted almost an entire chapter to the meeting of Jesus, the woman of Samaria, and the people of her city. See John 4.

7. Luke probably obtained much of his information from Joanna. J.R. Dummelow, *A Commentary of The Holy Bible*, New York: Mac Millan, 1978, 749.

8. "And many women were there beholding afar off, which followed Jesus from Galilee, ministering unto him" (Matthew 27:55; Mark 15:40–41).

9. Luke and John recorded that it was the next day, very early in the morning (Luke 24:1), while "it was yet dark" (John 20:1).

10. This story was told by Mary Ann Angel, the daughter of James William Angel and Phoebe Ann Morton, born June 8, 1803, in Seneca, Ontario, New York. She became the wife of Brigham Young, February 18, 1834, and the mother of six children: Joseph, Brigham, Mary Ann, Alice, Luna, and John. She died June 27, 1882 in Salt Lake City, Salt Lake, Utah. Susan Easton, *Membership of The Church of Jesus Christ of Latter-day Saints*, 1830–1848. Provo, Utah: Religious Studies Center Brigham Young University, 1984, vol. 2, 602–6.

11. Lydia Goldthwaite (Knight) was the daughter of Jesse G. Goldthwaite and Sally Burt. She was born June 9, 1812, in Sutton, Worcester, Massachusetts. She married Calvin Bailey in the fall of 1828, and Newel Knight on November 24, 1835, in Kirtland, Geauga, Ohio. To Lydia and Newel were born Sally, James, Joseph, Newel, Lydia, Jesse, and Hyrum. Lydia also married John Dalton on August 13, 1851, and later in her life is known to have married James McClellan. She died April 3, 1884, in St. George, Washington, Utah. Susan Easton, *Church Membership*, 1830–1848, vol. 18:616–18.

12. Susa Young Gates, *Lydia Knight's History*, Juvenile Instructor Office, Salt Lake City, 1883, 71–72.

13. Captain MacArthur's (second) handcart company left Florence,

Nebraska, July 24 1856, at 12 o'clock. McArthur, in his report to Wilford Woodruff, described this experience relating to Isabella Park that took place on August 16, 1856. LeRoy R. and Ann W. Hafen, *Handcarts to Zion* (Glendale, CA: Arthur H. Clark Co., 1960), 216–17. *LDS Journal History*, September 26, 1856. Susan Easton, *Members of the Ellsworth and McArthur Handcart Companies of 1856*, 1982, n.p.

14. Mary Elizabeth Rollins was the daughter of John Porter Rollins and Keziah Keturah VanBenthuysen. She was born April 9, 1818, in Lima, Livingston, New York. She married Adam Lightner in 1835 in Liberty, Clay, Missouri. She died December 17, 1917. Susan Easton, *Church Membership*, 1830–1848. *Utah Genealogical and Historical Magazine* (1926), vol. 17, 193–205, 250–60. N. B. Lundwall, *The Life and Testimony of Mary E. Lightner*. (n.p., n.d.), 44. *Journal of Mary Elizabeth Rollins Lightner*, located at the Harold B. Lee Library, Brigham Young University, Provo, Utah.

15. Lavina Fielding Anderson, "Kirtland's Resolute Saints," *Ensign*, January 1979, 49, 51.

16. Ibid.

17. *Lydia Knight*, 25.

18. LeRoy C. Snow, "Raised from the Dead," *Improvement Era*, (Sept. 1929): vol. 22, 881–86, 972–80.

19. Ibid.

20. Ibid.

21. By May of 1843 membership and attendance outgrew the brick store, and summer meetings convened in the Nauvoo grove and in the homes of the sisters.

22. Elizabeth Ann (Smith) Whitney was the daughter of Gibson Smith and Polly Bradley. She was born December 26, 1800, in Derby, New Haven, Connecticut. She married Newel Kimball Whitney on October 20, 1822, in Kirtland, Geauga, Ohio. Her children were Horace, Sarah Ann, Franklin, Mary Elizabeth, Orson, John, Joshua, Ann Maria, Don Carlos, Mary Jane, and Newel Melchizedek. She died February 15, 1882, in Salt Lake City, Salt Lake, Utah. Susan Easton, *Church Membership*, 1830–1848, n.p. *Women's Exponent*, 1878–79, 33, 41, 51, 71, 83, 91, 105, 191. Andrew Jensen, *LDS Biographical Encyclopedia*, vol. 3, 563–64.

23. D. Michael Quinn, "The Newel K. Whitney Family," *Ensign*, December 1978, 44.

CHAPTER THREE

The Beatitudes: Eight Qualities that Savor the Eternal Guest

Clark V. Johnson

In the New Testament, Jesus, after a long day of teaching multitudes of people, withdrew from them and "went up into a mountain; and when he was set, his disciples" joined him (Matthew 5:1). It was on this occasion that he taught the Sermon on the Mount. It was not taught to vast multitudes, but only to those disciples who followed him. Hence we may conclude that the Sermon on the Mount was a private sermon.[1]

In the forepart of the Sermon on the Mount Jesus spoke of eight characteristics that an individual must acquire to achieve spiritual perfection. In Jesus' greatest recorded sermon, he spoke concerning the attitude of his followers; thus, developing proper attitudes is an essential part of living the gospel.

The Savior taught that it is necessary to keep the commandments and to make covenants with the Lord through participation in the ordinances of the priesthood under the direction of those who have authority. In the Sermon on the Mount the Lord introduced another aspect of living the gospel. In addition to the outward display of keeping the commandments and of making covenants, a person must experience a change of heart, and develop the right attitude. Hence the Beatitudes are not just "ethical principles," but are part of the gospel and "are far more doctrinal than ethical in nature."[2]

President Spencer W. Kimball said, "Many members of the Church are dead to spiritual things. And I believe even many who are making pretenses of being active are also spiritually dead. Their service is much of the letter and less of the Spirit."[3] According to President Kimball, those who are spiritually dead live the letter of the law. A significant part of living the gospel is learning to live under the direction of the Spirit, which teaches us to do the right thing for the right reason. The Spirit instills within us a change of attitude.

The first step in changing our attitudes is changing our thoughts. Alma and Amulek taught the poor Zoramites that they would be judged not only according to their works and words, but also their thoughts (see Alma 12:14). It is the "thought" portion of the gospel that many disciples struggle with. We spend our time running from one meeting to another without thinking. Once we attend this or that required meeting, our religion is finished for the day and we have fulfilled the letter of the law. It is recorded several times in the New Testament that Jesus took time to be alone and to consult with his Father in prayer (see Matthew 14:23, 26:36; Mark 6:46; Luke 6:12). It is when we take time to be alone, to contemplate our mission, and to consult with our Heavenly Father that the Spirit will be able to work within us. At this point we will begin to cultivate the attitudes that Christ taught his disciples. These attitudes must be developed if a person is to understand and live his gospel.

The Beatitudes are often taught as a step-by-step process toward achieving a Christlike character. The problem with this approach is that these attitudes are not developed just once in life, but must be cultivated daily as a person struggles for perfection.[4] Thus the struggle for these qualities reoccurs daily in the life of a disciple of Jesus (see D&C 67:13).

I like to place the Beatitudes in a wheel,[5] thus taking them out of a step-by-step progression. A traditional wheel has three focal points: the hub, the rim, and the spokes.

The Hub of the Wheel

One key phrase the translators of the Bible left out of the Beatitudes is found in 3 Nephi, which contains the same sermon taught by the resurrected Savior to the Nephites. On that occasion he said to the Nephites, "Blessed are the poor in spirit, who come unto me, for theirs is the kingdom of heaven" (3 Nephi 12:3). The little phrase "who come unto me" is the hub for the Beatitudes.

Many living on earth today are poor in spirit, feel hopelessly lost, and have nowhere to turn. The key to the rewards offered with the Beatitudes is the Christ. Those who are poor in spirit who look to the Christ will inherit the kingdom of heaven. Thus, the hub or center of the Beatitudes is the Savior himself. As he said to his disciples, "Do that which ye have seen me do" is the model for anyone trying to live the gospel (see 3 Nephi 27:21).

The Rim and Spokes of the Wheel

The characteristics of being broken hearted, developing a contrite spirit, becoming sanctified, and enduring [to] the end form the rim of the wheel. These qualities ring the spokes, the eight Beatitudes, holding them in place after they are connected to the hub.

The Rim

In order to successfully draw near to him, the Savior instructed each person, "Come unto me with a broken heart and a contrite spirit" (see Psalm 34:18, Isaiah 66:2, 2 Nephi 2:7). Prior to his appearance to the Nephites, the resurrected Lord explained to them that the law of Moses had been fulfilled and that they were to come to him with a "broken heart and a contrite spirit" (3 Nephi 9:20). This constitutes the first two part of the wheel's rim.

An individual who is broken hearted is often frustrated with life, sees himself lacking in ability to keep gospel covenants, or is crushed by grief. As this disciple looks toward the Savior for direction, he recognizes that he is indeed poor in spirit.

Poor in Spirit

"Blessed are the poor in spirit who come unto me, for theirs is the kingdom of heaven" (Matthew 5:3; 3 Nephi 12:3). This disciple lacks spiritual dimension or quality. His spirit is poverty stricken and he recognizes the need to be "ever dependent upon the Lord."[6] He is destitute of those qualities that bring peace. At this point he mourns for his weakness, his lack of understanding, and his sins (see Matthew 5:3–4, 3 Nephi 12:3–4).

Mourn

"Blessed are they that mourn: for they shall be comforted" (Matthew 5:4, 3 Nephi 12:4). The person that mourns grieves over his weaknesses of character, his offenses against others, and his sins. This grief is godly sorrow (2 Corinthians 7:10). Late in life Nephi expressed it in these words: "O wretched man that I am! . . . My heart sorroweth because of my flesh; my soul grieveth because of mine iniquities" (2 Nephi 4:17). He ended this same soliloquy saying, "Awake my soul! . . . Rejoice . . . O Lord, I have trusted in thee, and I will trust in thee forever" (2 Nephi 4:28, 34). Nephi, like all disciples of Christ, realized the source of his strength, even though he was overwhelmed at times by his own weakness. In addition the mourner must lift another's burdens that they become light and must comfort those who need comfort (see Mosiah 18:8–9).[7]

Once an individual recognizes that he is broken hearted, he becomes poor in spirit and mourns because he is spiritually bankrupt. He realizes his only hope is in Christ, and he develops a contrite spirit, which is another section in the rim of the wheel. A person who has a contrite spirit is broken in spirit, meaning that he feels remorse at the recognition of past mistakes. In showing remorse we become meek.

Meek

"Blessed are the meek: for they shall inherit the earth" (Matthew 5:5, 3 Nephi 12:6). A synonym for *meek* is *humble*. To become humble is to lack pride, to be unpretentious, to be unassuming, or to be "not easily provoked or irritated."[8] When one becomes meek, or humble, he becomes teachable. This is the kind of meekness that causes a person to draw closer to the Lord because he desires to be taught by him. It is not the self-debasing meekness of the snivelers, who castigate themselves and look to the world for justification for their actions. President Harold B. Lee said, "Meekness is synonymous with weakness. The meek man is the strong, the mighty, the man of complete self-mastery."[9] When a person's focus is upon the Christ, he recognizes that there is strength in being teachable, and his soul desires to be taught by the Savior. Thus the meek hunger for spiritual truth.

Hunger and Thirst

"Blessed are they which do hunger and thirst after righteousness: for they shall be filled" (Matthew 5:6; 3 Nephi 12:6). Once again a critical phrase has been omitted in the biblical account, which the Book of Mormon includes: "they shall be filled with the Holy Ghost" (3 Nephi 12:6). Thus the desires of the meek are fulfilled. The Christ promised his disciples another Comforter, the Holy Ghost, when he would no longer be with them; he also promised them that the Holy Ghost would teach, instruct, and testify to them (see John 14:26; 16:7–8, 13). It is hungering and thirsting . . . which "prompts fervent prayer and leads our feet to holy temples."[10]

When the Holy Ghost enters into a person's life, subtle but significant changes begin to take place. That person enters the realm of sanctification, which is represented in another section of the outer rim of the wheel.

Sanctification is synonymous with *purification*. A person who is sanctified is dedicated, is consecrated, is free from sin, and is working toward perfection. Sanctification is a "state of saintliness, a state attained only by conformity to the laws and ordinances of the gospel." Elder Bruce R. McConkie further taught that "the plan of salvation is the system and means provided whereby men may sanctify their souls and thereby become worthy of a celestial inheritance."[11]

I think sanctification is the "grace" part of the Atonement of Christ. It is nothing we can earn but is part of the ransom paid by the Savior in Gethsemane and on the cross, when he suffered and died for each of us (see Alma 42:14–26; Mosiah 5:6–9, 16–20). It is a pure gift from God. On the other hand, as Elder McConkie pointed out, we must qualify ourselves for the gift through obedience to the laws and ordinances of the gospel.[12] Thus, as the Holy Ghost testifies to us, we qualify ourselves through meekness when we listen and follow his instructions.

Merciful

The next Beatitude that lies within the sphere of sanctification is "Blessed are the merciful: for they shall obtain mercy" (Matthew 5:7; 3 Nephi 12:7). Showing mercy is an act of showing compassion, clemency, or leniency toward another. In Nauvoo, the Prophet Joseph Smith taught the Saints, "If you will not accuse me, I will not accuse you. If you will throw a cloak of charity over my sins, I will over yours—for charity covereth a multitude of sins."[13] In other words, if I overlook your faults and weaknesses and you overlook mine, who is there that will stand to accuse us? A merciful person avoids harsh judgments of others and shows understanding and tolerance for others' predicaments. In addition, the merciful help others solve their problems, and they freely forgive trespasses made against them. From such actions, charity enters the human heart. "Charity suffereth long . . . is not puffed up . . . is not easily provoked, thinketh no evil . . . endureth all things" (1 Corinthians 13:4–8; see also Moroni 7:44–48).

Although a merciful person does not criticize, mercy does not overlook all acts. Sometimes to be merciful is to say, "No, that's not right," thus making the person accountable. Being merciful does not mean giving everyone everything they wish. Many a parent or teacher must say no to a child or student if they are merciful. The Savior did this in his earthly ministry. For example, even though he loved the people, he drove the money changers from the temple on at least two occasions (see Matthew 21:12–13; Mark 11:15–18). Their acts were wrong. On another occasion he challenged the rich ruler to give away all his wealth and follow him. The man hung his head and walked away, for his wealth was very great (see Luke 18:18–24; Mark 10:17–22). On the other hand, when the woman with the issue of blood touched his garment and hid within the crowd, he made her accountable for what she had done. Trembling, and with great fear at his request, she finally faced him, and he blessed her and rewarded her (see Mark 5:24–34). In each of these situations he was merciful. A merciful person has pure motives because he is at peace.

Pure in Heart

"Blessed are the pure in heart: for they shall see God" (Matthew 5:8, 3 Nephi 12:8). To be pure is to be cleansed from anything that adulterates, taints, or impairs.[14] To be pure in heart is to have clear and refined motives. Job was tried in every conceivable way. He lost his family, his home, his business, his farm, and his health; yet he refused to curse God and die (see Job 1:12–22, 2:9–10). He insisted that he had always done those things that were good and that his desires were pure. When his friends betrayed him and accused him of lying and hypocrisy, he insisted that God judge him (see Job 13:15; 20:5, 11). In this he was not disappointed, for God spoke to him out of a whirlwind (behind the veil), and Job accounted to him (see Job 38:1–7). Finally, when Job finished his accounting, the veil was rent and he said, "Mine eye seeth thee" (Job 42:5). He saw God. Job's trials sanctified him. Job's motives were pure; he became pure in heart through the trials he suffered, and he was ushered into the presence of God.

President Harold B. Lee taught:

> You can see only that which you have eyes to see. Some of the associates of Jesus saw him only as a son of Joseph the carpenter. Others thought him to be a winebibber or a drunkard because of his words. Still others thought he was possessed of devils. Only the

righteous saw him as the Son of God. Only if you are the pure in heart will you see God.[15]

A true disciple of Jesus Christ takes full advantage of all the Savior offers. As Elder McConkie pointed out, a true disciple conforms to "the laws and ordinances of the gospel." This means that not only are we baptized as Jesus was, but by our own choice we avail ourselves of those sacred blessings we receive in the temple. In the temple we not only receive the endowment (a gift of knowledge and power from God), but we also make more covenants with God that bind us to him. Once we have done all we can, then we must maintain a gospel standard of living based on the covenants we have made and the additional knowledge we have received. As we become sanctified, we desire that others have peace, so we teach others the gospel.

Peacemaker

"Blessed are the peacemakers: for they shall be called the children of God" (Matthew 5:9; 3 Nephi 12:9). A peacemaker makes peace or settles conflicts. The peacemaker, therefore, must have peace within. The only source of peace in his world is "adoption of the gospel of Jesus Christ, rightly understood, obeyed and practiced by rules and people alike."[16] A peacemaker in our family takes the form of a blonde, who upon entering our home after a hard day at school, announced to her mother, "I'm going upstairs to have a nervous breakdown!" Things had not gone well that day. A short time later she bounded downstairs toward the telephone. After several phone calls, she explained, "I'm over my nervous breakdown. Everything is all right. I got it straightened out." We never did learn what the crisis was. But we did learn that peacemakers are actors, not reactors. In the gospel sense, peacemakers act upon the situation with mercy and solve the problem by making things right. Whether or not it is to their advantage is unimportant; things must be made right and thus peace is restored. From pure thoughts with continued focus upon the hub, such a person becomes a child of God and develops a quality of calmness and tranquility. This strength allows one to meet life's defeats positively, because one acts upon situations rather than reacting to them.

The last part of the rim of the wheel falls into place when we realize that once we have received these blessings and made covenants, we must endure to the end. Recently, a middle-aged sister approached me after class and said, somewhat frustrated, "What am I going to do? I have been ward and stake Primary president twice, and I am serving as stake Relief Society for the second time. I have already served as ward Relief Society president three times." She explained that she was out of ideas and found no challenge in her Church calling because she had worked in it before. The answer to her concern lies in a revelation given to Nephi in Helaman 10, when the Lord said to his servant, "Blessed art thou Nephi . . . for . . . thou hast" served me with "unwearyingness. . . . Thou hast not sought . . . thine own life, but hast sought my will, and to keep my commandments" (Helaman 10:4) Through long and faithful service, Nephi had accessed God's mind, and God granted unto Nephi all power because he knew Nephi would "not ask that which is contrary to my will" (Helaman 10:5). Later this same sister wrote me a note saying, "I understand."

Persecution

The last spoke in the Beatitudes seems to be a prophetic promise to those who emulate Christ by acquiring these attitudes.

"Blessed are they which are persecuted for righteousness sake: for theirs is the kingdom of heaven" (Matthew 5:11; 3 Nephi 12:11). When people follow Christ, live his kind of life, and seek to become like him, they will be persecuted.[17] The scriptures are full of examples; Jeremiah knew nothing but persecution; the Jews sought Lehi's life because he testified of God (1 Nephi 1:19–20); the Pharisees and Sadducees constantly tried to entrap Jesus (Matthew 12:14, 18, 15:1–12, 19:3, 22:15; Mark 12:13; Luke 20:19); the Missourians sought Joseph Smith during the Nauvoo period of Church history; and the enemies of the Church tried to destroy it even after the Saints migrated to the Great Basin. In spite of persecution by outsiders, Christ's disciples continue to prosper.

However, there is another side of persecution that is more difficult to bear: persecution from within the Church or family, persecution from those who should be our greatest supporters. The Jews at Jerusalem did not cause Lehi his greatest problems; it was his eldest sons, Laman and Lemuel (1 Nephi 17). The Pharisees and Sadducees had no power over Christ until he was betrayed by Judas (Matthew 26:14–16, 47–50; Mark 14:43–46; Luke 22:47–48). The Carthage Greys may have pulled the triggers that murdered Joseph Smith, but it was betrayal by the Fosters, Higbees, Laws, and other Church members that compromised him into their hands.

Likewise, many disciples today are betrayed by those who supposedly love them. Many can attest they were driven from their homes or ostracized by family members when they joined the Church. Both Alma the elder and Alma the Younger commented upon persecution from within when they challenged those who wanted baptism to bear one another's burdens (Mosiah 18:8–10; Alma 5:53–56).

Conclusions

Those who struggle to develop the qualities of godliness as a part of their character change inwardly. They become the "salt of the earth" (Matthew 5:13; 3 Nephi 12:13) and "the light of the world" (Matthew 5:14–16; 3 Nephi 12:14–16). They build their lives upon Christ's "rock" (Matthew 7:24–29; 3 Nephi 11:39), and they become "childlike" (Mark 10:15; Luke 18:17).

When someone is referred to as the "salt of the earth," that person is the backbone of an organization. He can be relied on to perform difficult tasks with integrity. There are men and women in every ward and stake in the Church who are the salt of the earth. They are the "seasoning, savoring, preserving influence in the world, the influence which would bring peace and blessings to all others."[18] They are grounded in the gospel of Jesus Christ and are determined to serve him at all costs. Their value is immeasurable. They elevate every situation. They become examples of integrity to others.

Their light is the light upon a hill that shines. There is something about them that radiates what they are, and they do not have to say a word. Recently my wife and I took seventy-four BYU students to the Holy Land as part of a BYU Semester Abroad Program. When touring in the old city of Jerusalem for the first time, I became impressed with the shrewdness of the Arab businessmen. As we passed by their shops, they called out, "Hey, BYU, come here! Got a special deal for T-shirt! Only five dollars! Best deal in town!" Another yelled, "Hey, Mormon, come here! Special deal! New shirt only four dollars!" I thought to myself, "These guys are really something. They have these kids pegged." Several weeks passed and I found myself on the same street behind another group of students from the United States. The Arab shopkeepers seemed to ignore them. A block or two later I fell in with a small group of our students, and once again I heard the calls, "Hey, BYU! Hey, Mormon!" At that point I realized that our students were different. They shined. They radiated cleanliness, purity, and honesty. It was not the way we were dressed, but there is an aura around any Latter-day Saint who tries to live the gospel. He shines! Several times while traveling on busses, we were stopped by strangers asking about the "delightful young people" with whom we were associated. Always with pride we answered that they were from BYU and that they were Mormons.

People who try to incorporate the Beatitudes into their personal lives center their lives around Jesus Christ. They imitate him; they do what he did. Thus they begin to build their lives upon his rock, or revelation. When they pray, they expect answers. Prayer becomes a tool to obtain the information they need to live life better and not just a religious ritual. These people study the scriptures expecting insights that will improve their lives and help them live richly and more completely. They work with tragedy and trials. They grow toward eternity with assurance and stability.

These men and women are childlike. There is a difference between being childlike and childish. Recently in a grocery store I watched a child fall to the floor, screaming and kicking because his mother would not buy the candy bar that the youngster wanted. That is childish. Childish people throw temper tantrums, they swear, and they manipulate people to obtain anything they happen to want at the time.

A childlike person is one who can be taught. He is submissive and responds to others' needs. He is willing to submit to God, through God's servants, "in all things even as a child does submit to his father" (Mosiah 3:19). A childlike person is willing to forgive instantly.

The characteristics of the Beatitudes occur again and again in a person's life as he struggles to overcome pride and worldliness and to focus upon imitating the lifestyle of the Savior. Hence, they are not eight one-time exercitations toward spiritual perfection, but eight recurring attributes that bring peace and assurance in this life and the certainty that by continued effort the eternal quest may be savored. Centered in Christ, they form the constitution for a perfect life.[19]

Notes

1. A text restoration completed by Joseph Smith of Matthew 5 indicates that those who approached Jesus were seeking baptism, were committed to following the Savior and not just the curiosity seekers among the multitudes. (See Joseph Smith, The Holy Scriptures Inspired Version, [Independence: Herald House, 1974.)] Matthew 5:1–4.) The resurrected Jesus taught this same sermon to the Nephites.

He appeared to 2,500 people who were at the temple in Bountiful. They witnessed his first visit, and he taught them the Sermon on the Mount (3 Nephi 12:1–12; 17:25). The scriptures indicate that an "exceedingly great number" were present for his second visit (3 Nephi 19:3, 5). Still, his first teachings were limited to a relatively small number of people when compared to his second visit to the Nephites.

2. Bruce R. McConkie, *Doctrinal New Testament Commentary*, 3 vols. (Salt Lake City: Bookcraft, 1965–1973), 1:215.

3. Spencer W. Kimball, *Conference Report*, April 1951, 104–6.

4. JST, Matthew 5:48. "Ye are therefore commanded to be perfect, even as your Father who is in Heaven is perfect." The word *perfect* in this verse comes from the word *shalam*, which means whole, complete, ripe, full, mature, or fully developed. Thus perfection is an ongoing struggle as long as a person remains in mortality. The Lord told the leaders of the early church in 1831 that they should "continue in patience until ye are perfected" (D&C 67:13).

5. Kay P. Wuthrich, Seminary and Institute Administrative Assistant Director, U.S. for the Northern Plains, introduced to me several years ago the idea of placing the Beatitudes on a wheel.

6. Harold B. Lee, *Decisions for Successful Living* (Salt Lake City: Deseret Boo, 1973), 57.

7. Ibid. 58.

8. Ibid., 60.

9. Ibid.

10. Ibid., 59.

11. Bruce R. McConkie, *Mormon Doctrine* (Salt Lake City: Bookcraft, 1966), 675–76.

12. Ibid.

13. Joseph Fielding Smith, *Teachings of the Prophet Joseph Smith* (Salt Lake City: Deseret Book, 1967), 193–94.

14. *Webster's New World Dictionary of the American Language*. College Edition. s. v. "pure."

15. Lee, *Decisions,* 59.

16. Joseph F. Smith, *Gospel Doctrine* (Salt Lake City: Deseret Book, 1966), 21.

17. McConkie, *Commentary,* 1:216–7.

18. McConkie, *Mormon Doctrine,* 601.

19. Lee, *Decisions,* 57.

CHAPTER FOUR

The Book of Mormon: An Interpretive Guide to the New Testament

Dennis Largey

The Lord, through his prophet President Ezra Taft Benson, caught our attention with repetitive admonitions regarding the blessings of and our responsibilities toward the Book of Mormon. In the October 1986 general conference, President Benson called God's gift of the Book of Mormon "more important than any of the inventions that have come out of the industrial and technological revolutions" and "or greater value to mankind than even the many wonderful advances . . . in modern medicine." He also made the charge that "every Latter-day Saint should make the study of the [Book of Mormon] a lifetime pursuit. Otherwise he is placing his soul in jeopardy and neglecting that which could give spiritual and intellectual unity to his whole life."¹ In a First Presidency Christmas message, President Benson said that we should know the Book of Mormon better than any other text.²

In light of President Benson's statements and persistent charges to read the Book of Mormon, our challenge is to find where we can appropriately incorporate the message of the Book of Mormon into New Testament study. The intent is not to overshadow the first testament of Christ, but to magnify it through providing inspired commentary.

Does the New Testament Need Book of Mormon Clarification?

The eighth article of faith of The Church of Jesus Christ of Latter-day Saints states, "We believe the Bible to be the word of God as far as it is translated correctly." Joseph Smith wrote, "I believe the Bible as it read when it came from the pen of the original writers. Ignorant translators, careless transcribers, or designing and corrupt priests have committed many errors."[3]

In a vision Nephi learned that, when the Bible would first go forth from the Jews to the Gentiles, the record would be pure and would contain "the fulness of the gospel of the Lord." However, in the hands of the Gentiles, many plain and precious parts and also many covenants would be taken away. This deliberate effort would be to "pervert the right ways of the Lord" and "blind the eyes and harden the hearts of the children of men." Nephi then beheld that this incomplete record, missing precious parts and the plainness it once had, would cause an "exceedingly great many [to] stumble."

The angel then revealed to Nephi God's plan to alleviate the stumbling: Jesus would manifest himself and minister to the seed of Nephi. The Nephites would write "many things" which would be "plain and precious," the record would be "hid up" and come forth unto the Gentiles by the gift and power of the Lamb. The second record (the Book of Mormon) would therefore restore plain and precious gospel truths which had been taken from the first record (the Bible) (1 Nephi 13:24–40).

Nephi's revelation has significant application for Latter-day Saints. *Failure to incorporate the gospel plainness of the Book of Mormon into New Testament study is failure to understand one of the central purposes of the book's existence.*

It would be impossible within the scope of this paper to explore all the doctrinal contributions and insightful expansions available to those who read the New Testament by the light of the Book of Mormon. The intent, therefore, is to explore three areas which demonstrate the power of combining these two testaments.

First, we will compare and contrast a study of the gospel with and without Book of Mormon commentary.

Second, we will show, through selected examples, the corrective and explanatory contribution the Book of Mormon makes on various doctrines and issues, some of which are only briefly referred to in the New Testament.

Third, we will show how the Book of Mormon combines with the New Testament to confound false doctrine.

I. A Study of Gospel Doctrine with Book of Mormon Support

First, and most important, the Bible and the Book of Mormon are testaments of Jesus Christ and the gospel he preached. The first four books of the New Testament bear the descriptive introduction: "The Gospel According to . . ." The word *gospel* is not defined in the New Testament in any detail. The resurrected Christ appeared to his Nephite disciples and in conversation with them gave us one of the most definitive statements concerning the gospel in all scripture.

> Behold I have given unto you my gospel, and this is the gospel which I have given unto you—that I came into the world to do the will of my Father, because my Father sent me.
>
> And my Father sent me that I might be lifted up upon the cross; and after that I had been lifted up upon the cross, that I might draw all men unto me, that as I have been lifted up by men even so should men be lifted up by the Father, to stand before me, to be judged of their works, whether they be good or whether they be evil. (3 Nephi 27:13–18)

According to Jesus, then, the foremost elements of his gospel center in his redemptive mission in rescuing mankind from both spiritual and temporal death. The Atonement, enabling repentance, remission of sin, resurrections, and universal judgment, constitutes the core of gospel truths. As stated, parts of that core were eliminated.

In making a search from the Gospel of Matthew to the book of Revelation, one can find sixty-two passages that make *direct* reference to Jesus' sacrifice for the remission of sins. Of the sixty-two passages, fifty-six refer to the Atonement or the effects of the Atonement but are not sustained with definitive explanation. In other words, no scriptural passage precedes or follows to explain the doctrine. Combining the content of New Testament scripture related to redemption from sin, we learn that justification, sanctification, propitiation, intercession, reconciliation, and mediation come through Jesus Christ who offered himself, through the shedding of his blood, as a sacrifice for the sins of all those who believe.

In contrast, the Book of Mormon expands and defines doctrine and terminology which the New Testament briefly mentions. For example, while Paul referred to the intercessory role of Jesus in the offering of himself, Abinadi added that the Resurrection empowered Jesus to make intercession, in that he "ascended into heaven, having the bowels of mercy; . . . standing betwixt them and justice; having broken the bands of death, taken upon himself their iniquity and their transgressions, having redeemed them, and satisfied the demands of justice" (Mosiah 15:9).

While Paul stated that "Christ is the *end of the law* for righteousness to everyone that believeth" (Romans 10:4; italics added), Lehi explained that "by the law no flesh is justified." But the sacrifice of Christ answered the *"ends of the law,"* efficacious only for "those who have a broken heart and a contrite spirit; and unto none else can the ends of the law be answered" (2 Nephi 2:5, 7; italics added).

With clarity unparalleled, King Benjamin added that "his blood atoneth for the sins of those who have fallen by the transgression of Adam, who have died not knowing the will of God concerning them, or who have ignorantly sinned" (Mosiah 3:11).

While Paul taught that men are justified by the blood of Christ, which will save them from wrath, Amulek explained the doctrine of justification by teaching that the intent of Jesus' sacrifice was to initiate a plan of mercy which would overpower justice and enable men to have faith and repent. The result of this, Amulek continued, is that mercy can satisfy justice and encircle the repentant person in the arms of safety (thus saving him from the wrath Paul mentioned), while he that exercises no faith unto repentance is exposed to the whole law of the demands of justice" (Alma 34:15–16; see Romans 5:9).

While the Apostle John spoke of Jesus as the propitiation for our sins, Alma defined *propitiation* by using the synonym *appease*: "And now, the plan of mercy could not be brought about except an atonement should be made; therefore God himself atoneth for the sins of the world, to bring about the plan of mercy to appease the demands of justice, that God might be a perfect, just God, and a merciful God also" (Alma 42:15; see 1 John 4:10).

Interestingly the word *justice* is not mentioned in the New Testament, and neither is the word *plan* indicating a plan of salvation.

Luke recorded that the Master sweat great drops of blood in Gethsemane (see Luke 22:44). King Benjamin added that the anguish that caused our Lord to bleed from every pore was due to his suffering for the wickedness and abominations of his people (see Mosiah 3:7). With only the New Testament as a guide, the Christian world looks predominantly to the cross for the remission of sins. The Latter-day Saints, knowing the words of King Benjamin and having a further witness of the Savior's suffering recorded in the Doctrine and Covenants, believes the suffering began in the Garden of Gethsemane and was consummated on the cross (3 Nephi 27:13, 14).

Paul recorded that death and sin entered the world through Adam, and life through Christ (see 1 Corinthians 15:16–22). Lehi, in one chapter, enumerated conditions before and after the Fall; the necessity of opposition; the wisdom of Adam's fall; the freedom of man to choose between two enticing forces; the role of Satan; and Jesus' role as the great Mediator (see 2 Nephi 2).

Can one understand the redemption of man without the true doctrine in relation to the Fall of man? Other than the doctrine that Adam's fall brought death and sin and Christ brought life, a study of the Atonement from the New Testament will be in isolation from the Fall. Interestingly, Lehi, Jacob, Abinadi, Alma, King Benjamin, Aaron, Amulek, and Ammon all either make reference to, or offer doctrine and explanation concerning, the Fall while teaching the Atonement.

The New Testament message on the Atonement is largely descriptive of his atoning mission but not descriptive of the atoning doctrine. The New Testament tells us that there *was* an atonement for sin; the Nephite record explains with clarity and depth *why* one was necessary.

The Book of Mormon passages quoted are not isolated verses but are references embedded in masterful discourses which tie the doctrines of salvation together into what Amulek terms "the great plan of the Eternal god" (Alma 34:9).

Contributions to Our Understanding of the Resurrection

The Atonement of Jesus Christ offers redemption from physical death through the Resurrection. There are 104 references to the Resurrection in the New Testament. Of the 104 references, 79 are in context with either prophecy before the Resurrection, apostolic witness after the Resurrection, or the storyline of the New Testament. Therefore, there are twenty-five references we look to for doctrinal explanation.

From these verses we learn the following: (1) Jesus would rise on the third day (John 2:19) with a body of flesh and bone (Luke 24:36–39); (2) his resurrection would bring the resurrection of all men (1 Corinthians 15:22); (3) Jesus was raised for our justification (Romans

4:25); (4) each will be resurrected in his own order (1 Corinthians 15:23); (5) Jesus' resurrection will bring the resurrection of the just and unjust (Acts 24:15); (6) just as the sun, moon, and stars differ in glory, so will the resurrected bodies of men (1 Corinthians 15:39–42); (7) the second death will have no power over those worthy to come forth in the first resurrection (Revelation 20:6); and (8) the Resurrection brings a lively hope (1 Peter 1:3).

Almost in every case the Book of Mormon acts as a second witness to the New Testament doctrine on the Resurrection and then goes beyond to offer additional insights. For example, if one wrote down all doctrine gleaned from the New Testament on the subject of resurrection, one could then add the following information from the Book of Mormon: Details concerning the resurrection of the just and the unjust (2 Nephi 9:10–19); the fate of the spirit were it not for an infinite atonement (2 Nephi 9:7–9); a definition of the resurrection of damnation (Mosiah 16:11); specific qualifications to achieve the first resurrection (Mosiah 15:21–24, 18:9); the necessary relationship of resurrection to universal judgment (3 Nephi 27:13–18); information on the space of time between death and resurrection (Alma 40); the inseparability of the spirit from the body after resurrection (Alma 11:45); and a clear definition of what resurrection is (Alma 11:44; 40:23).

The Universal Judgment

Having discussed redemption from sin and death we now come to our third element of gospel study—the universal judgment.

From New Testament passages we learn that God will judge all men through Jesus Christ (John 5:22; Romans 2:16); according to their works (Revelation 22:12); on the appointed day (Acts 17:31); when every knee shall bow and tongue confess to God (Romans 14:11). Those who are worthy to be on the right hand of God will have right to the tree of life; they can enter the Holy City (Revelation 22:14) and can sit down on the throne of Christ (Revelation 3:21). Those found on his left hand will depart into a lake of unquenchable fire to be tormented day and night forever and ever (Revelation 20:10), which is the second death (Revelation 20:14).

Here the Book of Mormon again offers significant insight regarding a central gospel doctrine. Information unique to the Book of Mormon includes what the souls of men will confess at the judgment bar (Mosiah

16:1, 27:31); the fact that we will be judged not only according to our works but also according to the desires of our hearts (Alma 41:3, 5); that mankind will be judged from scriptural records (2 Nephi 29:11); a definitive statement concerning the second death (Alma 12:16–18); and that hell *is as* a lake of fire and brimstone, in that the unjust are "consigned to an awful view of their own guilt, which doth cause them to shrink into a *state* of misery and endless torment, from whence they can no more return" (Mosiah 3:24, 27; italics added).

The purpose of this comparison is not to cast any disfavor upon the New Testament but to show how the records can and should work in concert. Ezekiel prophesied that the stick of Judah and the stick of Joseph are to become one (Ezekiel 37:15–19). We have seen them become one under one cover with one footnoting system in our new editions of the scriptures. The challenge now is to use them as one. Nephi was told by an angel that "the words of the Lamb shall be made known in the records of thy seed, as well as in the records of the Twelve Apostles of the Lamb; wherefore they both shall be established in one; for there is one God and one Shepherd over all the earth" (1 Nephi 13:41).

The two testaments of Christ complement each other. The messages and sermons were given to different audiences for differing reasons, thus the varying content. Elder Neal A. Maxwell said: "Imagine, for a moment, where we would be without the New Testament's matchless portrait of the Savior. . . . Granted, much doctrinal fulness came later in 'other books' . . . but it remains for the New Testament to provide the portrait of the mortal Messiah." Elder Maxwell then went on to say: "Wonderful as the New Testament is, it is even stronger when it is joined with the other books of scriptures."[4]

Occasionally at lectures or forums, time is given at the end for questions and answers. Often during these sessions and dialogues the most significant learning takes place. Here explanations are given, elaborations are made, and terms are defined. The New Testament constitutes some of the greatest literature known to our world, yet with the myriad of misinterpretation and brevity on important subjects a question-and-answer period which elaborates concepts and defines terms would be of significant worth. The Bible contains many doctrinal statements that are pronounced, but no sustained with further discussion. The Book of Mormon comes to support the Bible by providing the sustained discussion, as would a question-and-answer period.

DENNIS LARGEY

For example:

> And Zeezrom began to inquire of them diligently, that he might know more concerning the kingdom of God. And he said unto Alma: *What does this mean* which Amulek hath spoken concerning the resurrection of the dead, that all shall rise from the dead, both the just and the unjust, . . . to stand before God to be judged according to their works? (Alma 12:8; italics added)

Alma then gave not only a description of the elements of judgment, but a chronological order of events (see Alma 12:9–37).

Consider the depth of the doctrine Abinadi offered the questioning priests of Noah, recorded in Mosiah 12–17. Amulek sought to answer the Zoramites' question, "whether the truth be in Christ," and by so doing restored plain and precious truth (see Alma 34). Alma's answers to the concerns of his wayward son Corianton makes available information on the spirit world, the law of restoration, and the interaction between the justice of God and the plan of mercy that are unrivaled for clarity and plainness of language (see Alma 40–42).

Perhaps Mormon, aware of the Savior's definition of the gospel (3 Nephi 27:13–18), and knowing the stumbling that would take place as plain and precious parts of the gospel were extracted by the great and abominable church (1 Nephi 13), searched the records available to him and then incorporated into his abridgment sermons that taught the gospel so plainly that no one could possibly err.

Alma invited his Zoramite listeners to:

> cast about [their] eyes and begin to believe in the Son of God, that he will come to redeem his people, and that he shall suffer and die to atone for their sins; and that he shall rise again from the dead, which shall bring to pass the resurrection, that all men shall stand before him, to be judged at the last day according to their works.
>
> And now, my brethren, I desire that ye shall plant this word in your hearts, and as it beginneth to swell even so nourish it by your faith. (Alma 33:22–23)

The seed, identified by Alma as the redemptive act of Jesus Christ, permeates the pages of the Book of Mormon. It was an intentional act by the great and abominable church to take out plain and precious gospel truths (see 1 Nephi 13:27) and it was an intentional act to replace them through the Nephite record (see 1 Nephi 13:35).

54

II. Additional Areas of Helpful Commentary

Example 1: The Book of Mormon offers interpretive commentary on New Testament passages.

When Jesus came to John the Baptist to be baptized, "John forbade him, saying, I have need to be baptized of thee. . . . Jesus answering said unto him, "Suffer it to be so now: for thus it becometh us to fulfill all righteousness" (Matthew 3:14–15). The New Testament student might be left puzzled inasmuch as there is no explanation offered as to what it means to fulfill all righteousness.

The prophet Nephi was blessed with a vision of the ministry of Christ. In the vision he was shown the prophet that would baptize the Savior. Years later, in one of his final sermons, Nephi discussed the baptism of Jesus and taught his people the meaning of Jesus' words to John:

> And now, if the Lamb of God, he being holy, should have need to be baptized by water, to fulfil all righteousness, O then, how much more need have we, being unholy, to be baptized, yea, even by water!
>
> And now, I would ask you, my beloved brethren, wherein the Lamb of God did fulfil all righteousness in being baptized by water?
>
> Know ye not that he was holy? But notwithstanding he being holy, he showeth unto the children of men that, according to the flesh he humbleth himself before the Father and witnesseth unto the Father that he would be obedient unto him in keeping his commandments. . . .
>
> And again, it showeth unto the children of men the straightness of the path, and the narrowness of the gate, by which they should enter, he having set the example before them. (2 Nephi 31:5–7, 9)

Example 2: The Book of Mormon restores words and phrases lost to the New Testament text.

Matthew 5–7 contains one of the most powerful sermons ever given—the Sermon on the Mount. Jesus repeated many of the same teachings to his people in the Americas. In comparing discourses, the Book of Mormon account contains additions which clarify to whom Jesus was speaking as he taught various segments of his sermon. The Beatitudes were for those who would come to Christ. To "blessed are the poor in spirit," the Book of Mormon adds, *who come unto me,* for theirs is the kingdom of heaven" (Matthew 5:3; 3 Nephi 12:3; italics added). In the New Testament the clarifying phrase "who come unto me" is omitted. It is not a blessed condition to be poor in spirit, as the Matthew account portrays; however, if one finds oneself poor in spirit, and as a solution to that condition comes to Christ, as the Book of Mormon suggests, his is the kingdom of God.

The Matthew account has Jesus telling the multitude to take no thought for their physical provisions. This seems in conflict with good sense and not in harmony with other words of the Master. In the Book of Mormon account we read that Jesus turned from the multitude, or the general audience, before he gave these particular instructions and "looked upon the Twelve whom he had chose" (3 Nephi 13:25). The meaning then becomes clear: those who were to devote themselves to full-time service, as the presiding Twelve, would have their daily needs taken care of by the Lord whom they served.

Example 3: The Book of Mormon expands upon doctrinal concepts briefly mentioned in the New Testament.

The Apostle Paul described himself as the apostle of the Gentiles (Romans 11:13). In his epistle to the Romans he referred to the Gentiles as being a wild olive tree, to be grafted into the natural tree (Israel), to partake of the root. He told the Gentile audience that the natural branches were broken off because of unbelief and warned them that since "God spared not the natural branches, take heed lest he also spare not the. . . . For I would not, brethren, that ye should be ignorant of this mystery, lest ye should be wise in your own conceits; that blindness in part is happened to Israel, until the *fulness* of the Gentiles be come in" (Romans 11:21, 25; italics added).

Here again there is no sustained discussion concerning his reference to the fulness of the Gentiles. By way of commentary, in 1 Nephi 15:7 we read: "And they [Laman and Lemuel] said: Behold, we cannot understand the words which our father hath spoken concerning the natural branches of the olive-tree, and also concerning the Gentiles." In reply, Nephi taught:

> Behold, I say unto you, that the house of Israel was compared unto an olive tree, by the Spirit of the Lord which was in our father; and behold are we not broken off from the house of Israel?
> And now, the thing which our father meaneth concerning the

grafting in of the natural branches through the *fulness of the Gentiles*, is, that in the latter days, when our seed shall have dwindled in unbelief, yea, for the space of many years, and many generations after the Messiah shall be manifested in body unto the children of men, then shall the fulness of the gospel of the Messiah come unto the Gentiles, and from the Gentiles unto the remnant of our seed. (1 Nephi 15:12–13; italics added)

Here Nephi not only answered his brothers' questions, but also gave the New Testament student a definitive statement of interpretation to Paul's references. In the latter days, the fulness of the gospel would come to the Gentiles, and the Gentiles would then take it to the house of Israel. This would cure the blindness, for as Nephi further taught, "They shall be brought out of obscurity and out of darkness; and they shall know that the Lord is the Savior and their Redeemer, the mighty One of Israel" (1 Nephi 22:12).

While the New Testament refers to the house of Israel and the Gentiles, the Book of Mormon restores the importance of the genealogical distinctions and shows their interrelationship in the gospel plan. For example, the Book of Mormon uses the term *gentile* 110 times. Sixty-four percent of the time the context of the passage concerns Gentiles living at or after the time of Restoration. Chief among the latter-day Gentiles was to be a man who would be named after Joseph of old (see 2 Nephi 3:15). Joseph Smith opened the dispensation of which Paul spoke to the Ephesians: "In the dispensation of the fulness of times he [will] gather together in one all things in Christ, both which are in heaven and which are on earth; even in him" (Ephesians 1:10).

Through the instrumentality of Joseph Smith the gospel is restored, Israel is gathering to Christ, and the New Testament is being adopted, or grafted in to the natural tree. Thus the Book of Mormon shows continuity in God's plan, connecting dispensations, proving to the world that he is active in its behalf, for he is the same God yesterday, today, and forever.

Example 4: The Book of Mormon serves as a corrective lens in reading difficult passages.

A good example of how the Book of Mormon helps in understanding difficult passages can be seen from a passage in Hebrews:

For this Melchizedek, king of Salem, priest of the most high

God, who met Abraham returning from the slaughter of the kings, and blessed him;

To whom also Abraham gave a tenth part of all; first being by interpretation King of righteousness, and after that also King of Salem, which is, King of peace;

Without father, without mother, without descent, having neither beginning of days, nor end of life; but made like unto the Son of God; abideth a priest continually. (Hebrews 7:1–3)

Here we are left with the impression that there was a man, a king, with no father, mother, genealogy, beginning, or end. In Alma 13, we have an expanded discourse on Melchizedek and the clarification that Paul was not referring to a man but to the high priesthood: "This high priesthood being after the order of his Son, which order was from the foundation of the world; or in other words, *being without beginning of days or end of years*, being prepared from eternity to all eternity, according to his foreknowledge of all things" (Alma 13:7; italics added).

Example 5: The Book of Mormon contributes key insights concerning the Jews who crucified Christ as well as the spiritual destiny of the Jewish nations.

The Nephite prophets offer us insights into the character of those who crucified their king. Nephi said: "The world, because of their iniquity, will judge him a thing of naught." Jacob taught that it was expedient that Christ come among the Jews, among those who are the more wicked part of the world, and "there is none other nation on earth that would crucify their God." Priestcraft and iniquity would be the causal factors, that they at Jerusalem would "stiffen their necks . . . that he be crucified." King Benjamin added, "They shall consider him a man, and say he hath a devil, and shall scourge him, and shall crucify him" (1 Nephi 19:9; 2 Nephi 10:3–5; Mosiah 3:9).

Nephi prophesied that, because the Jews would turn their hearts aside, they would "become a hiss and a by-word, and be hated among all nations" (1 Nephi 19:14–16). The cure would be to turn their hearts back to their Messiah and then would the covenant the Holy One made with Israel be remembered, that is, that all the people of the House of Israel would be gathered in.

How Would Judah Return to Christ?

After giving the parable of the wicked husbandmen, Jesus alluded to Psalms (18:22–23) as an interpretation for his listeners—which consisted of the chief priests and scribes: "The stone which the builders rejected, the same is become the head of the corner. Whosoever shall fall upon that stone shall be broken; but on whosoever it shall fall, it will grind him to powder." After he quoted this prophecy, the chief priests and scribes "sought to lay hands on him" (Luke 20:17–19). They supposed that the parable had been spoken against them.

The Book of Mormon prophet Jacob also quoted these verses and related them to the Jews:

> And now I, Jacob, am led on by the Spirit unto prophesying; for I perceive by the workings of the Spirit which is in me, that by the stumbling of the Jews they will reject the stone upon which they might build and have safe foundation.
>
> But behold, according to the scriptures, this stone shall become the great, and the last, and the only foundation, upon which the Jews can build.
>
> And now my beloved, *how is it possible that these,* after having rejected the sure foundation, can ever build upon it, that it may become the head of their corner? (Jacob 4:15–17; italics added)

In answering the question (how the Jews will return to Christ after rejecting him), Jacob restored to us the allegory of the ancient prophet Zenos. The allegory not only concerns itself with the Jewish remnant, but portrays God's dealings with all the house of Israel in gathering them after apostasy (see Jacob 5:1–77).

The Book of Mormon provides commentary on Judah's past and future. The Savior stated: "The fulness of my gospel shall be preached unto them; And they shall believe in me, that I am Jesus Christ, the Son of God, and shall pray unto the Father in my name" (3 Nephi 20:30–31).

III. The Book of Mormon Confounds False Doctrine

The last item in this examination is yet another role the Book of Mormon plays. Joseph Smith, in his search for a true church, resorted to the admonition of James, "to ask God" (James 1:5), because the ministers of his area "understood the same passages of scripture so differently as to destroy [his] confidence in settling the question by an appeal to the Bible" (Joseph Smith—History 1:12). Without additional light, gospel truths taught in the New Testament were intermingled with the precepts of men, doctrines differed, priests contended, and confusion reigned.

Lehi, in blessing his son Joseph, restored to us a prophecy made by his progenitor Joseph who was sold into Egypt: "Wherefore, the fruit of thy loins shall write; and the fruit of the loins of Judah shall write; and that which shall be written by the fruit of the loins of Judah, shall grow together, unto the confounding of false doctrines" (2 Nephi 3:12). It was to be the combined effort of two records that would counteract the wresting of scripture.

Undoubtedly Mormon's reading of the small plates influenced his abridgment of the large plates. He would have known the prophetic commission of combining testaments to confound false doctrine. He would also have read Nephi's vision where Nephi beheld that the record that would proceed forth from the mouth of a Jew had been altered from its purity, causing confusion among the Gentiles (see 1 Nephi 13:29).

How would he fulfill his responsibility, so that the last record (the Book of Mormon) would powerfully establish the truth of the first record (the Bible), confound false doctrine, and restore what was lost? Within the enormous library of plates, of which Mormon states he could not write "a hundredth part" (Words of Mormon 1:5), how would he know what was needed or what to include? A statement made by his son Moroni indicates a principle upon which Book of Mormon abridgers must surely have relief in their selection process. After describing the corruption of latter-day churches, Moroni spoke directly to his latter-day audience: "Behold, I speak unto you as if ye were present, and yet ye are not. But behold, Jesus Christ hath shown you unto me, and I know your doing" (Mormon 8:35).

The implication is that those responsible for the major work of compilation saw our day and, thus aided, selected what was needed, based upon what they saw. With this thought in mind, it is interesting to ask ourselves why certain parts of the Book of Mormon were included. For example, why would the abridger give us Alma 31, a story about an apostate people who would go to a particular spot once a week to offer up a repetitive creedal prayer which proclaimed God to be a spirit forever? The Zoramites believed they were "elected" to be saved, while others were "elected" to be damned. The belief in predestination to heaven or hell by the Zoramites predates Calvin and exposes this belief as a doctrine of the devil.

Through story, prophecy, and sermon, the Book of Mormon denounces paid clergy (Alma 1:3, 20:2; Nephi 26:31); infant baptism (Moroni 8); systems of religion that deny miracles, revelation, and prophecy (2 Nephi 28:4–6; 3 Nephi 29:5–6); systems that preach salvation based exclusively upon the law (Mosiah 13:27–37); being saved by grace alone (2 Nephi 25:23); and the philosophy that mercy can rob justice (2 Nephi 28:7–8). The Book of Mormon also denounces religion that restricts God to a single book of scripture (2 Nephi 29).

Summary

Numerous additional points could be made. Paul spoke of charity (1 Corinthians 13); Mormon gave us a formula on how to obtain it (Moroni 7, 8). John saw the New Jerusalem and described it (Revelation 21); Ether and Jesus told us where it would be built and who would build it (3 Nephi 21; Ether 13). While the New Testament tells of an apostle who would tarry until Jesus returns in his glory (John 21:20–23); the Book of Mormon contains a whole chapter on the nature of translated beings (3 Nephi 28). Again this information comes to us as an answer to a question. Mormon inquired of the Lord, the Lord responded, and Mormon recorded the answer for all to be enlightened. While Paul taught about election and predestination, doctrines which cause many to stumble (Romans 8–9), Alma taught that men were "called and prepared from the foundation of the world according to the foreknowledge of God, on account of their exceeding faith and good works; in the first place being left to choose good or evil; therefore they having chosen good, and exercising exceedingly great faith, are called with a holy calling" (Alma 13:3).

In Acts 8, we read about Philip and his meeting with the eunuch. The Ethiopian was sitting in his chariot reading the book of Isaiah. The Spirit told Philip to approach him and Philip responded by running to the chariot. As he heard the man read from the book of Isaiah, he asked: "Understandest thou what thou readest?" The eunuch answered, "How can I, except some man should guide me?" (Acts 8:29–31).

He then asked Philip to join him. The particular passage was from Isaiah 53: "He was led as a sheep to the slaughter; and like a lamb dumb before his shearer, so opened he not his mouth: In his humiliation his judgment was taken away: and who shall declare his generation? for his life is taken from the earth. . . . Then Philip opened his mouth, and began at the same scripture and preached unto him Jesus" (Acts 8:32–35).

The dialogue between Philip and the eunuch ended at this point. Philip identified the suffering servant as Jesus, but what else he said concerning this precious chapter is not told us. In Mosiah 14, Abinadi, in defense of his preaching concerning the condescension of God, quoted the entire fifty-third chapter of Isaiah to the wicked priests. The next chapter Abinadi devoted to the interpretation of his quote. In his commentary he revealed who constitutes the seed of Jesus Christ, and who it is that will declare his generation (Mosiah 15:10–13).

In short, as Philip in this story was to the eunuch, the Book of Mormon prophets are to us. We have a host of men to guide us in the interpretation of the sacred scripture.

To the reader of the New Testament aided by the Book of Mormon, the gospel drama unfolds prior to Matthew's declaration of the genealogy of Jesus. In approximately 550 BC, Nephi taught the doctrine of Christ and proclaimed his name as the only name whereby man can be saved (2 Nephi 31:21). During the year 124 BC, King Benjamin gave his people a new name, the name of Jesus Christ (Mosiah 5:8–12). Jesus is the God of Israel; his doctrine was taught before his birth. The characters in the messianic drama were known hundreds of years before their mortal births. King Benjamin taught that the Creator of all things would be called Jesus Christ, and his mother's name would be Mary (Mosiah 3:8). Nephi was told by an angel not to write a portion of his vision concerning the end of the world, because that stewardship belonged to an apostle whose name would be John (1 Nephi 14:18–22, 24–25, 27).

The story of Jesus is a two-continent story. He is actively concerned with both areas of the world, for as Mary and Joseph were making preparations for the advent of Jesus' birth in the manger at Bethlehem, Jesus was speaking to Nephi, giving comfort and instruction: "Lift up your head, and be of good cheer . . . on the morrow come I into the world, to show unto the world that I will fulfill all that which I have caused to be spoken by the mouth of my holy prophets" (3 Nephi 1:13).

The Lord said to Nephi: "I speak the same words unto one nation like unto another. And when the two nations shall run together the testimony of the two nations shall run together also" (2 Nephi 29:8).

In view of what has been presented, the following suggestions are made concerning study of the New Testament in conjunction with the Book of Mormon.

First, we should seek to fulfill President Ezra Taft Benson's directive and know the Book of Mormon better than any other text. If we do so, we will always have available to us the magnifying and corrective lens of the Book of Mormon as we read the Bible. Many of the plain and precious parts of the biblical text have been restored. However, that restoration is of no effect unless we personally restore those precious truths in our own study. Perhaps the command and understanding Joseph Smith had of the Bible can be attributed to the fact that he *first* translated the Book of Mormon.

Second, when reading and studying a particular standard work, either personally or in one of our church classes, we should incorporate the contribution of the other standard works where appropriate. The depth of our knowledge comes from the depth of our witness. With the Book of Mormon, the Doctrine and Covenants, and the Pearl of Great Price we are three-deep in backup testimony and clarification when studying the Bible. As teachers of the New Testament we keep waiting witnesses on the wings of our teaching stage to strengthen the concepts presented. Thus, the 500 who saw Jesus after his resurrection in the old world (1 Corinthians 15:4) are joined with 2,500 who saw, heard, and touched the Master in the land Bountiful (3 Nephi 11). The raising of Tabitha by Peter (Acts 9:40) is joined by the raising of Timothy by Nephi (3 Nephi 19:4), and so forth. Is it not common in the work of the Lord to call forth as many witnesses as one can to prove the truth of a righteous claim? Witnesses express themselves differently, even though they are speaking about the same events. Some have seen more, or were present longer, or were present in a different capacity. The people in Ammonihah rejected and ridiculed Alma and his message, *but became astonished* at the words of Amulek, "seeing that there was *more than one witness* that testified of the things whereof they were accused" (Alma 10:12; italics added). It was the *second* witness that astonished the people.

Third, consider our Bible-believing brothers and sisters across the congregations of Christendom who have inherited the creeds and doctrines passed down over the centuries by those disadvantaged by the loss of revelation, prophets, and priesthood. Many doctrines of men have been incorporated with Jesus' teachings forming the various sects of our day. We should be ambassadors of the plain and precious parts of the gospel. By knowing how to use the Book of Mormon as a missionary tool, we can disperse the darkness of false doctrine and restore to our investigating friends precious truth not available from any other source.

Testimony

Many who know the gospel and then go inactive do not, for the most part, join other churches. Perhaps one reason is that scripturally they know too much. Stop and think how much understanding of the gospel comes from the Restoration. It would be difficult to listen to a sermon about Jesus' "other sheep," where the one preaching identifies the other sheep as Gentiles. It would be difficult indeed, especially knowing that the Savior visited the Nephites in America and personally said to them, "Ye are they of whom I said: Other sheep I have which are not of this fold; them also I must bring" (3 Nephi 15:21).

A relative of the writer once attended a Protestant service, where the minister made a most interesting statement in the course of his sermon. He said: "Adam fell that men might be, and men are that they might have joy" (2 Nephi 2:25). The member approached the minister afterward and said, "I'm interested in that quote you used." The minister asked, "Are you a Mormon?" "Yes, I am." The minister then took him to his office and took down a copy of the Book of Mormon from his bookshelf. He said, "There is a lot of good stuff in here! I just don't tell them where it comes from."

There *is* a lot of good "stuff" in the Book of Mormon, and Latter-day Saints are most fortunate to know where it comes from. Having God's gift of the Book of Mormon and knowing of its truthfulness bestows upon every member of the Church a responsibility, for, as Lehi said: "Wherefore, how great the importance to make these things known unto the inhabitants of the earth" (2 Nephi 2:8).

Notes

1. Ezra Taft Benson, "The Book of Mormon—Keystone of Our Religion," *Ensign,* November 1986, 4–7.
2. First Presidency Christmas Message, satellite broadcast, December 1986.
3. Joseph Smith. (Salt Lake City: Deseret Book, 1976), 327.
4. Neal A. Maxwell, "The New Testament—A Matchless Portrait of the Savior," *Ensign,* December 1986, 21–24.

CHAPTER FIVE

Isaiah As Taught By the New Testament Apostles

Victor L. Ludlow

This paper will study the various ways in which the New Testament writers, especially the apostles, presented the prophecies and pronouncements of Isaiah. The purpose will not be to study the doctrines in any great depth, but to analyze the approach, context, and application of Isaiah's writings as they are found in the New Testament.

Where Is Isaiah in the New Testament?

Frequent readers of the New Testament recall that there are occasional references to the prophet Isaiah (or *Esaias*, as he is usually referred to in the King James Translation), which usually highlight some prophecy that was fulfilled by Jesus of Nazareth. Maybe these readers were like me in assuming that most of the remembered references seemed to be in the Gospel account of Matthew, since he frequently demonstrated how Jesus became the fulfillment of Isaiah's messianic prophecies. However, we find that other apostles also quoted from Isaiah. The Apostle Paul did so most frequently, three times as often as Matthew.

There are at least seventy-one passages in the New Testament in which Isaiah is either quoted or expressly referred to as his teachings are cited or paraphrased. Except for the book of Psalms (with eighty-nine references), no other Old Testament book is quoted or referred to more times in the New Testament. For those who like to keep more careful track of such references, Isaiah is quoted or referred to ten times in Matthew; seven times in Mark; six times in Luke; four times in John; five times in Acts; sixteen times in Romans; nine times in 1 and 2 Corinthians; one time each in Galatians, Ephesians, Thessalonians, and Hebrews; six times in 1 Peter; and four times in Revelation. Looking at it from another direction, thirty-one of Isaiah's sixty-six chapters are quoted in the New Testament, ranging from one to sixty-six, with the heaviest concentration coming from chapters 6, 8, 28, 29, 40, 49, 52, and 53.

The Isaiah passage quoted most often in the New Testament books is Isaiah 6:9–10, which is found in the first six books—namely, Matthew 13:14–15, Mark 4:12, Luke 8:10, John 12:40, Acts 28:26–27, and Romans 11:8. This passage refers to the difficulty most people have who have heard the word of the Lord but still do not understand it.

The favorite chapter of the New Testament writers is an obvious one—Isaiah 53, which prophesies of the suffering servant or the Messiah and is referred to in Matthew 8:17, Mark 15:28, Luke 22:37, John 12:38, Acts 8:32–33, Romans 10:16, and 1 Peter 2:22–24. Another favorite Isaiah chapter is the fortieth, which talks about the power and glory of the Lord, especially in conjunction with the message of a forerunner preparing for his coming to a transformed earth with references in Matthew 3:3, Mark 1:3, Luke 3:4–6, John 1:23, Romans 11:34, 1 Corinthians 2:16, and 1 Peter 1:24–25.

As can be summarized from the references above, more than one-third of the Isaiah passages quoted in the New Testament come from just twenty-one verses: Isaiah 6:9–10; 40:3–8; 13 and 53:1–12. (For a full list of Isaiah passages in the New Testament, see "Quotations" on page 758 in the Bible Dictionary of the LDS version of the Bible.)

How Did Matthew Teach From Isaiah?

More passages from Isaiah are found in Matthew than in any other of the Gospel accounts. Six of the ten references from Isaiah in Matthew are also found in one or more of the other Gospels, and four of the Isaiah passages are unique to the writings of Matthew.

The favorite presentation used by Matthew as he quoted from Isaiah was: "That it might be fulfilled which was spoken by Esaias the prophet, saying . . ." He used this phrase to introduce verses from Isaiah, which he gave as evidence for the messianic calling of Jesus. This phrase is found with all four passages from Isaiah that Matthew quoted but are not found in any other of the Gospel accounts (Matthew 1:22–23; 4:14–16; 8:17; 12:17–21).

Two passages from Isaiah are found in all four Gospel accounts. The first, from Isaiah 40:3, refers to the voice of one crying in the wilderness, "Prepare ye the way of the Lord." This scripture applied to John the Baptist, who used it as he preached in the Judean wilderness near the Jordan River. It is interesting to note four different ways this scripture is used in the Gospel accounts as each writer applied it in a slightly different context. Matthew said that John was the person prophesied by Isaiah whose voice would cry in the wilderness (Matthew 3:3). Mark simply said that it was written in the prophets that a messenger would precede the Messiah, that the messenger's voice would cry in the wilderness, and that John did preach in the wilderness (Mark 1:3). Luke wrote that John was preaching in the country about Jordan, as it is written in Isaiah about the voice of one crying in the wilderness, and then quoted verses 3–5 (Luke 3:4–6). John noted that John the Baptist referred to himself as the voice crying in the wilderness as Isaiah had promised (John 1:23). In other words, Matthew used the Isaiah passages as a proof for John's calling; Mark roughly tied John and the Isaiah scripture together by association; Luke implied that John used the Isaiah prophecy in his teachings or at least was the embodiment of it; and John specifically stated that John the Baptist said he was the fulfillment of Isaiah's promise.

The other passage found in all four Gospel accounts comes from Isaiah 6:9–10, where it is promised that many who hear the word of the Lord will not understand it.

This passage is also applied in different contexts by the different writers. Matthew states that Jesus used the passage to tell his disciples why many could not perceive his message. According to Matthew, Jesus specifically referred to Isaiah and quoted the passage in great depth (Matthew 13:14–15). Mark and Luke are similar in that they paraphrase or briefly quote the Isaiah passage in the context of Jesus' talking to his disciples, but neither account mentions Isaiah as the earlier source of this teaching (Mark 4:12; Luke 8:10). John, on the other hand, uses the Isaiah ideas to back up his own explanation as to why many Jews could not understand Jesus and be converted. He does not mention that Jesus used these ideas but uses them to explain why many did not believe in Jesus (John 12:39–41).

There is one Isaiah passage found in the three synoptic Gospels, but not in John. The brief reference comes from the first half of Isaiah 56:7, which Jesus used to describe how the house of the Lord should be a house of prayer, but the moneychangers had made it into a den of thieves. The fact that this description comes from Isaiah is not even mentioned in any of the accounts (Matthew 21:13; Mark 11:17; Luke 19:46).

Three Isaiah passages found in Matthew are also found in one other Gospel account. Matthew and Luke both record how Jesus told the disciples of John the Baptist to return to their master and tell him how they had witnessed Jesus as he performed miracles among the blind, the lame, the leprous, the deaf, and the dead. In recounting these types of miracles, Jesus used promises from the prophecy found in Isaiah 35:6–7 (Matthew 11:5; Luke 7:22).

Matthew and Mark share the same concepts and context as they record how Jesus chastised the hypocrites by telling them that they were the fulfillment of the words of Isaiah 29:13, which is about how people would draw near to the Lord with their lips, but their hearts would be far from him (Matthew 15:8–9 and Mark 7:6–7).

Matthew and Mark also shared parallel accounts as they told of the teachings of Jesus concerning Jerusalem and the last days. Jesus borrowed some phrases from Isaiah 13:10 about the sun being darkened and the moon not giving her light as one of the signs of the times. Neither account gave any specific reference to Isaiah (Matthew 24:29; Mark 13:24).

In summarizing how Matthew used Isaiah in this teachings, one notes that he has more references from Isaiah than any other Gospel writer. Of the ten passages, four are distinct to Matthew's account, while the other six are also found in various other Gospel accounts. In his own distinct references to Isaiah, Matthew always specifically mentioned that he was using Isaiah and in the shared references Matthew was also more inclined to mention specifically that the quoted passages came from Isaiah. Thus he uses Isaiah as an authoritative source for his teachings as he bears witness of Jesus the Messiah.

How Was Isaiah Taught in the Other Gospel Accounts?

Although Mark and Luke were not apostles in Christ's early church, as far as we know, it is of value to see how they also taught from Isaiah. John the Apostle also has a few references to Isaiah in his Gospel account.

Mark and Luke share one brief Isaiah passage from chapter 53, verse 12, concerning Christ's being numbered among the transgressors, but they apply it in completely different contexts. Luke wrote that shortly before Gethsemane Jesus told the apostles that he must fulfill the prophecy that the Messiah, or suffering servant, must be reckoned among the transgressors, referring perhaps to the approaching atonement or intercession for the transgressors which Jesus would shortly suffer (Luke 22:37). Mark uses this same passage from Isaiah in describing events shortly after Jesus was placed upon the cross. He wrote that the prophecy was then fulfilled in that Jesus was crucified between two thieves, or in other words, "he was numbered with the transgressor" (Mark 15:28).

Mark makes reference to one Isaiah scripture which is not found in the other Gospel accounts. In chapter 9, starting with verse 43, Jesus taught about severing ourselves from those elements, even parts of our body, which might lead us to hell. He specifically referred to our hands, feet, and eyes. The basic teaching was that if our hand, foot, or eye should offend us and lead us to hell, then we should separate it from us. After each item is mentioned, Mark records Jesus' teaching that hell is "where their worm dieth not, and the fire is not quenched" (Mark 9:44, 46, 48). This quote echoes the very last verse in Isaiah, where he teaches that those who transgress against the Lord will be in a miserable state, "for their worm shall not die, neither shall their fire be quenched" (Isaiah 66:24). In his Inspired Version, Joseph Smith kept the first and last references but dropped the middle one (JST, Mark 9:41–48). Although Matthew also taught about separating oneself from evil hands, feet, and eyes, he did not include the specific phrase found in Isaiah 66:24 (Matthew 18:8–9). It is interesting that Mark not only includes it, but repeats it three times, and the whole teaching is found with more detail in his account (especially as recorded in the Joseph Smith Translation) than in Matthew. With the repeated use of the phrases found in Isaiah 66, it seems that this teaching episode was clearly impressed upon Mark so that he recorded it in more depth.

Luke also has one important quote from Isaiah not recorded in the other Gospel accounts. In chapter 4, verses 17–19, Luke states that Jesus began his public ministry in the Nazareth synagogue by quoting from the prophet Isaiah. We find the words Jesus quoted in Isaiah 61:1–2 which refer to a messianic calling. As Jesus applied this prophecy to himself, the townspeople wanted to cast him off the cliff. These words of Isaiah got Christ's ministry off to a rocky start. It is interesting to note that not all of verse two was quoted; Jesus did not mention that he was coming to proclaim the day of vengeance of our God or perhaps his reception may have been even more severe. Besides, his first coming was to bring redemption through an "acceptable year of the Lord," and the "day of vengeance of our God" would more closely combine with his second coming.

John also includes a couple of distinctive Isaiah passages in his writings which are not found in the other Gospel accounts. In John 6:45 he records that Jesus included an Isaianic teaching in the famous "bread of life" sermon. Without mentioning Isaiah by name, Jesus stated that it was written "in the prophets" that all people shall be taught of God. In Isaiah 54:13 we find the same specific concept.

In the twelfth chapter of John, John gave some detailed commentary on why many Jews did not accept Jesus and believe on him. He referred to two specific pronouncements found in Isaiah to explain this rejection. He first referred to Isaiah 53:1, which asks: Who would believe our report and to whom has the arm of the Lord been revealed? John says this scripture was fulfilled by those who saw the many miracles performed by Jesus, but still did not believe in him. John then referred to the passage in Isaiah 6:9–10 about how people's eyes and hearts would be blinded to the truth. John said that his saying of Isaiah also explained why many Jews did not believe in Jesus (John 12:38–41).

To summarize the use of Isaiah in the Gospel accounts of Mark, Luke, and John, we find that most of the passages are in the context of various teachings of Jesus, who used Isaiah as he taught. In the main, these quotations or references by Jesus are straightforward and to the point of supporting and verifying his teachings. However, John did use some Isaiah material to reinforce his commentary about the hard hearts of many people who listened to Jesus but did not accept him.

How Did Paul Teach from Isaiah?

More passages from Isaiah are found in the writings of Paul than in the records of any other New Testament writer. Of the 32 such references in the teachings of Paul, the heaviest concentration is found in Romans 9–11, three reference are in Acts, and the rest are scattered throughout his epistles.

In Antioch, Paul taught the Jews from the writings of Isaiah as he testified about the resurrection of Jesus and said that it was the "sure mercies of David" as promised by Isaiah 55:3. To the same audience

Paul also said that if they rejected him, then he, as a spokesman for the word of God, was also to be a "light of the Gentiles," as prophesied in Isaiah 49:6 (Acts 13:34, 47).

The last apostolic teachings recorded in Acts were the words of Paul in Rome as he commented on why many Jews in Rome did not believe his message. He used Isaiah 6:9–10 and said that his audience was a fulfillment of Isaiah's inspired words about people hearing but not understanding the word of God (Acts 28:26–27).

The most concentrated use of Isaiah in the New Testament is found in Paul's epistle to the Romans. After a couple of brief references from Isaiah (which were simply blended within the context of his teachings: Isaiah 52:5 in Romans 2:2, and Isaiah 59:7–8 in Romans 3:15–17), Paul started an extensive series of thirteen quotes from Isaiah starting with Romans 9:27 and continuing for the next two and one-half chapters. The chart below shows where the Isaiah passages are found:

Isaiah Passages in Romans   **Parts of Romans with Isaiah Quotes**

Isaiah 1:9	Romans 9:29	Romans 9:27–29	Isaiah 10:22–23
Isaiah 6:9–10	Romans 11:8	Romans 9:29	Isaiah 1:9
Isaiah 8:14	Romans 9:32–33	Romans 9:32–33	Isaiah 8:14, 28:16
Isaiah 10:22–23	Romans 9:27–28	Romans 10:11	Isaiah 28:16
Isaiah 27:9	Romans 11:27	Romans 10:15	Isaiah 52:7
Isaiah 28:16	Romans 9:33, 10:11	Romans 10:16	Isaiah 53:1
Isaiah 29:10	Romans 11:8	Romans 10:20–21	Isaiah 65:1–2
Isaiah 40:13	Romans 11:33–34	Romans 11:8	Isaiah 6:9–10, 29:10
Isaiah 52:7	Romans 10:15	Romans 11:26–27	Isaiah 59:20–21
Isaiah 53:1	Romans 10:16	Romans 11:27	Isaiah 27:9
Isaiah 29:20–21	Romans 11:26–27	Romans 11:33–34	Isaiah 40:13
Isaiah 65:1–2	Romans 10:20–21		

As can be seen from the chart above, Paul quoted from twelve different chapters of Isaiah in just two and one-half chapters of his own writings. A whole symposium presentation could be delivered using this material as a basis. Suffice it to say that Paul used these many and varied passages from Isaiah to back up his teachings to the Romans about how Israel had been chosen to receive the covenant blessing of the Lord, but she had forfeited them. These covenant opportunities and blessings were not being offered to the Gentiles and they could be heirs to them, depending upon their faith and righteousness. Indeed, the faithful Gentiles could be grafted into the house of Israel and the gospel would go preferentially to them until their time was fulfilled. These chapters contain a masterful discourse of Paul about the covenant relationship between the Lord and the house of Israel, including those righteous Gentiles who would become a covenant part of Israel. He used a number of other scriptures in this discourse, but half of them came from Isaiah.

Later in Romans, Paul quotes Isaiah three more times as he declares: (1) that everyone will come before Christ and know him (Isaiah 45:23 in Romans 14:11), (2) that Christ as the root of Jesse will reign over the Gentiles (Isaiah 11:10 in Romans 15:12), and (3) that people separated from the place and events of Christ's life could come to understand him and his gospel (Isaiah 52:15 in Romans 15:21).

In his epistle to the Corinthians, Paul uses nine scattered references from Isaiah, particularly at the beginning and end of his first epistle. Almost all these quotes are in sets of two each, as seen in chapters 1, 2, and 15 of 1 Corinthians and in chapter 6 of Corinthians. In 1 Corinthians 1:19–20, Paul quotes two Isaiah passages to illustrate that the wisdom of the world is foolishness before God, and what the world finds as foolish in the gospel is the true wisdom of God (Isaiah 29:14, 33:18).

Two Isaiah passages are in the second chapter also, and both of them illustrate that although the wisdom of the Lord is hard for mortals to comprehend, through the Spirit and mind of Christ, people can be instructed by God (Romans 2:9 and Isaiah 64:4; Romans 2:16 and Isaiah 4:13).

A lone Isaiah reference in 1 Corinthians 14:21 where Paul paraphrases Isaiah 28:11–12 tells of a stammering, foreign speaker not being understood even though the message was of great value. Paul applies this reference to the gift of tongues to reinforce his teaching that the gift of tongues is not as important as the gifts of faith and belief.

Two verses from Isaiah found in 1 Corinthians 15:32, 34, are also paraphrased by Paul. In teaching about the Resurrection, Paul compares his own spiritual readiness to face death with the attitude of "eat and drink for tomorrow we die" which Isaiah used to describe the people in Jerusalem (Isaiah 22:13). Later he promises that the sting of death will be swallowed in the victory of the Resurrection, borrowing some phraseology found in Isaiah 25:8.

The two Isaiah passages in 2 Corinthians are both in the sixth chapters. Paul uses Isaiah 49:8 and 52:11 to back up his invitation to the Gentiles to come out of the world and accept the salvation of Christ (2 Corinthians 6:2, 17).

Four single references from Isaiah are scattered in four other epistles of Paul. In Galatians 4:27 he uses Isaiah 54:1 to tell the Gentiles that they too are the children of promise even though they are not literal descendants of Israel. Continuing his theme of comforting the Gentiles, he uses Isaiah 57:19 in Ephesians 2:17 to tell those far from Jerusalem that the gospel message of peace is also to come to them through the Spirit of God. In 2 Thessalonians 2:8 Paul addresses a different theme as he borrows Isaiah 11:4 to promise that at the Second Coming the Lord will reveal and consume the wicked in the brightness of his coming. Finally, Paul uses one phrase from Isaiah 8:18 in his epistle to the Hebrews. In Hebrews 2:13 he testifies of his trust in Christ and those fellow Christians whom God had given to Christ as his children.

In summary of Paul's use of Isaiah, we find that he not only used passages from all parts of Isaiah's writings, but he also varied from paraphrasing to using specific, exact quotations. His scripture quotations were often bunched together, so we usually find clusters of Isaiah references in the same chapter. Most of his emphasis was upon the covenant relationship between people and the Lord. He used Isaiah to illustrate both why Israel forfeited her role as the chosen people and why the Gentiles had a spiritual right to the blessings promised to Israel. He also applied Isaiah passages to teachings about the Atonement, the Resurrection of Christ, and some key events surrounding his later Second Coming. In short, Paul found wide and varied applications of Isaiah in his writings.

How Did Peter Teach From Isaiah?

In the few brief writings of Peter, we find some important applications of some prophecies of Isaiah. He concludes what we now have as chapter 1 of his writings with a poetic description of man's temporary, transitory nature which he undoubtedly borrowed from Isaiah 40:6–8 (1 Peter 1:24–25).

Peter's most important and numerous references from Isaiah are found in the second chapter of his first epistle. As he testifies of Jesus Christ as the chief cornerstone of the gospel, he quotes from the scriptures, and particularly from Isaiah 28:16, which is mentioned twice (1 Peter 2:6, 8). At the end of this chapter, Peter testifies about the purity of Christ and his atoning sacrifice as he borrows important phraseology from Isaiah 53 (1 Peter 2:22–24).

One last possible but weak reference from Isaiah is found in the third chapter of the same first epistle. At best, this passage might be a loose paraphrase from Isaiah 8:12–13, where Judah was commanded to be brave and to sanctify the Lord. In 1 Peter 3:14–15, Peter tells the early Saints to not be afraid but to sanctify the Lord in their hearts.

In brief summary, Peter basically uses the pronouncements of Isaiah to reinforce his testimony about Jesus as the chief cornerstone and as the pure sacrifice for sin.

How Much of Isaiah Is Found in Revelation?

Actually, surprisingly little of Isaiah is found in direct reference in the writings of John the Revelator. Only four specific references seem to come from the writings of Isaiah. One passage from Isaiah 44:6–7, where the Lord of Israel states that he is the first and the last, is clearly echoed in Revelation 1:17–18 and 2:8. Indeed, the combination of three scriptures from Isaiah in Revelation reinforces the doctrine that the Lord of Israel and of the Old Testament is also the Christ and Lord of the New Testament.

Another specific Isaiah passage is found in the third chapter of Revelation, where the keys of David are mentioned as a symbol of the power and authority of Christ (compare Revelation 3:7 with Isaiah 22:22). The last clear Isaiah reference is from Isaiah 49:10, where the righteous are promised that they will neither hunger or thirst as they will be protected from the sun and heat. This same promise is found in Revelation 7:16 where those before the throne of God are given the same blessing.

Although one does not find a number of specific quotations from Isaiah, thoughtful readers of the Bible sense that major portions of John's revelations from his grand visions are similar to Isaiah's apocalyptic visions. It is as though they both have seen the same events in the last days but each had drawn from the vision and recorded those perspectives which they felt to be the most distinctive and valuable. I feel particularly this way as I read chapters 24–27 of Isaiah and compare his insights with those of John in Revelation 6–9, or Isaiah 6 with Revelation 5, Isaiah 51 with Revelation 11, and so on.

How Did the Apostles Differ in Their Use of Isaiah's Writings?

Matthew and Peter quote specifically from Isaiah to support their declarations that Jesus is the Messiah. Paul inserts Isaiah as a subtle reinforcement to his teachings about the covenant relationship of the house of Israel. John uses Isaiah to reinforce his testimony and commentary about Jesus in his Gospel account. Then, in his book of Revelation, he duplicates Isaiah's perspective because he seems to have seen the same or similar visions and thus repeats some of what is in Isaiah's apocalyptic writings. Thus we have a progression from a "Bible bash" scriptural foundation to a "reinforced teaching" approach to a "shared vision" concept of relating the pronouncements of Isaiah to their own contemporary teaching situations. What does this mean for us today?

How Can We Use Isaiah Today?

The apostolic teachings from Isaiah in the Gospel accounts often were simply a reflection of Jesus using the Isaiah material in his teachings. However, some writers, especially Matthew, specifically note that Isaiah was being quoted whereas others would simply quote or paraphrase the Isaiah material in the general context of Jesus' teachings.

There is no general, uniform pattern with which the apostles used Isaiah in their teachings. I looked for such a pattern, but instead I found diversity. Maybe this means that each of us has to approach and use Isaiah from the framework of our own background and adapt his teachings in the context of our own personality for the purposes of the particular teaching situation, as inspired by the Holy Spirit. It appears, from the example of the ancient apostles as recorded in the New Testament, that we are allowed a fair amount of flexibility in our use and application of the profound writings of the ancient prophet Isaiah.

The classical example of using Isaiah in a flexible teaching situation is found in the New Testament, but it has not been mentioned earlier because it did not involve one of the apostles. The episode is found in Acts, chapter 8, where the evangelist Philip was inspired to ask the visiting dignitary from Ethiopia if he understood the teachings from Isaiah which the Ethiopian was reading. Using Isaiah 53 as the foundation, Philip taught him from the scriptures, and the Ethiopian was baptized later that same day. I guess one never knows when a good teaching situation will arise where the teachings of Isaiah will help convert someone, so all students of the scriptures need to study his profound writings an have them available to teach and help others.

Chapter Six

We Have Found the Messiah, Which Is the Christ

Robert J. Matthews

The purpose of scripture is to bear witness of Christ. Jesus challenged even his detractors to "search the scriptures; for . . . they are they which testify of *me*" (John 5:39). We have done some of that searching in this book.

I have selected as a topic a passage from the testimony of John. They are the words of Andrew, Simon Peter's brother. On that day he had talked with Jesus, and he was so excited that the first thing he did was find his brother Peter to tell him about it. He said: "We have *found* the Messias, which is, being interpreted, the Christ" (John 1:41; italics added).

Although the passage does not tell in detail of the background and what these men had talked about previously, there is a clue in the way the sentence is worded to show us that finding the Messiah was important to them and must have been something they had talked about on earlier occasions.

To get the full impact of what it meant to them to "find the Messiah," we need to look at the extended passage. In order to catch the force of these words, please notice the frequency of such words as *seek, findeth, come and see,* and *we have found.* I will quote from Joseph Smith's translation because it is a richer account. The setting is this: John the Baptist had taught a special delegation of the Jewish leaders that the Messiah was on the earth, among them, but that they had not recognized him. Beginning with John 1:35, we read:

> Again, the next day after, John stood, and two of his disciples,
>
> And looking upon Jesus as he walked, he said; Behold the Lamb of God!
>
> And the two disciples heard him speak, and they followed Jesus.
>
> Then Jesus turned, and saw them following, and saith unto them, What seek ye? They said unto him, Rabbi (which is to say, being interpreted, Master); Where dwellest thou?
>
> He said unto them, Come and see. They came and saw where he dwelt, and abode with him that day; for it was about the tenth hour.
>
> One of the two who heard John, and followed Jesus, was Andrew, Simon Peter's brother.
>
> He first findeth his own brother Simon, and saith unto him, We have found the Messias, which is, being interpreted, the Christ.
>
> And he brought him to Jesus. And when Jesus beheld him, he said, Thou art Simon, the son of Jonas, thou shalt be called Cephas, which is, by interpretation, a seer, or a stone. And they were fishermen. And they straightway left all, and followed Jesus.
>
> The day following, Jesus would go forth into Galilee, and findeth Philip, and saith unto him, Follow me.
>
> Now Philip was at Bethsaida, the city of Andrew and Peter.
>
> Philip findeth Nathanael, and saith unto him, We have found him, or whom Moses in the law, and the prophets, did write, Jesus of Nazareth, the son of Joseph. (JST, John 1:3–45)

There is an underlying awareness, almost taken for granted, that all these brethren were cognizant of the things Moses and the prophets had written about the Messiah. They placed a high value on those words of the prophets and considered it of greatest importance to find that Messiah who was so highly spoken of in the scriptures. Notice the joy, the sense of fulfillment, when a person is able to say, "We have found the Messiah."

The discovery by these brethren, Andrew, Simon, Philip, and Nathanael reminds us of the words of the Lord to Jeremiah:

> Then shall ye call upon me, and ye shall go and pray unto me, and I will hearken unto you.
>
> And ye shall seek me, and find me, when ye shall search for me with all your heart.
>
> And I will be found of you, saith the Lord. (Jeremiah 29:12–14)

This same idea has perhaps become more familiar to many of us through Felix Mendelssohn's oratorio "Elijah," in which it is beautifully expressed this way: "If with all your heart ye truly seek me, ye shall ever surely find me, thus saith our God."

In the writings of Moses to scattered Israel, we find this promise:

> But if from thence thou shalt seek the Lord thy God, thou shalt find him, if thou seek him with all thy heart and with all thy soul. (Deuteronomy 4:29)

And Father Abraham, after a marvelous personal manifestation and blessing from the Lord, reflected on his great experience and wrote of it as follows:

> Now, after the Lord had withdrawn from speaking to me, and withdrawn his face from me, I said in mine heart: Thy servant has sought thee earnestly; now I have found thee; . . . and I will do well to hearken unto thy voice. (Abraham 2:12–13)

Let it be remembered and noted that his Messiah, this Jesus whom the fishermen of Galilee had found in *their* day and in *their* country, was the same being, the same God, whom Moses, Abraham, Elijah, Isaiah, Jeremiah, and many others had sought for and found in their day, whose name was Jehovah. Jesus, the Messiah in the New Testament, is the same being known as Jehovah in the Old Testament.

The heart of righteous men and women hunger for more contact with their Savior and to find him is manna to the soul. To be in his favor is even more refreshing than drinking cool water in a thirsty land or finding a covering from the sun in time of heat. Knowledge and testimony of Christ are food for the hungry spirit, just as meat and potatoes are food for the hungry body.

Heaven, knowing the proper price to put on all its goods, has so arranged things that one has to seek and search in order to really *find* the Messiah. The Lord has to be searched for and found, discovered, as it were, by each person individually. Information *about* the Savior can be found almost everywhere, but there is a significant difference between knowing the Lord and only knowing about him. We may learn *about* the Savior by reading or listening, but must obey his commandments to *know* him and understand much about him. The Lord himself has promised to unveil his face and be made known by his servants but he has told us that it must be in his "own time," and in his "own way," and according to his "own will."

I will quote from Doctrine and Covenants 88:63–68:

Draw near unto me and I will draw near unto you; seek me diligently and ye shall find me; ask, and ye shall receive; knock, and it shall be opened unto you.

Whatsoever ye ask the Father in my name it shall be given unto you, that is expedient for you;

And if ye ask anything that is not expedient for you, it shall turn unto your condemnation.

Behold, that which you hear is as the voice of one crying in the wilderness—in the wilderness, because you cannot see him—my voice, because my voice is Spirit, my Spirit is truth; truth abideth and hath no end; and if it be in you it shall abound.

And if your eye be single to my glory, your whole bodies shall be filled with light, and there shall be no darkness in you; and that body which is filled with light comprehendeth all things.

Therefore, sanctify yourselves that your minds become single to God, and the days will come that you shall see him; for he will unveil his face unto you and it shall be in his own time, and in his own way, and according to his own will.

We may think that, because we live so long after the mortal life of the Savior, what is being talked of in these verses—a personal visit by vision or divine manifestation—is considerably different than seeing Jesus on the roads and byways of Galilee or the streets of Jerusalem. But it is not entirely different. If we had lived at that time, in that place, and had seen him in the mortal flesh, we would not have known that he was the Messiah or that he was anything more than a man unless the Holy Spirit whispered it to our own spirit. Many saw him, but knew not who he was. John the Baptist knew him and declared plainly that he was the Messiah, the Son of God—but also explained—"There standeth one among you whom ye know not" (John 1:26). It is only by the testimony of the Spirit that anyone can recognize the difference between the Messiah and any other man. This is one of the functions of the Holy Ghost, to bear witness of the Father and the Son (Moses 5:9). The scriptures testify of Christ, and the Holy Ghost bears record that those scriptures are true.

The lengthy passage quoted from the first chapter of John showed that two of the disciples of John the Baptist subsequently became apostles of the Lord Jesus. These two are Andrew and John, who was later known as John the Beloved or John the Revelator, the son of Zebedee. However, other passages suggest that perhaps most, if not all, of the Twelve were tutored by John the Baptist, and that it was from him that they learned their earliest lessons about the Messiah who had already come to earth and actually lived in their neighborhood.

In Acts 1:21–22 we read a statement of Peter at the time of the choosing of Matthias as a new member of the Twelve. Peter says that from among the believers who had "companied with" the apostles all the time, "beginning from the baptism of John, unto that same day that he [Jesus] was taken up from us, must one be ordained to be a witness with us of his resurrection." This sounds significantly as if most of the Twelve had been followers of John the Baptist and from him they had learned that Jesus of Nazareth was the Messiah. John's mission was a forerunner to prepare the way for the Savior and to prepare a people to receive him. What more effective way than for John to actively tutor and start on their way those who later became Jesus' chief witnesses. He taught them the right way to find the Messiah and introduced many of them first to the doctrines of the Lord and then to the Lord in person.

Let us now review from the scriptures what one finds when and if he finds the Messiah. The shepherds near Bethlehem, being prompted by the angels of heaven, found the Messiah as a little babe "wrapped in swaddling clothes, lying in a manger" (Luke 2:12, see 8–18). He looked like other babies in outward appearance, but because the shepherds knew who he was, they worshipped him and could hardly wait to tell others of it.

About forty days later when Joseph and Mary brought the infant Jesus to the temple to fulfill the rites of purification according to the laws of Moses, they met a righteous and devout man whose name was Simeon. To him it had been revealed by the Holy Ghost that before his death he should see the Messiah. He recognized the baby Jesus as the Messiah, the "Hope of Israel," took him in his arms and blessed him. This man was made happy because by the Holy Spirit he had seen, understood, and found the Messiah (see Luke 2:25–35).

At that same instant, Anna, a righteous woman of great age, who had been left a widow more than eighty-four years after only seven years of marriage, came into the room. She saw the child, knew who he was, and gave thanks that she had seen the Messiah (Luke 2:36–38).

The wise men, being led by his star—not just a star, or *the* star, but as the scripture says—*his* star—a special star, found Jesus in a house as a young child, for it was a year or two since his birth. He no doubt looked like other children, but the wise men, being spiritually endowed and having knowledge, knew he was wonderfully different, and they brought him gifts and worshipped him (see Matthew 2:1–12; JST, Matthew 3:1–12). In the King James Version the wise men came seeking him that was born to be king, but from the Joseph Smith Translation we see an additional dimension and learn that they were seeking not only a *king* who would *rule* but the *Messiah* who would *save*. You see, he who looks for and finds the *Messiah* is wiser even than he who only looks for and finds a king.

Later, when Jesus was twelve, he was taken to the temple in Jerusalem by his parents, according to the requirement of the law of Moses for the Passover observance. When the formalities were over, Joseph and Mary were returning to Galilee and had journeyed about a day from Jerusalem when they discovered that Jesus was not with them. I have often reflected on the fear, the sorrow, the near-panic emotions that must have surged through Joseph and Mary's souls, to have lost track of that son in such a large and crowded city as Jerusalem at the time of Passover.

Such an experience would be almost overwhelming for any of us with our natural children. Mary and Joseph would have had the same pain we would have, but more in addition, for they had lost the very Son of God. That is worse than losing 116 pages of manuscript or almost anything else that could have happened to them. After three days of searching they found him. What did they really *find* when they found him? A normal twelve-year old boy? They found him teaching the learned doctors of the scripture. The account given in Luke 2:46 reads as follows in the King James Version:

> And . . . after three days they found him in the temple, sitting
> in the midst of the doctors, both hearing them, and asking them
> questions.

I suppose that it is something to write about any time a twelve-year-old boy will sit for three days and listen to a discussion of the scriptures and even ask questions. However, that is only the lesser part of the story. The Joseph Smith Translation reads as follows:

> They found him in the temple, sitting in the midst of the doctors,
> and they [the doctors] were hearing him, and asking him questions.

With this clarification, the next verse then takes on more meaning: "And all that heard him were astonished at his understanding and answers" (v. 47).

What did the learned doctors find when they "found" the Messiah in the temple courts? They found a young man who looked like other boys but with wisdom, knowledge, and more understanding of the spiritual things of life and the scriptures than they had been able to acquire through study and years of experience.

How did Jesus come by such wisdom at so early an age? When he was born, a veil was placed over his mind and his memory the same as it has been with us, but he had the power of the Spirit, the Holy Ghost. In John 2:24–25 we read that Jesus "knew all things, and needed not that any should testify of man; for he knew what was in man" (JST, John 2:24–25), and in John 3:34, we read that the Father giveth him the Spirit in unlimited abundance and not "by measure."

The Joseph Smith Translation adds yet another passage that allows us a glimpse of the unusual ability and personality of the Messiah as a young man. I will quote from Joseph Smith Translation, Matthew 3:24–26 (in the King James Version this would be inserted just at the end of Matthew).

> And it came to pass that Jesus grew up with his brethren, and waxed strong, and waited upon the Lord for the time of his ministry to come.
>
> And he served under his father, and he spake not as other men, neither could he be taught; for he needed not that any man should teach him.
>
> And after many years, the hour of his ministry drew nigh.

We often hear it said that we do not know anything about the Savior's early life, but we can see from these passages that we do know something.

Let us read now from the scriptures the words of those who knew Jesus as an adult man and who found him to be the Messiah. What did they say they found when they found the Messiah? As we have already read, they identified him as the one of whom Moses and the prophets had written. Many other people, when they saw him and heard him, thought he was one of the ancient prophets come back to earth again—perhaps Elijah, Jeremiah, or one of the other prophets (Matthew 16:14). Herod, upon hearing of his miracles and wonderful works, but having never seen him, thought he was John the Baptist risen from the dead (Matthew 14:2).

There is not a single case in the four Gospel records that represents Jesus as impatient, critical, or unkind to people who were repentant, teachable, and willing to change their lives. He forgave transgressions and mingled with publicans and sinners on condition of their repentance. He cast out devils, healed the lame, raised the dead, fed the hungry, opened the eyes of the blind, gave hearing to the deaf, and restored the sick to health if they but had the faith that he could do it. But he was a terror to the workers of iniquity and those who were self-righteous, deceptive, or hypocritical. In dealing with the repentant, he was kind and gentle, yet firm: the promised Messiah. To the proud, the haughty, and the arrogant, he was absolutely indomitable and irrepressible and a threat to their craftiness.

A few years ago I made a list of Jesus' teaching methods as illustrated in the four Gospels and discovered that his methods were adapted to the need and the occasion. The idea for this search was first suggested to me by a former faculty member, Glenn Pearson, in his master's thesis, so I am indebted to him for some of this material. I have listed twenty-three methods as follows:

1. Using simple exposition. Matthew 5–7; John 7:14–18.
2. Spoke with forthrightness and authority, not secondhand. Matthew 7:28–29.
3. Performed miracles. Matthew 12:9–13.
4. Used irony (almost sarcasm). Matthew 9:10–13; Mark 2:15–17; Luke 5:27–32; 15:1–7.
5. Used subtlety and wile. John 4:15–19.
6. Prophesied. Matthew 12:36–42; 24:3–51
7. Appealed to Old Testament for precedence. Matthew 12:1–8
8. Quoted from the Old Testament. John 10:34; Matthew 19:3–6; 22:31–32.
9. Taught with parables. Matthew 13.
10. Used logic. Matthew 12:24–28
11. Used object lessons. Matthew 18:1–6; 22:16–22; Luke 5:4–10.
12. Asked questions. Matthew 16:13–15; Luke:24–26.
13. Asked questions of those who asked him. Luke 10:25–28.
14. Bargained by means of questions. Matthew 21:23–27.
15. Used invective. Matthew 11:20–24; 23:1–39
16. Used repartee. Matthew 22:15–46.
17. Posed a problem. Matthew 22:41–46.
18. Candidly corrected those who were in error. Matthew 22:29.
19. Used debate and argument (beyond mere discussion). John 7–8, 20.
20. Was selective in what he taught to different groups. Matthew 7:6, 10.
21. Refused to give signs. Matthew 12:38–40.
22. Changed the subject, thus avoiding the full force of the issue. Matthew 22:30–31.
23. Sometimes refused to say anything. Luke 23:7–11.

But what did the Jewish *rulers* find when the encountered the Messiah? They saw him as a threat to their way of life. They were amazed at his strength of character and endless wisdom. He had *not* gone through their training and curriculum or their schools, and yet he knew much about the scriptures and about men and many other things. Once, in what appears to be a mixture of surprise and dismay over Jesus' success as a teacher, they marveled and cried out, "How knoweth this man letters, having never learned?" Jesus answered them and said, "My doctrine is not mine, but his that sent me" (John 7:15–16). John records: "And there was much murmuring among the people concerning him: for some said, He is a good man: others said, Nay; but he deceiveth the people" (John 7:12).

Three days before his crucifixion Jesus spent the entire day in a vivid confrontation with the Jewish rulers. They found that in defense of truth he was superb. He was righteousness coupled with facts—an unbeatable combination. They learned the truth of Job's expression, "How forcible are right words" (Job 6:25). I will read only a portion of what the record tells us took place on that day. Jesus had just one day previously cast the moneychangers out of the temple. When he came into Jerusalem and to the temple the next morning, the chief priests and the elders approached him as he was teaching and asked:

> By what authority doest thou these things? and who gave thee this authority?
>
> And Jesus answered and said unto them, I also will ask you one thing, which if ye tell me, I in like wise will tell you by what authority I do these things.
>
> The baptism of John, when was it? from heaven, or of men? And they reasoned with themselves, saying, If we shall say, From heaven; he will say unto us, Why did ye not then believe him?
>
> But if we shall say, Of men: we fear the people; for all hold John as a prophet. And they answered Jesus, and said, We cannot tell.
>
> And he said unto them, Neither tell I you by what authority I do these things. (Matthew 21:23–27)

Discussion then ensued and Jesus pointed out to them several flaws in their character, such as greed, perfidy, spiritual blindness, and such everyday things. Then the Pharisees held a meeting to see how they might entangle him in his talk (Matthew 22:15).

> And they sent out unto him their disciples with the Herodians, saying, Master, we know thou art true, and teachest the way of God

in truth, neither carest thou for any man; for thou regardest not the person of men.

This was to be a trap. No matter which way Jesus answered, they could challenge him about it and seek to discredit him.

> Tell us therefore, What thinkest thou? Is it lawful to give tribute to Caesar, or not?
>
> But Jesus perceived their wickedness, and said, Why tempt ye me, ye hypocrites?
>
> Shew me the tribute money. And they brought unto him a penny.
>
> And he saith unto them, Whose is this image and superscription?
>
> They say unto him, Caesar's. Then saith he unto them, Render therefore unto Caesar the things which are Caesar's; and unto God the things that are God's.
>
> When they had heard these words, they marveled, and left him, and went on their way. (Matthew 22:16–22)

On the very same day the Sadducees came to him, also to refute him and if possible to embarrass and discredit him publicly. They had a "hard question" to ask him about marriage and about the resurrection. It is important to note that the Sadducees do not believe there is any resurrection from the dead. We need to know that so we can understand that this question is not asked in good faith or with a desire to seek the truth but is in reality the setting of another trap.

> The same day came to him the Sadducees, which say that there is no resurrection, and asked him,
>
> Saying, Master, Moses said, If a man die, having no children, his brother shall marry his wife, and raise up seed unto his brother.
>
> Now there were with us seven brethren: and the first, when he had married a wife, deceased, and, having no issue, left his wife unto his brother:
>
> Likewise the second also, and the third, unto the seventh.
>
> And last of all the woman died also.
>
> Therefore in the resurrection whose wife shall she be of the seven? for they all had her.
>
> Jesus answered and said unto them, Ye do err, not knowing the scriptures, nor the power of God.
>
> For in the resurrection they neither marry, nor are given in marriage, but are as the angels of God in heaven.
>
> But as touching the resurrection of the dead, have ye not read that which was spoken unto you by God, saying,

I am the God of Abraham, and the God of Isaac, and the God of Jacob? God is not the God of the dead, but of the living.

And when the multitude heard this, they were astonished at his doctrine. (Matthew 21:23–33)

This passage is usually the one that non-LDS people use to refute our doctrine of eternal marriage because of the words "for in the resurrection they neither marry nor are given in marriage." A *casual* reading might lead a person to think that is a denial or a rejection by the Savior of the eternal marriage doctrine. But a *careful* reading will show that this is one of the strongest examples in the Bible showing that Jesus plainly taught the doctrine of eternal marriage.

I had an experience that will illustrate this point. As a seminary teacher, I found that friendly, playful high school students would sometimes put whisky bottles, cigarette cartons, and the like on my front porch during the night. Sometimes they put cigarettes under the windshield wipers on my car. Why did those students do those particular things? Was this not a reaction to my teaching about the Word of Wisdom in seminary class? They did not put milk cartons or soft-drink bottles—only liquor and tobacco items. Now, I tell you the truth! Once as an experiment, I said in class that some people feel that the eating of chocolate is contrary to the Word of Wisdom. And do you know what was under the windshield wipers the next day? A chocolate candy bar. I was not astute enough at the time but I have often thought since, I should have told them that "the love of money was the root of all evil."

Now return to Jesus and the Sadducees. Since the Sadducees did not believe in the resurrection anyway, and since it was a hostile audience and encounter, is it not easy to see that these clever men were trying to give the Messiah a hard question about marriage and resurrection that they supposed he could not answer? And why do it on the subject of marriage in the resurrected state unless it was widely known that he had been teaching such a doctrine? They were reacting to what he had said. His answer simply was that this woman and her seven husbands had not been married by the proper power and authority, and hence, there was no problem at all, since none of her marriages would be eternal. I say this passage, when read in its context, is one of the strongest evidences that Jesus taught both eternal marriage and resurrection from the dead and everyone there knew it, but the Sadducees did not like it.

The chapter ends with one more encounter between Jesus and the Pharisees. After they were properly rebuffed for their deliberate neglect and lack of understanding, the scripture says:

And no man was able to answer him a word, neither durst any man from that day forth ask him any more questions. (Matthew 22:46)

Now in closing, let us ask, what do men and women find today when they discover the true Messiah? Finding the Messiah is the greatest of all discoveries. If we were to discuss the most important thing about Jesus the Messiah, what would it be? If we were to go home today to our families and say, "We have found the Messiah!" what would we say about him? What is the most important thing about him that we could tell another person? Would it be his height or weight, the color of his hair, the style of his clothes, the tone of his voice? Everything about Jesus is important, and any true detail or concept would be worth knowing, but what would be the single most important thing to find out about him? I could answer that as to my own opinion, but let us take a clue from what the scriptures say about him.

I think it can be summarized in John 3:16: "For God so loved the world, that he gave his only begotten Son, that whosoever believeth in him should not perish, but have everlasting life."

While that is the central concept, it takes a considerable amount of study to know what that one verse means. I'll tell you what I have learned about the Messiah from the scriptures and the whisperings of the Holy Ghost.

The greatest message about Jesus Christ is that he has conquered death—both spiritual and physical death. He is literally the light and the life of the world (D&C 10:70).

We are given a plain discussion of the redeeming role of the Savior in the following scriptures:

From Paul:

For as in Adam all die, even so in Christ shall all be made alive. (1 Corinthians 15:22)

From Jacob:

For it behooveth the great Creator that he suffereth himself to become subject unto man in the flesh, and die for all men, that all men might become subject unto him.

For as death hath passed upon all men, to fulfill the merciful plan of the great Creator, there must needs be a power of resurrection, and the resurrection must needs come unto man by reason of the fall; and the fall came by reason of transgression; and because man became fallen they were cut off from the presence of the Lord.

Wherefore, it must needs be an infinite atonement—save it should be an infinite atonement this corruption could not put on incorruption. Wherefore, the first judgment which came upon man must needs have remained to an endless duration. And if so, this flesh must have laid down to rot and to crumble to its mother earth, to rise no more.

O the wisdom of God, his mercy and grace! For behold, if the flesh should rise no more our spirits must become subject to that angel who fell from before the presence of the Eternal God, and became the devil, to rise no more.

And our spirits must have become like unto him, and we become devils, angels to a devil, to be shut out from the presence of our God, and to remain with the father of lies, in misery, like unto himself. (2 Nephi 9:5–9)

And from Nephi:

Behold, my soul delighteth in proving unto my people the truth of the coming of Christ; for, for this end hath the law of Moses been given; and all things which have been given of God from the beginning of the world, unto man, are the typifying of him.

And also my soul delighteth in the covenants of the Lord which he hath made to our fathers; yea, my soul delighteth in his grace, and in his justice, and power, and mercy in the great and eternal plan of deliverance from death.

And my soul delighteth in proving unto my people that save Christ should come all men must perish. (2 Nephi 11:4–6)

Do we understand that Jesus made payment with his blood in order for mercy to satisfy justice? No other person, no human being, could redeem us; the redemption could be made only by a God, as explained by Amulek:

Behold, I say unto you, that I do know that Christ shall come among the children of men, to take upon him the transgressions of his people, and that he shall atone for the sins of the world; for the Lord God hath spoken it.

For it is expedient that an atonement should be made; for according to the great plan of the Eternal God there must be an atonement made, or else all mankind must unavoidably perish; yea, all are hardened; yea, all are fallen and are lost, and must perish except it be through the Atonement which it is expedient should be made.

For it is expedient that there should be a great and last sacrifice; yea, not a sacrifice of man, neither of beast, neither of any manner of fowl; for it shall not be a human sacrifice; but it must be an infinite and eternal sacrifice.

Now there is not any man that can sacrifice his own blood which will atone for the sins of another. Therefore there can be nothing which is short of an infinite atonement which will suffice for the sins of the world.

Therefore, it is expedient that there should be a great and last sacrifice.

And that great and last sacrifice will be the Son of God, yea, infinite and eternal. (Alma 34:8–14)

What does this mean to us? It means that our association with the Messiah is not optional or casual. It is critical.

By the Fall of Adam, all mankind has suffered two deaths—a spiritual alienation from God, and a physical death. We have all suffered the first—the alienation. We will yet, with no exceptions, suffer the physical death. We are thus dominated by death because of the Fall of Adam. It is absolutely necessary that we understand that Jesus, in order to be the Messiah, had to be divine, that he had to be the literal, biological Son of God, and thus was not dominated by death and sin as is all the rest of humanity. Had he not been the Only Begotten, he could not have been able or worthy to pay the debt of the Fall of Adam and of our own individual sins. The infinite atonement required the life and the death and the sacrifice of a God, not of a man.

The plan of salvation is equally real. Adam was a living person in time and in space. The Fall is so real that, if we knew the details, we could place on a calendar the time when he fell. Also, if we knew the details, we could mark on a map the location where he ate the "forbidden" fruit.

In the very same manner, the Atonement of Jesus Christ is so vital and so necessary in time and in space, that if we had the facts, we could place on a calendar the date of his birth, the date of his suffering in the Garden of Gethsemane, the date of his death, and the date of his resurrection. In like manner we could mark on a map the place of his birth, suffering, death, and resurrection. These are all events in time and geography. This is the Messiah I have found, and I believe it to be the greatest message in the world. It is the message of John 3:16 in its expanded form.

When that morning comes that any of us stands in perfection of body and spirit, resurrected, cleansed, and with eternal life in the presence of God, we will then know with full meaning what we perceive only in part today when we say, "I have found the Messiah!"

CHAPTER SEVEN

Special Witnesses of the Birth of Christ

Joseph Fielding McConkie

Two events within holy writ exceed all others in importance—Christ's birth and his Resurrection. If it could be legitimately shown that the testimony of either was suspect, the very foundations of Christianity would be cracked. Of necessity, the Nativity story must establish the divine sonship of Christ, while the Easter story must establish his victory over death and the actuality of his resurrection. The testimony of these two stories must stand unimpeached if the world is to be held responsible to accept Jesus of Nazareth as the promised Messiah, the Son of God, our Savior and Redeemer.

This paper will confine itself to a brief review of the Nativity story. The attention of the paper will center on the testimony of those who in the providence of heaven were chosen to be the special witnesses of the birth of God's Son. We find within the New Testament account of Christ's birth the testimony of twelve witnesses. Each will be briefly examined. Of the four Gospel writers only Matthew and Luke tell the story. Would that they all had, but two are sufficient to comply with the law of witnesses. Each will be briefly examined. Of the twelve witnesses within our two Gospel accounts, we have the testimony of heaven and earth, of man and of woman, of the wicked and of the pure, of the youthful and the aged, of the humble within society and of those who could command audience with kings. Indeed, as we shall see, our story is of all stories most perfect.

Twelve Witnesses of Christ's Birth

Gabriel

Properly, our first New Testament witness of the birth of Christ is a messenger from the presence of God. Appropriately, he makes his initial appearance in the temple to a faithful priest of the Aaronic order, one who is performing the ritual function in behalf of his nation of burning incense on the altar within the Holy Place. In the performance of this duty, Zacharias represented the combined faith of Israel. His prayer was their prayer, and that prayer was for an everlasting deliverance from all their enemies at the hands of their promised Messiah. The ascending flames of incense symbolized the ascension of that united prayer. As Zacharias prayed within the Holy Place, so his fellow priests and all within the walls of the temple united their amens to his appeal.[1]

In response to Israel's prayer, an "angel of the Lord" appeared before Zacharias. He stood on the right side of the altar of incense and identified himself as Gabriel, one who stood "in the presence of God" (Luke 1:11, 19). By modern revelation we know Gabriel to be Noah, that he "stands next in authority to Adam in the Priesthood,"[2] and that he holds the keys of "the restoration of all things." The keys held by Gabriel make of him an Elias to prepare the way before the Lord (D&C 27:6–7). The name Gabriel, by which Noah performs his angelic duties, means "man of God," though it has also been interpreted as "God is my champion," or "God has shown himself valiant."[3]

Gabriel is mentioned twice in the Old Testament; both instances are appearances to Daniel. The first was to interpret Daniel's vision of the ram and the he-goat, and the second was while Daniel prayed, confessing his sins and those of his people. In the second instance, Gabriel revealed that after seventy weeks (a symbol for an unknown period of time), Israel and Jerusalem would be restored and an atonement made for their sins. Gabriel promised that an everlasting righteousness would be accomplished in their behalf (see Daniel 8–9).

Six months after his visit to Zacharias, Gabriel also visited Mary to announce to the beautiful virgin girl of Nazareth that she was to become the mother of God's Son (Luke 1:26, 32). Thus the pattern of Gabriel's visits appears to be that of "fellow-servant" of the Saints, bearing messages of comfort and glad tidings.

In both Jewish and Christian traditions Gabriel is spoken of as an archangel.[4] The *Ascension of Isaiah* announces "Gabriel, the angel of God, and Michael, chief of the holy angels," as the two angels who were to open the sepulcher of Christ.[5] Jewish theology accords Gabriel a place second only to that of Michael, as do the Latter-day Saints.[6] We, of course, know Michael to be Adam (see D&C 27:11).

As to Luke's account of Gabriel's appearance and prophecy to Zacharias, we are compelled to say the story is perfect. How more properly could the birth of the Son of God be announced than by a heavenly Elias, one from the presence of God himself? One who comes first to consecrate the birth of the earthly Elias who will announce the Messiah to the chosen nation. To whom ought our heavenly emissary appear? Why, to a priest, of course, for the sacerdotal office itself was a prophecy that the Son of God would yet come. What of the place? Jerusalem must be our answer. The Holy City from which the word of the Lord was to go forth. Not Hebron, not the hill country of Judea where Zacharias lived. Where within the city? The answer is obvious to all: the temple, the place where God is to be sought. Most specifically, where within the temple? The Holy Place at the altar of incense, the symbolic place of the ascending prayers of Israel. At what time of day should this heaven-sent announcement come? At the solemn hour of public prayer, that time designated for those of faith to plead with the heavens that their Messiah be sent. And finally, what confirming sign? The striking of Zacharias dumb. What better symbol of the day when every tongue of disbelief shall be silenced?

Zacharias

Who then was this Zacharias to whom Gabriel appeared? He was a descendant of Abia (Hebrew *Abijah*). His name meant "remembered of Jehovah."[7] He was married to a woman named Elisabeth, whose fathers, like Zacharias', had also been priests (see Luke 1:5). Her name was that of Aaron's wife, of whom she was a descendant (see Exodus 6:23). It means "God is my oath," or "consecrated to God."[8] Thus this noble couple, "consecrated to God" long before their births, were, in the Nativity story, to be "remembered of Jehovah," as the promise was granted to them that they at long last should become the parents of a child—a child destined to be the earthly forerunner of the Messiah.

Of the parents of John the Baptist we read: "They were both righteous before God, walking in all the commandments and ordinances of the Lord blameless" (Luke 1:6). Zacharias and Elisabeth honored the law of their fathers not only in letter, but in spirit. Their righteousness entitled them to God's favor. Zacharias, who held that priesthood which entitled him to receive the administration of angels, was worthy of, and received, that sacred privilege (see D&C 84:26–27; 67:10–13).

Elisabeth

If we read of John, as we do, that he would be "filled with the Holy Ghost, even from his mother's womb," it tells us something of the purity of the temple in which his body was housed (Luke 1:15). Indeed, Elisabeth was a prophetess in her own right. None could tell the story more beautifully than Luke.

> When Elisabeth heard the salutation of Mary, the babe leaped in her womb; and Elisabeth was filled with the Holy Ghost: and she spake out with a loud voice, and said, Blessed art thou among women, and blessed is the fruit of thy womb. And whence is this to me, that the mother of my Lord should come to me? For, lo, as soon as the voice of thy salutation sounded in mine ears, the babe leaped in my womb for joy. And blessed is she that believed: for there shall be a performance of those things which were told her from the Lord." (Luke 1:41–45)

John the Baptist

What a marvelous scene it must have been—John, yet within his mother's womb, filled with the Holy Ghost and leaping for joy in an unspoken testimony of the divine Sonship of the unborn child that Mary carried; Elisabeth greeting her cousin Mary in the Spirit of prophecy and Mary responding by that same Spirit. Again we are compelled to say, how perfect! The testimony of two women: the aged Elisabeth and the youthful Mary; each bearing a child conceived under miraculous circumstances, rejoicing together.

As Christ was born the rightful heir to David's kingdom, so John was born the rightful heir of the office of Elias that he had been promised by Gabriel. Robert J. Matthews identifies that heirship in this language:

The things of the law of Moses, especially with regard to the qualifications of the priests and their functions in the offering of various animal sacrifices, were designed by revelation to prefigure and typify the Messiah and to bear witness of him. Heavy penalties were affixed to the performance of sacred rites and duties without the proper authority. It was, therefore, essential that when the Messiah came in person as the Lamb of God, John, the forerunner and witness of the Lamb, should be of the proper lineage to qualify for the mission. If it was necessary for a priest to be of the lineage of Aaron in order to labor with the sacrificial symbols, which were only prefigures of the Messiah, how much greater the necessity that John, the forerunner of the Messiah in person, be of the proper priestly lineage and authority.[9]

Mary

There could be no more perfect mortal witness of Christ's divine Sonship than his mother, Mary. From Gabriel she received the promise that she would conceive in her womb "the Son of the Highest" (Luke 1:31–32). Following that marvelous event she testified, saying: "He that is mighty hath done to me great things; and holy is his name" (Luke 1:49). Nephi gave us the perfect scriptural account of this most sacred event. Our eternal Father, he told us, condescended, that is, he came down from his royal court on high, and in union with the beautiful virgin girl of Nazareth, fathered a son "after the manner of the flesh." "And it came to pass," Nephi wrote, "that I beheld that she was carried away in the Spirit; and after she had been carried away in the Spirit for the space of a time the angel spake unto me, saying: Look! And I looked and beheld the virgin again, bearing a child in her arms. And the angel said unto me: Behold the Lamb of God, yea, even the Son of the Eternal Father!" (1 Nephi 11:19–21). Alma, testifying of the birth of Christ, said, "He shall be born of Mary, at Jerusalem which is the land of our forefathers, she being a virgin, a precious and chosen vessel, who shall be overshadowed and conceive by the power of the Holy Ghost, and bring forth a son, yea, even the Son of God" (Alma 7:10).

Joseph

We have no scriptural record of any words spoken by Joseph, the foster father of Jesus. Despite the lack of words, Joseph's testimony as to Christ's divine Sonship is most eloquent. He was, we are told,

JOSEPH FIELDING McCONKIE

a "just man," meaning that he lived the law of Moses with exactness and honor. We know that he dreamed dreams and entertained angels. Further, we know that as he was faithful in keeping the law of Moses, so he faithfully heeded each divine direction that was given to him. Surely his unquestioning obedience is evidence of his belief. It included taking Mary, who carried another's child, as his wife, and "knowing her not till she had brought forth her firstborn son;" naming him Jesus; fleeing by night with Mary and the holy child to Egypt; remaining in Egypt until directed to return; and then upon their return living in Galilee rather than in Judea (see Matthew 1:19–21, 25; 2:13–23). Each action witnessed anew Joseph's conviction that this child was indeed the Hope of Israel, the Son of God.

The Shepherds

On the eve of Christ's birth in the stable at Bethlehem, there were in the fields not far distant shepherds watching over their flocks. The fact that they were in the field by night gives us some indication of the season of the year in which Christ was born. It was the custom among the Jews to take their sheep to the fields about the time of Passover and bring them home at the coming of the first rains—thus they would be in the fields from about April to October.[10] Of these shepherds Elder Bruce R. McConkie has suggested:

> These were not ordinary shepherds nor ordinary flocks. The sheep there being herded—nay, not herded, but watched over, cared for with love and devotion—were destined for sacrifice on the great altar in the Lord's House, in similitude of the eternal sacrifice of Him who that wondrous night lay in a stable, perhaps among sheep of lesser destiny. And the shepherds—for whom the veil was then rent: surely they were in spiritual stature like Simeon and Anna and Zacharias and Elisabeth and Joseph and the growing group of believing souls who were coming to know, by revelation, that the Lord's Christ was not on earth. As there were many widows in Israel, and only to the one in Zarephath was Elijah sent, so there were many shepherds in Palestine, but only to those who watched over the temple flocks did the herald angel come; only they heard the heavenly choir.[11]

That the testimony of one apostle does not stand alone relative to the character of these shepherds, I cite that of another, Alma, who announced the principle that angels would declare the glad tidings of the Messiah's birth to "just and holy men" (Alma 13:26, 22–25).

The special witness that these "just and holy men" bore relative to the birth of Christ was not limited to the night of the Savior's birth, but was for each of them a lifetime calling. Their story was to be told to family, friends, and neighbors. It was to be told in the courts of the temple, and from there it was to find itself told among all nations of the earth.[12] Luke tells us that after the shepherds had seen the "babe lying in a manger," they "made known abroad the saying which was told them concerning this child" (Luke 2:16–17). Such was the commission of the angel who stood before them that holy night declaring "good tidings of great joy" which were to go to "all people" (Luke 2:10).

The Heavenly Choir

When the heavens were opened to the shepherds, they first saw an angel of the Lord—we would suppose Gabriel—saying: "Fear not: for, behold, I bring you good tidings of great joy, which shall be to all people. For unto you is born this day in the city of David a Saviour, which is Christ the Lord" (Luke 2:10–11). Then "suddenly," according to the King James account, "there was with the angel a multitude of the heavenly host praising God, and saying, Glory to God in the highest, and on earth peace, good will toward men" (Luke 2:13–14).

In the telling of the Christmas story there is an occasional objection to the idea that Christ's birth was heralded to the shepherds by a heavenly choir. This objection is on the grounds that the text of the Bible does not say their message was sung. In response, I first observe that there are responsible Bible translations that report the heavenly host "singing the praises of God;"[13] second, it would be contrary to the order of worship in heaven for the host to do other than sing, as a host of scriptural texts attest;[14] and third, we have record of the appearance of heavenly choirs on other occasions of rejoicing.[15] Musical ability ranks among the talents with which one might be born and which one can take with him into the worlds to come. Bruce R. McConkie frequently preached the doctrine that those with great musical talents are laboring on the other side of the veil to prepare the music and the choir that will attend the return of Christ.

As to the choir that sang to the humble shepherds of Judea, perhaps they had engagements the world over to herald the Savior's birth among the scattered remnants of Israel. "Yea, and the voice of the Lord, by the mouth of angels, doth declare it unto all nations," Alma wrote, "yea, doth declare it, that they may have glad tidings of great joy; yea, and he doth sound these glad tidings among all his people, yea, even to them that are scattered abroad upon the face of the earth; wherefore they have come unto us" (Alma 13:22).

The Christmas hymn "It Came upon the Midnight Clear" is an announcement of the very hour of the appearance of the heavenly choir to the shepherds. This hymn has as its roots a text from the Wisdom of Solomon, a part of the Old Testament Apocrypha. The passage states that the "night in its swift course was now half gone," and refers contextually to the destruction of the firstborn of the Egyptians at the time of the Exodus. This, however, has not prevented Christian writers from seeing it as a reference to the time of Christ's birth (see Wisdom of Solomon 18:14–15).

Simeon

Our attention now turns to Jerusalem and its temple. There an aged man, described by Luke as "just and devout," one who in faith had awaited the coming of the Messiah and who had received the promise of the Lord that he would not die until he had seen the Savior, was moved upon by the Holy Ghost to go to the temple. His is the first testimony within the sacred walls of the temple of which we have record that announces the birth of Christ. Appropriately, he bore the name Simeon, which means "God has heard" (Genesis 29:33); indeed God had heard his righteous plea and now his prayer was to be answered.

Thus Simeon was there to greet parents and child as they entered the temple—Mary for the ritual of cleansing, and Joseph to pay the tax which is paid to redeem the firstborn from priestly service. Simeon took the child in his arms and, praising God, said, "Lord, now lettest thou thy servant depart in peace, according to thy word: For mine eyes have seen thy salvation, which thou hast prepared before the face of all people; a light to lighten the Gentiles, and the glory of thy people Israel" (Luke 2:29–32). Simeon's declaration, which came by the spirit of prophecy, reached far beyond the understanding and hope of those of his nation—for he saw the universal nature of Christ's ministry and attested that he was Savior to Jew and Gentile alike. Had his words fallen upon the ears of a Pharisee, they would have been greeted with shouts of heresy!

Then Simeon blessed Joseph and Mary and said to Mary: "Behold, this child is set for the fall and rising again of many in Israel: and for a sign which shall be spoken against; (Yea, a sword shall pierce through thy own soul also,) that the thoughts of many hearts may be revealed." Would that we knew all else that he spoke, including the words of blessing pronounced upon the couple in whose custody the Child was placed. Always—as we shall see throughout this whole work—there was more uttered orally to those who then lived, usually far more, than was recorded and preserved for those who should thereafter hear the accounts. At least we know that Simeon foresaw that Jesus and his message would divide the house of Israel; that men would rise or fall as they accepted or rejected his words; that he was a sign or standard around which the righteous would rally; and that Mary, who now had joy in the growing life of the infant son, would soon be pierced with the sword of sorrow as she saw him during his waning hours on the cross of Calvary.[16]

Anna

In the providence of God the marvelous testimony of Simeon was not to stand alone. Anna, an aged widow, a devout and saintly woman who worshipped constantly in the temple with fasting and prayer both day and night, now approached the holy family. As Simeon was a prophet, so she was a prophetess, and her voice now joined his as a special witness of the birth of the Christ. Anna, whose name means "full of grace,"[17] bore testimony to all in Jerusalem who "looked for redemption" (Luke 2:36–38). Through the countless hours she had spent within the walls of the temple she was undoubtedly well known to those of the Holy City who also faithfully sought the coming of the Messiah. All such would hear her testimony of his birth (Luke 2:36–38).

The Wise Men from the East

There has been more speculation about, and more legends created concerning, the so-called Magi who visited Joseph and Mary in their house in Bethlehem than about almost any other biblical event. There is an air of mystery here that appeals to the speculative mind, and the fictional accounts—as to who they were, whence they came, and the symbolic meaning of what they did—fill volumes.

They are presumed to be kings because of the richness of their gifts; it is said they were Gentiles, showing that all nations bowed before the newborn King; it is thought they were masters of some astrological cult that could divine great happenings from the stars. They are even named, identified, and described; their ages are given, and the color of their skin; and one can, or could in times past, at least, even view their skulls, crowned with jewels, in a cathedral in Cologne [Germany]. They are thought to have dealt in magic, to be magicians of a sort, and they have become great heroes of the mystical and unknown.[18]

In the scriptural account, Matthew alone makes reference to the coming of the wise men. He simply says, "there came wise men from the East to Jerusalem" (Matthew 2:1). The more terse the text, it seems, the more voluminous the traditions. We do not know their number, we do not know whether they rode camels, we do not even know if they traveled together. Yet if we are to assume that the Lord will continue to follow the pattern we have seen in his choice of each of the others who have been privileged to testify of the birth of the Savior, we can safely say of them that they were devout, just, and holy, that they knew of Christ's birth by the revelation of heaven, and that they were destined to be lifetime witnesses of it. It would follow, then, as night follows day, that they came from a people of faith and would return to that people to testify of that which they had done and seen. All evidence within the story sustains such a conclusion.

This we know: the "wise men" were ignorant of the political situation in Jerusalem. Surely they would not have knowingly endangered the life of Christ by seeking his whereabouts from Herod. No one who knew Herod would have asked such a question of him. We know that they were visionary men, for they were "warned of God in a dream that they should not return to Herod" and that "they should depart into their own country another way" (Matthew 2:13). We also know from the Joseph Smith Translation of the Bible that they came seeking "the Messiah of the Jews" (JST, Matthew 3:2). "The probability is," wrote Elder McConkie, "that they were themselves Jews who lived, as millions of Jews then did, in one of the nations to the East."[19] It is hard to suppose that others would come seeking the Jewish Messiah. Though men of all nations are subject to the light of Christ, the God of heaven commissions only those within the household of faith to be special witnesses of his Son. Admittedly, an Egyptian pharaoh dreamed dreams relative to the destiny of his nation, but let it not be forgotten that none but Joseph, the Lord's prophet, could interpret them (see Genesis 41). In like manner, Belshazzar was permitted to see the hand of the Lord as the message of his destruction was given him, yet Daniel alone could interpret it (see Daniel 5).

Who, then, were these wise men from the East? We can only assume that they were prophets of the true and living God, that they held the priesthood, that they knew the prophecies of Christ's birth—including prophecies now lost to us—and that they were directed by the light of heaven in their journey.

Herod

Our concluding witness is a most unlikely and reluctant one; a fiend in human body, a man who had drenched himself in the blood of the innocent, a man whose deeds were enough to cause hell itself to shudder—none other than Israel's king, Herod the Great. Herod had made his alliance with the powers of the world; his friends were Augustus, Rome, and expediency. He had massacred priests and nobles; he had decimated the Sanhedrin; he had caused the high priest, his brother-in-law, to be drowned in pretend sport before his eye; he had ordered the strangulation of his favorite wife, the beautiful Hasmonaean princess Mariamne, though she seems to have been the only person he ever loved. Any who fell victim to his suspicions were murdered, including three sons and numerous other relatives.

Such is the irony of history that the most wicked man "ever to sit on David's throne was its occupant in the very day when He came whose throne it was, and who would in due course reign in righteousness thereon."[20] It was to this man, who personified the wickedness of the world and the corruptions of the earth, that the wise men from the East went and bore their testimony that Israel's rightful king and ruler had been born. Such a testimony would not have been heeded had it come from Simeon or Anna or from simple shepherds, but coming as it did from these eastern visitors, whose credentials, whatever they were, established them as men of great wisdom, it was given credence by Herod.

Of a truth, the kingdom of God will never go unopposed in the days of earth's mortality, the period of Satan's power. The question as to whether Herod really believed that Israel's king had been born is of little moment. What is of importance, that which makes the Nativity story complete, is evidence of the anger and wrath of hell at the birth of God's Son. The glad tidings of heaven have no such effect on the prince of darkness and his legions. Herod responded to the testimony of the wise men with murderous wrath. As Satan's chief apostle, with all the cunning of hell, he sought to destroy the Christ child. Thus the decree went forth that "all the children that were in Bethlehem, and in all the coasts thereof, from two years old and under," according to the time that Herod had inquired of the wise men, were to be slain (Matthew 2:16).

Conclusion

Of the restoration of the gospel in the meridian of time Paul said, "This thing was not done in a corner" (Acts 26:26). As was true of the spreading of the gospel, it was true of its most sacred historical events: the birth and Resurrection of Christ. As to the story of Christ's birth, Alma tells us that it was heralded by angels to those who were "just and holy" among all nations (Alma 13:22, 26). To those in the Americas Samuel had prophesied that there would be "great lights in heaven, insomuch that in the night before he cometh there shall be no darkness, insomuch that it shall appear unto man as if it was day. Therefore, there shall be one day and a night and a day, as if it were one day and there were no night." Thus that people were to witness the rising and setting of the sun without the coming of the darkness of night. Further, they were promised that a new star would arise, the likeness of which they had never seen, and that it would be attended by other signs and wonders in the heavens (Helaman 14:3–6).

In the nation of Christ's birth the testimony was also to go forth in ever-widening circles. Again our story finds its fulfillment among those who were blameless in keeping the commandments and ordinances of the Lord, those who were "just and devout," those who were filled with the Holy Ghost. There is no evidence that these special witnesses were randomly chosen, but rather that they were called and prepared even before the foundations of the earth were laid. As one evidence of their foreordination, we cite the perfect harmony of their names with the peculiar circumstances that called forth their testimony: Zacharias, the aged priest who obtained the promise of a son and whose name meant "remembered of Jehovah"; Elisabeth, whose name meant "consecrated to God," who was the faithful wife of Zacharias, and who was destined in her advanced years to become the mother of the Elias who would prepare the way before the Christ; Mary, the mother of the Christ Child, of whom Simeon prophesied that the sword of sorrow would pierce her soul, whose name meant "she shall weep bitter tears"; Jesus, the son of Mary and the Eternal Father, whose name, which meant "Jehovah saves," was given by the angel; John, his forerunner, whose name was also announced by Gabriel, its meaning being "Jehovah is gracious"; Simeon, the aged prophet who had been promised that he would not taste of death until he had seen the savior, whose name meant "God has heard"; and Anna, the widowed prophetess whose name meant "full of grace," who would testify to the faithful of Jerusalem of the salvation that was theirs through Christ.

As the story unfolds, every appropriate element appears in its proper place, which is all the more remarkable because of its coming from two writers, each telling different parts of the story. Properly, it begins with an angelic announcement within the Holy Place of the Temple to a priest whose prayers have ascended to heaven in behalf of his nation imploring the very event. With equal propriety it ends with the announcement of Herod's satanic designs upon the life of the Christ child. Within the story we see the heavens opened to priest and layman, to man and woman, to old and young, to the mighty and the humble, and we see each called to be a lifelong witness of the most beautiful of stories ever told.

For us of the latter days, the Nativity story is more than a perfect witness of the birth of the Savior. In it we find the pattern by which the knowledge of God is to be restored and go forth once again among all the nations of the earth (see JS—M 1:31). How will it go forth? By special witnesses, witnesses called and prepared in the councils of heaven. Who will they be? The old and the young, women and men, the learned and the unlearned, but in it all they will be those who "walk in all the commandments and ordinances of the Lord blameless," those who dream dreams, entertain angels, and are filled with the Holy Ghost. So it has ever been, so it must ever be.

Notes

1. On this matter Elder Bruce R. McConkie has written: "What prayers did Zacharias make on this occasion? Certainly not, as so many have assumed, prayers that Elisabeth should bear a son, though such in

days past had been the subject of the priest's faith-filled importuning. This was not the occasion for private, but for public prayers. He was acting for and in behalf of all Israel, not for himself and Elisabeth alone. And Israel's prayer was for redemption, for deliverance from the Gentile yoke, for the coming of their Messiah, for freedom from sin. The prayers of the one who burned the incense were the prelude to the sacrificial offering itself, which was made to bring the people in tune with the Infinite, through the forgiveness of sins and the cleansing of their lives. 'And the whole multitude of the people were praying without at the time of incense'—all praying, with one heart and one mind, the same things that were being expressed formally, and officially, by the one whose lot it was to sprinkle the incense in the Holy Place. The scene was thus set for the miraculous event that was to be." (*The Mortal Messiah* [Salt Lake City: Deseret Book, 1979], 1:307–8.)

2. *Teachings of the Prophet Joseph Smith,* Joseph Fielding Smith (Salt Lake City: Deseret Book, 1976), 157.

3. *The Interpreter's Bible,* 12 vols. (New York: Abingdon Press, 1965), 6:487.

4. William Smith, *Dictionary of the Bible,* 4 vols. (New York: Hurd and Houghton, 1868), 1:848.

5. L. LaMar Adams, *The Living Message of Isaiah* (Salt Lake City: Deseret Book, 1981), 110.

6. Jan Comay and Ronald Brownrigg, *Who's Who in the Bible,* 2 vols. (New York: Bonanza Books, 1980), 2:116.

7. Joseph Fielding McConkie, *Gospel Symbolism* (Salt Lake City: Bookcraft, 1985), 189–90.

8. Ibid.

9. Robert J. Matthews, *A Burning Light—The Life and Ministry of John the Baptist,* (Provo, Utah: Brigham Young University Press, 1972), 18.

10. Adam Clark, *Clark's Commentary,* 3 vols. (Nashville: Abingdon, n.d.), 3:370.

11. Bruce R. McConkie, *Mortal Messiah,* 347.

12. Ibid., 348.

13. *See,* for instance, *The New English Translation* and *The Jerusalem Bible.*

14. When the heavens were opened to Lehi he saw "numberless concourses of angels . . . singing and praising their God" (1 Nephi 1:8). At his death King Benjamin prayed that his spirit might "join the choirs above in singing the praises of a just God" (Mosiah 2:28).

Isaiah twice records the Lord's injunction that the heavens herald the redemption in song: "Sing, O ye heavens; for the Lord hath done it; shout, ye lower parts of the earth: break forth into singing, ye mountains, O forest, and every tree therein: for the Lord hath redeemed Jacob, and glorified him in Israel" (Isaiah 44:23; *see also* 49:13). Singing is an eternal part of the divine system of worship (*see* D&C 25:12, Job 38:7; D&C 133:56).

15. Temple dedications would be one such illustration. For other illustrations *see* Fredrick W. Babbel, *To Him That Believeth* (Salt Lake City: Bookcraft, 1982), 57–58.
16. Bruce R. McConkie, *Mortal Messiah*, 354–55.
17. *Webster's Dictionary of First Names* (New York: Galahad Books, 1981), 112.
18. Bruce r. McConkie, *Mortal Messiah* 357.s
19. Ibid., 358.
20. Ibid. 362.

CHAPTER EIGHT

Jesus and Josephus Told of the Destruction of Jerusalem

Keith H. Meservy

At various times during his ministry, Jesus predicted the divine judgments that eventually befell Jerusalem and the Jews. During his last week of mortal life, he not only identified for his disciples the time and the kinds of problems incident to that dark day, but also the ways by which they could avoid suffering the consequences.

The Jews took their major step toward the prophesied destruction when they revolted against the Romans in AD 66. Merely four years later, sword, famine, and fire had leveled the city of Jerusalem; soldiers of Rome had leveled Jewish homes vacated recently by the dead and the captives; Jerusalem itself was desolate. Only forty years had passed since Jesus had predicted it. Undoubtedly, many of those who died on Jerusalem's streets had heard Jesus' warning of disaster and his instructions on how to avoid it.

Today, the hour of God's judgments is being announced again in the land. For this generation at risk it is reassuring to see how God saves those who listen to him.

Many accounts of that war were written, but the only one that has survived was written by Josephus, a twenty-nine-year-old commander-in-chief of the Galilean sector, who was in an admirable position to write about it. He knew much of the thinking that had produced it and was an eyewitness to many of its events. He knew the major Jewish leaders and, after his capture, knew also the Roman commanders, Vespasian and Titus. He observed the progress of the war from within the Roman camp and kept track of its details by regular interviews with Roman and captured Jewish participants. He saw the fall of Jerusalem, the burning of its temple, and the leveling of the city. Consequently, his firsthand knowledge of that war makes his record an excellent source for studying the fulfillment of Jesus' prophecy. Especially so, since he felt that God had inspired him to understand what was happening and had preserved his life so that he could tell it.

Josephus, Divine Recorder of the War, Understood It

As the Galilean general, Josephus faced the Romans at the city of Jotapata. When it finally fell after a forty-day siege and he surrendered, he recalled many dreams that he had recently had but had not understood. Referring to himself in the third person, he said: "There came back into his mind those mighty dreams, in which God had foretold him the impending fate of the Jews and the destinies of the Roman sovereigns." As a priest, he knew how to interpret dreams and knew the prophecies in the scriptures. At that hour he was inspired to read their meaning. Recalling the dreadful images of his recent dreams, he

> offered up a silent prayer to God. "Since it pleases thee . . . who didst create the Jewish nation, to break thy work, since fortune has wholly passed to the Romans, and since thou hast made choice of my spirit to announce the things that are to come, I willingly surrender to the Romans and consent to live; but I take thee to witness that I go, not as a traitor, but as thy minister."[1]

Josephus' interpretation of the war is so consistent with the prophecy of Jesus that it seems as though he had Jesus' prophecy in front of him as he wrote. I see *no* evidence, however, that this was the case. And this lack of evidence suggests that, as Josephus said, he really was inspired to understand the meaning of the war.

Eusebius, early church historian, felt that the similarity between the prophecy and Josephus' history was so striking that it was a testimonial of Jesus' foreknowledge. "How can one fail to be amazed," he wondered, "and to admit how truly divine and surpassingly marvelous our Savior's prescience and foretelling were?"[2] I echo his questions. To understand the prophecy, therefore, one must read Josephus' account of the fulfillment. To understand the fulfillment, one must understand the prophecy.

Divine Judgments Came When Love Waxed Cold and Iniquity Ripened

Divine judgments befall the wicked whenever they reject the words and warnings of God's prophets, ripen in iniquity, and experience the withdrawal of God's Spirit (see Ether 2:8–11, 15; 2 Nephi 25:9; 26:11). Two phrases used by Jesus—*iniquity will abound* and *love wax cold*—show why the coming day would be a generation of judgment. When Josephus described that day (his own), one sees the face of a generation wherein iniquity abounded and love waxed cold. Josephus concluded that had the Romans "delayed to punish these reprobates," God would have sent an earthquake, flood, or thunderbolt to wipe them out. "For it produced a generation far more godless than the victims of [those former] visitations" (because wickedness enveloped the whole nation).[3]

Jewish Robberism Destroyed the Jewish Nation

One might simplify very complex issues by saying that Jewish efforts to plumb the depths of iniquity began, when, Cainlike, they set their hearts on the things of this world and used robberism, or organized force, to get gain. That kind of robberism, according to Josephus, became the chief plague affecting the nation and leading to its destruction.[4]

By the time robberism had fully matured, gangs of robbers were waging a form of war on Jewish communities. They plundered cities, slaughtered citizens, and forced anarchy upon the country. When the robbers opted for war against Rome, they either encouraged or forced all others to adopt the same course. Finally, at Jerusalem, long before Romans arrived, they were themselves devastating the sacred city. They were the first to burn up the grain supply, bloody the temple courts, and put the torch to sacred precincts. Their unyielding resistance to the Romans contributed to the desolation of the city. Overall, Josephus held them responsible for the destruction of their country, Jerusalem, its temple, and its people.

The Robberism That Destroyed the Nation was Based on Lust for Power

Robberism was an old problem. At least a century earlier in the time of Herod, robbers were at work plundering the country. The infamous Barabbas, "who for a certain sedition made in the city, and for murder, was cast into prison" (Luke 23:19), was a robber (*lestes* [John 18:40] a term used by Josephus for robbers or brigands). By the time of Florus, robbers were flourishing throughout the country. The robbers' common goal was to free themselves from Roman rule, but the ultimate goal of each was to gain the power to control the country.

Such robberism, said Josephus, was not based on patriotism but upon lust for gain and power:

> When raids are made by great hordes of brigands and men of the highest standing are assassinated, it is supposed to be the common welfare that is upheld, but the truth is that in such cases *the motive is private gain.*[5]

Robberism Spawned Iniquity Worthy of Divine Judgments

Materialism, anarchy, and depredations by robbers were all signs of abounding iniquity. That period became "so prolific of crime of every description amongst the Jews, that no deed of iniquity was left unperpetrated, nor, had man's wit been exercised to devise it, could he have discovered any novel form of vice."[6]

Jesus and John both recognized the power and threat of the evil that was even then rearing its head. Jesus called that generation an adulterous and evil one, one that loved darkness rather than light, one that satisfied the lust of its murderous father. Both agreed that it was "a generation of vipers" (see Matthew 12:24, 34, 38–39; 13:4; John 8:44; Luke 11:29).

Love Waxed Cold and Iniquity Abounded

After forty years of ripening, Josephus said that the brigand bands who converged on Jerusalem, "abstained henceforth from no enormities."[7] Governed by:

> an insatiable lust for loot, they ransacked the houses of the wealthy; regarded the murder of men and the violation of women as a sport; they caroused on their spoils, with blood to wash them down.[8]

Satiated with these activities, they imitated effeminate dress in their hairstyling, clothing, perfumes, and makeup. They even imitated

> the passions of women, devising in their excess of lasciviousness unlawful pleasures and wallowing as in a brothel in the city, which they polluted from end to end with their foul deeds. Yet, while they wore women's faces, their hands were murderous.[9]

They vied with each other to open "up new and unheard of paths of vice. They paraded their enormities and exhibited their vices as though they were virtues, striving daily to outdo each other in being the worst."[10] Josephus, in tears, concluded that no other city

> ever endured such miseries, nor since the world began has there been a generation more prolific in crime. . . . It was they who overthrew the city, and compelled the reluctant Romans to register so melancholy a triumph.

Killing their high priest along with many of the priests and thousands of citizens, they gloried in their deeds. Josephus concluded that God had condemned the city to destruction and wanted "to purge the sanctuary by fire." Consequently, he "cut off [the priests] who clung to [the temple and its altar] with such tender affection."[11] The green tree had become dead and dry, ready for the burning.

God Never Destroys Without Warning

One generation earlier, John the Baptist had warned them that judgments were impending and wondered who had warned that generation of vipers to "flee from the wrath to come." The axe already was being laid at "the root of the trees: every tree therefore which bringeth not forth good fruit is hewn down, and cast into the fire" (Luke 3:7, 9). The Messiah, whom they yearned for, was coming as to a threshing floor with fan in hand. He would "throughly purge his floor" and "gather the wheat into his garner; but the chaff he will burn with fire unquenchable" (Luke 3:17).

Jesus Warned of Jerusalem's Desolation, Its Pain and Agony

Seeing what awaited the coming generation, Jesus, during his triumphal entry into Jerusalem, "beheld the city and wept over it." Said he:

The days shall come upon thee, that thine enemies shall cast a trench about thee, and compass thee round, and keep thee in on every side. And shall lay thee even with the ground, and thy children within thee; and they shall not leave in thee one stone upon another; because thou knewest not the time of thy visitation. (Luke 19:41–44)

Later, at the temple, Jesus told the parable of the wicked farm tenants to warn conspiring Jews that God would destroy them for killing his servants. As a householder, he had let out his vineyard to wicked husbandmen, who would, in turn, beat, kill, and stone the servants sent to receive the fruits of the vineyard. When they finally killed the son of the householder to "seize on his inheritance," Jesus wanted to know what would happen to the husbandmen.

The Jews in his audience concluded that the Lord of the vineyard would "miserably destroy those wicked men" (Matthew 21:41). Jesus allowed their judgment to stand, but changed the metaphor to one of a stone rejected by builders that became the chief cornerstone. Whoever shall fall on this stone, he warned, "shall be broken: but on whomsoever it shall fall, it will grind him to powder" (see Matthew 21:44; 33–46).

Destroyed for Fighting Against God and His Servants

Jesus censured Jews who hated light and loved darkness, killed true prophets and upheld false ones. Such Jews were struggling to eliminate God's influence from their lives. Lusting for Jesus' blood, they would soon satisfy the lusts of their father, known as "a murderer from the beginning" (John 8:44).

They Fought Against the True Prophets

Jesus tried to show those who claimed to reverence dead prophets that they really had prophet-killing hearts. In his parable of the wedding feast, they were the ones who refused the royal invitation to the wedding, who mistreated and killed the royal servants, but were themselves killed when the king sent forth his armies to destroy those murderers and burn up their city (Matthew 22:1–7).

His opponents knew, of course, how determined they were to kill him but seem not to have understood that their determination qualified them as prophet-killers. How surprised they must have been when he told them to fill "up then the measure of your fathers. Ye serpents,

ye generation of vipers, how can ye escape the damnation of hell?"
(Matthew 23:32–33). That unique generation spilled not only the blood
of the prophets but also the blood of the Son of God. So God would
require of them "the blood of all the prophets, which was shed from the
foundation of the world" (Luke 11:50; see also Matthew 23:35). The
spirit that had produced every martyrdom since the world began—the
desire to fight God—was fully alive and vibrant in that generation.
Therefore, said he to Jews of Jerusalem, "Your house is left unto you
desolate" (Matthew 23:38; Luke 13:35). Any house without God in
residence is desolate.

Conversely, he had to warn his faithful prophets that in such a
generation, some of them would suffer martyrdom (see Matthew 24:9).
The names of John the Baptist; Jesus; Stephen; James, the apostle; and
James, the Lord's brother, show how successful that generation was in
fighting God.[12]

Those Who Kill True Prophets Love False Ones

By slaying true prophets, Jews became vulnerable to false ones—
the "ravening wolves." "Take heed that no man deceive *you*," Jesus had
warned, "For many shall come in my name, saying—I am Christ—and
shall deceive many. . . . Many false prophets shall [also] arise, and shall
deceive many" (Joseph Smith—Matthew 1:5–6,9).

As Josephus shows, false prophets from the time of Christ until the
time Jerusalem fell periodically deceived many Jews. Their influence
was critical enough that it contributed greatly to the destruction of the
nation. Although there seems to be no evidence that they came using
the name or title *Christ* (Messiah), there is every indication that several
came in this role. All prophets, true and false, come in the Lord's name.
The false prophets identified by Josephus came to lead people to victory,
and that, of course, was the role of the messianic prophet. Therefore, one
would conclude that those prophets must have thought of themselves as
messiahs in order to elicit the kind of support they got. Thus, whether
Josephus called them messiahs (christs) or not is irrelevant. They came
in that role.

By their fruits—promising deliverance but delivering no one—they
showed themselves to be false messiahs. And their disciples, believing
but undelivered, all too often ended up dead. Jesus warned his disciples
to identify and reject such deceivers. If Jews had followed his counsel,

they too would have survived. Several examples are cited by Josephus:

During the time when Fadus was procurator of Judaea, AD 40–46,

> a certain impostor named Theudas persuaded the majority of the masses to take up their possessions and to follow him to the Jordan River. He stated that he was a prophet and that at his command the river would be parted and would provide them an easy passage. With this talk he deceived many. Fadus, the procurator, simply cut his head off, slew many of his followers, and took many prisoners.[13]

When Felix was procurator in AD 52–54, deceivers and impostors, claiming divine inspiration, fostered change by revolution and persuaded the multitude to "act like madmen, and led them out into the desert under the belief that God would there give them tokens of deliverance." Felix slew many of them.[14]

Next an Egyptian charlatan claiming to be a prophet "collected a following of about thirty thousand dupes." He came from the desert to the Mount of Olives expecting to overpower the Roman garrison and "set himself up as tyrant of the people." He escaped, but his forces were killed or imprisoned.[15] By arousing hopes falsely, they led hundreds of thousands to death in the fall of their country rather than to victory as they had promised.

False prophets were active through the final days of the city. Six thousand women, children, and others were incinerated atop the last portico of the temple. *"They owed their destruction to a false prophet,"* who told them that "God had commanded them to go up to the temple court, to receive there the tokens of their deliverance."[16] The Romans simply burned them alive. There were no survivors of that false plan of salvation. Finally, to check desertions and encourage hope, numerous prophets "were suborned by the tyrants to delude the people, by bidding them await help from God" rather than fall to the enemy.[17]

Why were the Jews so gullible as to believe in so many different false prophets? As a people, they believe in true prophets and this, ironically, made them susceptible to false ones. Their scriptures also promised them that a special prophet would come and bring the kingdom back to them. In that kind of environment, Josephus said,

> What more than all else incited them to the war was an ambiguous oracle, likewise found in their sacred scriptures, to the effect that at that time one from their country would become ruler of the world.

This they understood to mean someone of their own race, and many of their wise men went astray in their interpretation of it.[18]

Josephus called the oracle ambiguous because he thought it applied to Vespasian. But, it is clear that both oracle and scriptures assured Jews that "at that time one from their country would become ruler of the world."

This suggests a terrible irony. Jews, as Josephus stated, had many prophecies in their scriptures that one of them would rise to rule the world (see Isaiah 9:6–7; 11:1–5; Deuteronomy 18:15, 18; Micah 5:2). He was popularly known as the Messiah (the Anointed One). Such scriptural prophecies of his coming provided an environment of expectation. Roman oppression provided the need. But, what oracle confirming the scriptures was Josephus speaking about? He doesn't specify. Is it, therefore, merely coincidence that contemporary records in the Gospels tell us that God did in fact give oracles through shepherds and wise men that the Messiah (Luke 2:11) or King (Matthew 2:2–3) had been born? And that this news was broadcast abroad, for "when [the shepherds] had seen [the baby], they made known abroad the saying which was told them concerning this child [that their Messiah, their Lord and Savior had been born]" (Luke 2:17). And, when the wise men came into the heart of Jewry and asked: "Where is he that is born King of the Jews?" Then Herod was "troubled, *and all Jerusalem with him*" (Matthew 2:2–3; italics added).

Given the significance of the messianic promise to the Jews, their need for a deliverer, the smallness of their country, and the fact that angels and a star had announced to that generation of Jews that the Messiah/King had come, there need be no question that the good news of the shepherds went like wildfire throughout the country. Within days, we must assume, all Jews of that generation knew that the Messiah had come. But, since he was merely a baby, they obviously knew that they must await patiently the time of his royal advent. When sufficient time had passed and John burst on the scene, "the people were in expectation and all men mused in their hearts of John, whether he were the Christ [the Messiah], or not" (Luke 3:15). When he denied that he was and died, they were left to find someone who fit their own mold. But, having rejected the true Messiah, they became vulnerable to all other messianic pretenders. As successive prophets arose and left believers wanting, Jews kept looking. By Josephus' time, they were sure he was still out there somewhere. When the Roman government, therefore, became bankrupt, they felt that they must make a beginning. Convinced by scriptural promises and some oracle, that "at that time" he would come, they struck boldly for freedom. How ironic that the revelation that the true Messiah had come seems to have made them vulnerable to false prophets who led them to destruction.

"Thus it was," said Josephus, "that the wretched people were deluded at that time by charlatans and pretended messengers of the deity." Yet, "as if thunderstruck and bereft of eyes and mind, [they] disregarded the plain warnings of God [see below]."[19] Jesus also marveled: "If thou hadst known, even thou, at least in this thy day, the things which belong unto thy peace! *But now they are hid from thine eyes*" (Luke 19:42; italics added).

We tend to think that Jesus' warnings about false prophets apply only to false prophets within the Christian Church, but Josephus made it clear that following false prophets led to the destruction of the whole Jewish community. Like corrupt trees, they, along with their fruits, were hewn down and cast into the fire (see Matthew 7:15–21).

It Was Prophesied that the City Would Be Destroyed When Faction Reigned

Other aspects of Jesus' prophecy show that the temple would be leveled. There shall not, said he, "be left here, upon this temple, one stone upon another that shall not be thrown down" (Joseph Smith—Matthew 1:3). Josephus said that many prophets predicted that the city and its temple would be destroyed, but robbers scoffed at these "oracles of the prophets as impostors' fables" and, consequently, brought about the fulfillment of the prophecies against it. One prophecy in particular stated that "the city would be taken and the sanctuary burnt to the ground by right of war, whensoever it should be visited by sedition, and native hands should be the first to defile God's sacred precincts."[20] Josephus shows how this happened when robbers became guilty of both sedition and defiling the sacred precincts.

When the time for the burning of the temple finally came, Josephus concluded that it was God and not the Romans who put it to the torch. Contrary to Titus' orders, "[a soldier] awaiting no order . . . moved by some supernatural impulse snatched a brand from the burning timber and . . . flung the fiery missile through a low gold door" and set the temple ablaze—all, said Josephus, because God had sentenced the temple to the flames.[21]

Because of "the height of the hill and the mass of the burning pile, one would have thought that the whole city was ablaze" and that the "temple-hill was boiling over from its base, being everywhere one mass of flame." Many died defending it.[22] The surrounding buildings, remnants of the porticos, and temple gates were then put to the torch.[23]

The City Was Leveled and the Inhabitants Within

While the temple blazed, the victors plundered everything that fell in their way and slaughtered wholesale all who were caught. No pity was shown for age, no reverence for rank; children and greybeards, laity and priests, alike were massacred; every class was pursued and encompassed in the grasp of war, whether suppliants for mercy or offering resistance. . . . The slain [were] more numerous than the slayers. For the ground was nowhere visible through the corpses; but the soldier had to clamber over heaps of bodies in pursuit of the fugitives.[24]

In addition to those who died by the sword, Romans discovered many houses that were "packed with bodies of the victims of the famine."[25]

Not One Stone Left on Another

Titus ordered:

the whole city and the temple to be razed to the ground, leaving only the loftiest of towers, Phasael, Hippicus, and Miramme, and the portion of the wall enclosing the city on the west. . . . All the rest of the wall encompassing the city was so completely leveled to the ground as to leave future visitors to the spot no ground for believing that it had ever been inhabited.[26]

The House Was Left Desolate

With the leveling of the temple, the city, and its inhabitants, another prophecy was fulfilled: "Behold, *your house is left unto you desolate*" (Matthew 23:38; italics added; see also Matthew 23:29–37; Luke 13:33–35). Any house in which love waxes cold, iniquity abounds, and God's Spirit withdraws is, by definition, a desolate house. But, the physical desolation of the Jewish house was pervasive.

Cities and villages throughout Galilee and Judaea were desolated by the ravages of robbers and soldiers. The countryside was desolate. The gardenlike environs of Jerusalem were desolated. "Trees and parks [were] reduced to an utter desert and stripped bare of timber." For a ten-mile radius around Jerusalem, all timber was cut to build siege platforms and towers.[27] Obviously, Jesus' beloved Garden of Gethsemane contributed its share of wood to the Roman attack on Jerusalem.

Jerusalem was leveled and desolated. The temple was desolated: robbers made the temple their den, polluted its precincts, plundered its gold, and profaned its courts with the blood of worshippers.[28] When Jewish blood was mingled with their sacrifices, another prophecy of Jesus was fulfilled. He had warned his hearers that unless they repented, then like Galileans "whose blood Pilate had mingled with their sacrifices," they too would "likewise perish" (Luke 13:1–3). They hadn't repented and, like Galileans, their blood also was mingled with their sacrifices.

Jewish lives also were desolated. The tribulation sent upon the inhabitants of Jerusalem, said Jesus, would be greater than at any time "since the beginning of their kingdom until this time; no, nor ever shall be sent again upon Israel" (Joseph Smith—Matthew 1:18). Jesus charged the women who "bewailed and lamented him" as he travailed his way onto Golgotha, "Daughters of Jerusalem, weep not for me, but weep for yourselves, and for your children," for in the coming days you "shall say, Blessed are the barren, and the wombs that never bare, and the paps which never gave suck. Then shall they begin to say to the mountains, Fall on us; and to the hills, cover us" (Luke 23:27–31). This prophecy was fulfilled many times over. Josephus, for example, said, "Such terror prevailed [at one point] that the survivors deemed blessed the lot of the earlier victims, now at rest, while the tortured wretches in the prisons pronounced even the unburied happy in comparison with themselves.[29]

Thus, all that housed whatever the Jews held dear—land, cities, gardens, fields, woods, their capital, their holy temple, the priesthood organization, their mosaic religion based on temple worship, and their lives—had become desolate.

How Did Jesus Save His Disciples?

Jesus obviously knew in detail the forces that would bring destruction. His warnings and counsel helped people prepare in specific ways to cope with the problems he had identified. They took his forewarnings and were forearmed. For example, having shown them that iniquity would abound and love wax cold, he assured them that "he that remaineth steadfast and is not overcome, the same shall be saved" (Joseph Smith—Matthew 1:10–11).

The unprecedented breakdown in law and order, the plunder and violence, the murder and rape described by Josephus, would frighten even the stalwart. But, degenerating conditions when a man's enemies would be they of his own house must not seduce disciples away from their simple faith, their strong moral commitment, and their deep level of love for one another. Seeing others succeed by violence and dishonesty must never entice them to succeed by the same means.

Steadfastness in the right builds character to withstand evil. So, when the world filled up with iniquity, when love fled and decency went away, ancient Saints steadfastly stood by their covenants.

Stand in the Holy Place

> When you . . . see the abomination of desolation, spoken of by Daniel the prophet, concerning the destruction of Jerusalem, then you shall stand in the holy place; whoso readeth let him understand. Then let them who are in Judea flee into the mountains. (Joseph Smith—Matthew 1:12–13)

"Stand in the holy place . . . then let them who are in Judaea flee." How can one *stand* in the holy place and *flee*? Obviously neither the temple nor Jerusalem were places of refuge. *Standing* apparently means here *to take one's stand*. By standing with holy feet on whatever ground, one stands in a holy place. Holy feet sanctify polluted ground just as polluted feet pollute holy ground. Standing steadfast, *saints* sanctify the places where they live. Thus, came the promise, "he that remaineth steadfast and is not overcome, the same shall be saved" (Joseph Smith—Matthew 1:11). How reassuring!

Know the Signs of the Times and Recognize the Divine Portents

God gives adequate signs so that his children may know the times in which they live. Jesus chided Jews who prided themselves on being able to look at winds and clouds and then predict the weather, but were unable to "discern this time" (Luke 12:54–56). Along with Josephus, one is amazed at how many special signs of impending disaster the Lord gave them that they ignored. But, loving darkness, they rationalized away the light and took no warning.

For example, during the winter of AD 66–67, when war preparations in Galilee and Jerusalem were being made, "there were omens, which to the friends of peace boded ill, although those who had kindled the war readily invented favourable interpretations of them."[30]

False prophets played a role in this misinterpretation. They deluded "the wretched people" into believing in deliverance, despite God's foretelling them of their desolation. "But as if thunderstruck and bereft of eyes and mind, they disregarded the plain warnings of God." These warnings consisted in a star resembling a sword that stood over the city; a comet seen for a year; and, for half an hour in the middle of the night, at the feast of unleavened bread, a light shining as bright as day around the altar and the sanctuary. Some thought the light to be a good one, but sacred scribes interpreted it as a message of disaster. Also, at that feast, a sacrificial cow gave birth to a lamb in the midst of the court of the temple. Then, the massive brass gate of the inner temple courts, fastened by iron bars and bolted into the stone threshold, swung open of its own accord at the sixth hour of the night. It was a favourable omen to some, but to the learned the "opening of the gate meant a present to the enemy." Then, after the festival and throughout the country, people saw chariots and armed battalions hurtling through the clouds and encompassing the cities. At Pentecost, priests inside the inner court of the temple reported a commotion and a din at night followed by a voice as of a host, "We are departing hence." Finally, at the Feast of Tabernacles, "four years before the war, when the city was enjoying profound peace and prosperity," Jesus, son of Ananias, stood in the temple, and cried out, "A voice against Jerusalem and the sanctuary . . . a voice against all the people." Despite being chastised and scourged by officials, he continued day and night for seven and a half years to say: "Woe to Jerusalem!" When woe had finally come upon the city, he pronounced his last woe on the city as well as on himself and was then struck by a stone and died.

Reflecting on these things one will find that God has a care for men, and by all kinds of premonitory signs shows His people the way

JESUS AND JOSEPHUS TOLD OF THE DESTRUCTION OF JERUSALEM

of salvation, while they owe their destruction to folly and calamities, of their own choosing. . . . Some of these portents, then, the Jews interpreted to please themselves, others they treated with contempt [until it was too late].[31]

Those kinds of signs given to the Jews fascinate Latter-day Saints who have been assured that they, too, will see many signs in the heavens and earth to identify the last days (see for example, D&C 29:14; 88:87–93.) They are urged to look for such signs (see D&C 39:23; 45:16). Seeing them will fill them with hope and expectation (see D&C 68:10–11).

Flee to Live!

Jews regarded Jerusalem not only as a sacred city but also as the best fortified one in the country. Consequently many fled to the city for refuge. Christians, knowing that the city was doomed, rejected popular wisdom and prepared to flee *from* it. Jesus said,

> When ye shall see Jerusalem compassed with armies, then know that the desolation thereof is nigh . . .
> Let them which are in the midst of it depart out; and let not them that are in the countries enter thereinto.
> For these be the days of vengeance, that all things which are written may be fulfilled. (Luke 21:20–22)

Ironically, while the Lord led the Saints out of Jerusalem, Josephus suggests that "by fate" the whole nation was brought within its walls before it fell. For having converged upon Jerusalem for the Feast of Unleavened Bread, they "found themselves suddenly enveloped in the war."[32] It was as though "the whole nation had been shut up by fate as in a prison, and the city when war encompassed it was packed with inhabitants."[33] Josephus estimated that 1,100,000 died during the siege and that 97,000 prisoners were taken.[34]

Christian disciples, who knew that old things had passed away and all things had become new in Christ, did not go to Jerusalem to observe the Feast of Unleavened Bread and the Passover, and therefore, were not caught by the Roman army and confined within Jerusalem. Their once-and-for-all Passover Lamb had already warned them to flee and to pray that

> your flight be not in the winter, neither on the Sabbath day; for then, in those days, shall be great tribulation on the Jews, and upon the

inhabitants of Jerusalem, such as was not before sent upon Israel, of God, since the beginning of their kingdom until this time; no, nor ever shall be sent again upon Israel. (Joseph Smith—Matthew 1:17–18)

Flight From Plundering Jews in Judaea

Roman soldiers, however, were not the only enemy from whom Jews had to flee. Jesus must have known that Jewish robbers would also slaughter, ravage, and plunder fellow Jews. And that in doing so they would show no mercy to those not fleet enough to outrun them. For example, Jewish bandits from Masada attacked unsuspecting Jews in the Judaean city of Engedi during the Feast of Tabernacles. The Jewish defenders were driven from town before they could seize arms. "Those unable to fly, women and children numbering upwards of seven hundred were massacred." The bandits carried their spoil to Masada and then wasted the whole district.

> Throughout the other parts of Judaea, moreover, the predatory bands, hitherto quiescent, now began to bestir themselves . . . each gang after pillaging [its] own village made off into the wilderness . . . There was, in fact *no portion of Judaea* which did not share in the ruin of the capital.[35]

Jesus' specific counsel to Judaean disciples was to get out of their cities and into the mountains. "Then let them which are *in Judaea* flee to the mountains" (Luke 21:20–21; italics added). Speed of departure was important, but, in that plundering society, they must be willing to abandon prized possessions. Robbers otherwise would have reason to pursue them. Also, carrying possessions would retard their flight. If they survived, survival would be the prize. Thus, more specific counsel:

> Let him who is on the housetop flee, and not return to take anything out of his house; neither let him who is in the field return back to take his clothes. (Joseph Smith—Matthew 1:14–15)

Flight Was Retarded by Children

One robber band after another converged on Jerusalem. Thus, John of Gischala and his band fled there from Galilee. The circumstances of their flight show something of Jesus' concern for the pregnant and those with small children. As John and his men fled and their wives and children could not keep up with them, they abandoned them despite their pleas for them to wait. Love had waxed cold. John gallantly promised to have his "revenge on the Romans for any left behind, if they are caught."[36] Six thousand stragglers were killed, and three thousand women and children were brought back by Titus' men.[37] Jesus recognized such problems when he said: "Woe unto them that are with child, and to them that give suck, in those days!" (Luke 21:23). Flight on wintry days or Sabbath would also have posed special hardships (see Matthew 24:17).

Jerusalem Saints Fled the City When God Told Them to Do So

Thus, throughout Judaea, those who failed to flee to the mountains suffered from the robbers. Those who fled to Jerusalem suffered the agonies of that dying city. But those who fled from Judaea to the mountains and from Jerusalem to a refuge city survived. Christians continued to carry on church business from Jerusalem for many years after Jesus had gone. Obviously they depended upon the Lord to tell them when the right time for them to flee had come. Thus, when the time was right, the true prophets led them out. Eusebius, the ancient Christian historian, tells us how

> the people of the church at Jerusalem, in accordance, with a certain oracle that was vouchsafed by way of revelation to approved men there, had been commanded to depart from the city before the war, and to inhabit a certain city of Peraea. They called it Pella. And when those who believed in Christ had removed from Jerusalem, as if holy men had utterly deserted both the royal metropolis of the Jews itself and the whole land of Judaea, the justice of God then visited upon them all their acts of violence to Christ and His apostles, by destroying that generation of wicked persons root and branch from among men.[38]

Josephus himself knew of the time when many fled the city. It occurred when the momentum for peace was shifting to that for war, when the Jewish victory over Cestius made Jews drunk with hope, when the war had not really begun because Vespasian had not yet arrived to begin the Romans' initiative. At that time, said he, "many distinguished Jews abandoned the city as swimmers desert a sinking ship."[39] It is not likely that Josephus regarded the Christians as "distinguished Jews."

But, it may be that Christian departures triggered an exodus of other distinguished Jews that was big enough to catch Josephus' attention.

We do not know what happened to the Christians thereafter, except that by going to Pella they survived, as Eusebius said. It got them out of the inferno.

The Horrors Were Not Over When the City Fell

According to Josephus, 97,000 prisoners had been taken during the war, 1,100,000 died within the city, the weak and old prisoners were executed, the strong men were sent to the mines, and the great number of women and children prisoners glutted the slave market.[40] Thousands of men were kept to fight as gladiators for the amusement of the Romans.[41]

Jesus said of the Jews after Jerusalem's fall: "All things which [had] befallen them [would be] only the beginning of the sorrows which [would] come upon them" (Joseph Smith—Matthew 24:19). Jerusalem itself would then be "trodden down of the Gentiles, until the times of the Gentiles be fulfilled" (Luke 21:24).

Unprecedented Tribulation Came Upon The Jews

Jesus knew that the tribulation experienced by the Jews would be unprecedented—"such as was not before sent upon Israel, of God, since the beginning of their kingdom until this time; no, nor ever shall be sent again upon Israel" (Joseph Smith—Matthew 1:18). Josephus concluded as much by his own observation. He said that Jerusalem

> suffered such calamities during the siege, that, had she from her foundation enjoyed an equal share of blessings, she would have been thought unquestionably enviable; a city undeserving, moreover, of the great misfortunes on any other ground, save that she produced a generation such as that which caused her overthrow.[42]

Correlating what Jesus predicted with events as described by Josephus shows again why sin is sin, how it feeds upon itself, how hurtful and deadly its effects are, and how the abomination of sinfulness desolates any people. It shows how well God knows what takes place on earth; how much he wants his children to avoid painful encounters; how adulterous, wicked lives maturate into violence and horror; how God uses the sword of the wicked to destroy the wicked; and how his righteous purposes are fulfilled in his judgments. It shows that those things that really pollute and defile lives are not unwashed hands but "evil thoughts, murders, adulteries, fornications, thefts, false witness, blasphemies" (Matthew 15:19–20). Jesus identified the undisciplined thought; Josephus catalogued the deeds.

Throughout the Gospels there is a sad awareness that Jesus, who knew with precision what would happen, knew also how to stop the desolation of human lives and save anyone who would listen to him. Repeatedly he tried to gather and protect his tender chicks. His prophecy and Josephus' record of fulfillment show that "the righteous that hearken unto the words of the prophets, and destroy them not, but look forward unto Christ with steadfastness for the signs which are given, notwithstanding all persecution—behold, they are they which shall not perish" (2 Nephi 26:8, see also 3 Nephi 10:14–16).

Notes
1. *Josephus the Jewish War* (hereafter referred to as *War*, trans. H. St. J. Thackeray, Harvard University Press, 1976, III: 351–354. Vol. I–III, published in 1976; Volumes IV–VII published in 1979.)
2. *Eusebius: The Ecclesiastical History and the Martyrs of Palestine*, III.7.6 trans. Hugh Jackson Lawlor and John Ernest Leonard Oulton, London, SPCK, 1954, 74.
3. *War* 5:566.
4. I discussed at the 1986 Pearl of Great Price Symposium my conviction that Jewish robberism was identical in type, motive, and works to the Gadiantonism exhibited among the Nephites.
5. *Josephus: Jewish Antiquities*, XVIII: 7–8, trans. Louis H. Feldman. London: Harvard University Press, 1969.
6. *War* 7:259–62.
7. *War* 4:138.
8. *War* 4:560–61.
9. *War* 4:561–63.
10. *War* 5:401–3, 417–20.
11. *War* 4:314–25.
12. Eusebius, *op. cit.*, III.5.2.
13. *Antiquities* 20:97–99. Cf. Acts 5:36.
14. *War* 2:258–60.
15. *War* 2:261–65.
16. *War* 6:285.
17. *War* 6:285–87.

18. *War* 6:312–13.
19. *War* 6:288.
20. *War* 4:385–88.
21. *War* 6:250–53.
22. See *War* 6:271–72, 275.
23. See *War* 6:281.
24. *War* 6:271–72, 276.
25. *War* 6:354–55.
26. *War* 6:1, 3.
27. See *War* 6:5–8.
28. See *War* 4:241–42, 258, 261–62; 5:14–19.
29. *War* 4:385–86.
30. *War* 2:648–50.
31. *War* 6:285–315
32. *War* 6:421.
33. *War* 6:428.
34. This number, Josephus claimed, was not excessive. On an earlier occasion, priests by count had sacrificed 255,600 lambs for the Passover, and, since no fewer than ten might eat one lamb, this meant that at least 2,700,000 partook of the Passover (War VI:422–425). Modern historians feel that the number is excessive. Joachim Jeremiah, for example, calculates that there were no more than 180,000 participants (55,000 citizens of Jerusalem and 125,000 pilgrims) in the Passover feast and probably fewer. (*Jerusalem in the Times of Jesus*, Fortress Press, Philadelphia, 1969, 77–84.)
35. *War* 4:406–409; italics added.
36. *War* 4:115
37. *War* 4:106:11. 38. Eusebius, *op. cit.*, III.5.3.
39. *War* 2:556.
40. *War* 6:384, 386.
41. *Wars* 7:96.
42. *War* 6:404–8.

CHAPTER NINE

Jude: A Call to Contend for the Faith

T. John Nielsen II

The epistle of Jude has been labeled "the most neglected book in the New Testament."[1] Why is it neglected? Why does it seem to be overlooked by the majority of Christians? What of Jude's authenticity? What of Jude's standing in the early church, his use of the apocryphal text, and his strange (to the major Christian religions) doctrines? Should Jude really be canon? All these questions have caused post-New Testament debate for centuries.

Modern revelation has shown to the living prophets that Jude is a valuable epistle, and, like other prophetic writings, it has been preserved through generations of theologians for us. Through modern revelation the Latter-day Saints easily understand the apocryphal statements made by Jude. They accept apocryphal texts as they conform to scripture—both ancient and modern. Only Jude spoke of our pre-existence as our "first estate,"[2] and only Jude referred to Enoch's prophecy of the Second Coming of Jesus Christ.

Modern revelation thus illuminates Jude's writings, and members of Christ's earthly kingdom are given valuable information about our past life and our world history. Jude wrote as a distant voice of warning to each Latter-day Saint who has been called to prepare for Christ's Second Coming. Jude, in verse 18, referred to the time just preceding the Second Coming as the "last time":

> How that they told you there should be mockers in the last time, who should walk after their own ungodly lusts.

His message is vital to us today, for he saw and understood the plan of God in this, the last day.

Let's move through the textual outline and see what Jude's message was to the Meridian-day Saints and why it is a valuable message for the Latter-day Saints. For convenience of study, Jude is divided into seven sections.

1. Introduction (1–2)
2. Purpose (3–4)
3. Reminder of the war with Satan (5–9)
4. Kinds of deceivers (10–13)
5. Prophecies: Enoch (14–16)
   Quorum of the Twelve (17–19)
6. Counsel and encouragement (20–23)
7. Testimony of hope and conclusion (24–25)

Introduction (v. 1–2)

Who was Jude, and what authority did he have to write to the early Saints? The answer to these questions would help us to also see the importance of his message to the Latter-day Saints. Jude first introduced himself as "called of Jesus Christ" (JST, Jude 1:1), and further identified himself as the "brother of James" (Jude 1:1). Luke 6:16 lists one of the apostles as "Judas of James," which translated from Greek means "Jude, brother of James."[3] Galatians 1:19 tells us that the Apostle James was the brother, or, more literally, the half-brother of Christ (Matthew 13:55–56). Therefore, Jude's humble introduction as the "Brother of James" (Jude 1:1) helps us to know him as an apostle and half-brother of the Savior. This James is not to be confused with the son of Zebedee or the son of Alphaeus. James, the Lord's half-brother, was bishop at Jerusalem and some time after the resurrection was called to serve as an Apostle (Acts 15:21). Jude "quite naturally . . . identified himself with his better known brother."[4] (McConkie 1973, 416). He reverentially documented his sayings as being in accord with the original Quorum of the Twelve.

> But, beloved, remember ye the words which were spoken before of the apostles of our Lord Jesus Christ. (Jude 1:17)

Though Jude can be accepted as an apostle, many Bible scholars struggled with Jude because of his words.

> Modern objections to the authorship of the letter by a half-brother of Jesus include the fact that its language seems very Hellenistic for an author who grew up in Galilee. In addition, the vocabulary abounds in ornate and rare words (there are thirteen words not found elsewhere in the New Testament).[5]

These scholars struggled because Jude used the Jewish apocalyptic writings of Enoch (v. 14), and the Assumption of Moses (v. 9).

Many Bible scholars of today lack the background that Jude assumed the reader had of the Jewish scriptures used by New Testament Saints. This is probably one reason why this book is "the most neglected book" by the majority of Christians. They are not familiar with the language of the members of Christ's original Church. Jude referred to doctrinal insights assuming the readers knew what he was talking about. Apostasy and the loss of apostolic revelation left Christendom without the pure doctrines of Christ and his true Church. Though the early Christian Saints knew those doctrines, the apostates and the later self-styled clergymen did not.

Jude used the Greek *Iesosis* as the God who saved the people in Moses' time. Iesosis is translated Jesus Christ. Centuries later theologians wrestled with the idea of Christ being the God of the Old Testament.

> Despite the weighty attestation supporting Iesosis (Jesus) . . . a *majority* of the committee *was of* the opinion that the reading was difficult . . . due to the well-attested early Christian desire to attribute to Jesus a role in the events of the Old Testament History.[6]

Apostasy and time had changed the doctrines of Christ's premortal life. Lost to later theologians was the true nature of Jesus Christ. The New Testament Christians attributed to Jesus his proper premortal role. John declared Christ as the God of the Old Testament and the Creator of man and earth (see John 1:1–3; 6:62; 8:58; 17:5). Scholars tried to reconcile Jude, struggling with Christ's role in the Old Testament and their own doctrines.

> Jude's use of apocryphal writings . . . occasioned doubts and reservations about the Biblical authority of this epistle. . . . The Syrian Church excluded it and many Christians . . . feel uneasy with the presence of Jude! They have difficulty reconciling Jude's use of

apocryphal writings with their concept of Biblical inspiration and truth.[7]

Some scholars tried to reconcile their difficulties by saying apostles were only men and thus erroneously used myth and slavonic legends.

> In the inspired books of the Old and New Testaments, we have God's word articulated in the words of men. These writers, like all human beings, were influenced in their thinking and expression by the culture and concepts of their day. They lived in a prescientific age. Many of their concepts, because of the limitation of their knowledge, were erroneous, indeed to us fantastic. God took these men as they were, and through their writings communicated.[8]

Although some scholars have tried to explain away Jude's letter because he used unique examples, modern revelation illuminates and validates this junior apostle's letter. What these scholars did not know they tried to disregard, discounting the knowledge a man gains from God as "erroneous." In reality God is not limited by man's weaknesses.

The Purpose (3–4)

Jude wrote with compelling desire to remind the Saints to "contend for the faith" (Jude 1:3). He reminded them of their brotherhood because of the "common salvation" which God has graciously allowed all men to partake of through baptism. Jude also told of his concern about those evil and designing followers of Satan and his angels (Jude 1:4). Satan has sought from premortal life to destroy God's plan of salvation. His demonic temper has caused him to despise all those who have inherited the second estate by choosing to follow the foreordained Savior in their first estate. Lucifer sought God's honor and power in the pre-existence (Moses 4:1–4), and Satan still seeks to destroy our Heavenly Father's plan and His only mortal Son, Jesus Christ (2 Nephi 2:17–18; Jacob 4:11; Revelation 12:9, 12, 17).

Jude's understanding was similar in many ways to Lehi's.

> Wherefore, men are free according to the flesh; and all things are given them which are expedient unto man. And they are free to choose liberty and eternal life, through the great Mediator of all men, or to choose captivity and death, according to the captivity and power of the devil; for he seeketh that all men might be miserable like unto himself. (2 Nephi 2:27)

Jude pleaded with us to contend for that original faith and to be aware of Satan's intention.

Reminder of the Premortal War With Satan (5–9)

Jude moved into a short doctrinal reflection of the devil's plan from the beginning by reminding us of our war against Satan (see D&C 76:29). One may have been saved by baptism and still lose the war against Satan. He reminded the Saints of the Israelites who thought they were saved, but because of their lack of obedience they were destroyed (Deuteronomy 1:35). Jude reminded them of the angels in heaven that followed Satan; though they were in the presence of God, they left their first estate, followed Satan, and became eternally damned. This damnation stopped them from going on to the second estate, or earth life. They could not gain a body of flesh and bones (see Abraham 3:22–28).

Jude used the examples of this war and its continuation on earth to remind the reader of the outcomes of those who have followed Satan:

A. The Israelites, after leaving Egypt, sought to worship idols and were destroyed.
B. Lucifer and his angels sought God's power and authority and lost their second estate.
C. The people of Sodom and Gomorrah sought after "strange flesh," that is, immorality, perverting the divine nature of sexual relationships, and thus they suffered death by eternal fire.

There is a proper way to fight Satan, and Jude reminded the Saints of Michael's dispute about the body of Moses. Satan desired the death of Moses, claiming that Moses was a murderer. If Moses had murdered the Egyptian, Satan would have had claim on him because of that sin. Michael, the archangel, remembered the Savior (the Holy One) as he who has power over Satan. Michael, known as Adam in the flesh[9] won the dispute for Moses' body by calling on the Lord. The war with Satan will come to an end, and it will be Michael who leads the last great battle (Revelation 12:7–9; D&C 78:16). Jude pointed out that as great as Michael was, he called on Christ, the great Deliverer. Michael showed us by example the need to call on Christ for strength against Satan.

In using this example of Michael's dispute with Satan, Jude created problems for the self-styled Christian. He quoted from the Assumption of Moses, an apocryphal Jewish text, and, though fragments have been found of the Assumption of Moses, this story has not been found. Some scholars would discount Jude for the lack of physical evidence. Ironically, verse 19 of Jude talked of those who are willing to understand only by physical things, excluding the spiritual. Jude told the Saints that it is in and through Jesus Christ that they will find safety, and not to heed those who have not his Spirit. Jude's message is important to use today, for man has placed most of his faith in the sterile scientific method and not in the Lord's prophets. Through Joseph Smith we learn that Enoch was a great prophet, and Jude's reference to Enoch was from Jude's personal visit with Enoch.

Kinds of Deceivers (10–13)

Jude describes the kinds of deceivers Satan employs, referring to these false teachers as "dreamers or *enypniazomenoi*." The Greek word *enypniazomenoi* refers to pretensions of prophecy.[10] By mentioning the false teachers, Jude helps make us aware of the growth of gnosticism already within the church at his time. These gnostics claimed to have new, more insightful, and special knowledge, claiming special powers and authority to perform secret ordinances. They defiled the flesh with sexual sins, promoting lasciviousness and immorality as godly worship. They hated the church leaders and spoke "evil of dignitaries," using gossip and lies to undermine the importance of the Lord's anointed servants in the church.

Jude condemned these perverters for repeating the sins of Cain, Balaam, and Korah. Cain murdered for gain. These false teachers were spiritually murdering Saints for personal gain and the praise of their own followers. Balaam sought to be paid for his use of the gifts of the spirit just as the false teachers of Jude's day sought to make money by prostituting a testimony for a sense of spirituality. Korah's gainsaying was equal to those false teachers' denials of true doctrines as taught by Christ and the apostles. Jude called these deceivers "spots in your feasts of charity" (JST, Jude 1:12). "Trees without fruit, twice dead, who came alive with baptism and were now dead because of apostasy, and hence are destined . . . to die permanently."[11]

The Saints of the twentieth century are plagued by the same sins as Jude's meridian-day Saints. People scheme and cheat for personal gain and fame. False evangelists, pastors, and spiritualists preach of Christ for money and political power. Other self-called religionists sell the blessings of God for a price. Doctrines are discarded for expediency and popular trends. The end result for the deceivers of today is eternal damnation, the same fate as those followers of Satan in the premortal life.

John the Revelator and Jude referred to Satan's followers as stars (Revelation 12:4). Jude described these stars as having lost their premortal luster; they wander in "the blackness of darkness for ever" (Jude 1:13).

Prophecies Enoch (14–16) and the Quorum of the Twelve (17–19)

Jude quoted from Enoch and the Apostles concerning the prophecies of their day. He also compares those prophecies to the last day (14–19). Though theologians have questioned Jude's reference to the writings of Enoch, modern revelation helps us know of its truthfulness. Through modern prophets our understanding of this great prophet is increased. The book of Moses says Enoch walked with God, finally being translated "and he was not; for God took him" (see Genesis 5:24–25).

We know that Enoch was powerful in his preaching, that he performed many great miracles and received numerous revelations. Not all his account in this life is available to us, but Enoch's full record will be had in the last days for the Saints to read and study (see D&C 107:53–57). All we have of Enoch today is in fragmented form. Jude must have had more than we do. But Jude did not have to rely on the apocryphal sources we have today, for the Prophet Joseph Smith taught that Enoch appeared and ministered unto Jude.[12]

Joseph Smith's revelation is completely contrary to one biblical apologist, Marvin R. Vincent, who said that the book of Enoch shows no Christian influence, is highly moral in tone, and imitates the Old Testament myths. Modern scholars have agreed that the book of Enoch was considered scripture by the first century (Meridian-day) Saints. The fourth century brought apostasy and the abandonment of earlier scriptures.

In verse 16, Jude identified the ungodly sinners as having the following qualities:

> Murmurers, complainers, walking after their own lusts; and their mouth speaketh great swelling words, having men's persons in admiration because of advantage. (Jude 1:16)

These qualities, all devoid of the Holy Spirit, were spoken of by Paul (see Acts 10:29; 1 Timothy 4:1; 2 Timothy 3:1–5). The false attitude of religious pomp was found by the prophet Alma among the Zoramites (see Alma 31). They dressed and worshipped to gain the praise of men.

Counsel and Encouragement (20–23)

Jude started to close his short epistle with counsel and encouragement. He told us to build our faith, "praying in the Holy Ghost." Elder Bruce R. McConkie said, "Praying by the power of the Holy Ghost, so that all requested petitions are granted, because 'it shall be given you what you shall ask' (D&C 50:29–30)."[13]

Jude's second suggestion was to keep yourself in the "love of God."

> Keep yourselves in the love of God, looking for the mercy of our Lord Jesus Christ unto eternal life. (Jude 1:21)

Jude's use of words here correlates beautifully with Lehi and Nephi's understanding of the "love of God." Lehi, while called as a prophet in Jerusalem about 600 BC, saw in vision Christ inviting him to partake of the fruit of the tree of life. Lehi described his partaking of this tree's fruit:

> And it came to pass that I beheld a tree, whose fruit was desirable to make one happy.
>
> And it came to pass that I did go forth and partake of the fruit thereof; and I beheld that it was most sweet, above all that I ever before tasted. Yea, and I beheld that the fruit thereof was white, to exceed all the whiteness that I had ever seen.
>
> And as I partook of the fruit thereof it filled my soul with exceedingly great joy; wherefore, I began to be desirous that my family should partake of it also; for I knew that it was desirable above all other fruit. (1 Nephi 8:10–12)

Lehi's son Nephi, upon inquiring of the Lord, discovered that this tree and its fruit represent the love of God (see 1 Nephi 11:22). Both prophets saw the fruit "was desirable above all other fruit" (1 Nephi 8:12). Jude's previous caution about mockers and his plea to "keep yourselves in the love of God echoes the description of Lehi and Nephi of what they had seen.

> They were in the attitude of mocking and pointing their fingers towards those who had come at and were partaking of the fruit.

> And after they had tasted of the fruit [the love of God] they were
> ashamed, because of those that were scoffing at them; and they fell
> away into forbidden paths and were lost. (1 Nephi 8:27–28)

Jude encouraged increased fellowship and gave sound advice to
leaders and other Saints who contend for the faith. He asked them to
have compassion (v. 22) with those who are weak in testimony. Lehi
demonstrated this principle with his sons Laman and Lemuel. They
would not partake of the love of God (fruit), but he "did exhort them
with all the feeling of a tender parent" (1 Nephi 8:37).

With others, Jude said, "Save with fear" (v. 23). We hear this same
counsel from God in modern scripture. The Doctrine and Covenants
reads, "Reproving betimes with sharpness, when moved upon by the
Holy Ghost" (121:43). There are times when we must be patient and
there are times when rebuke is appropriate.

Next, Jude said, "Hating even the garment spotted by the flesh," we
pull them out of the fire (Jude 1:23). The fire denotes the final judgment
and is found several places in the scriptures (see D&C 135:6; Amos
4:11; 2 Peter 3:10–18). We understand this principle by reading D&C
36:6:

> Save yourselves from this untoward generation, and come forth
> out of the fire, hating even the garments spotted with the flesh.

Though not used a great deal in the scriptures, the expression
"spotted in the flesh" refers to the fact that one should avoid the mere
appearance of evil. We should be completely disassociated from all sin,
thus avoiding contaminations as if it were any other dreaded disease
(see Leviticus 15:4–17).

Testimony of Hope and Conclusion (24–25)

In closing, Jude bore his witness of the Savior's power to save the
Saints, saying that they could be presented before God faultless and
joyous (v. 24). His message reaches nineteen hundred years ahead to our
day with just as much fervor to "contend for the faith" (v. 3).

Twentieth century conditions have caused other apostles to quote
from Jude as a warning in our own day. On August 16, 1985, Elder
Dallin H. Oaks of the Quorum of the Twelve, addressed teachers of the
Church Educational System and warned them of evils of our day. We
have biased historians, writers of half-truths, and news media specialists

who convey erroneous information. He said, "the fraud of the so-called Hitler diary convinces us to be cautious."[14] Elder Oaks quoted Jude 1:8, which condemns those who speak evil of dignitaries—the Lord's anointed ones.[15]

In 1983 President Gordon B. Hinckley said:

> We have those critics who appear to wish to cull out of a vast panorama of information those items which demean and belittle some of the men and women of the past who worked so hard in laying the foundation of this great cause. They find readers of their works who seem to delight in picking up these tidbits, and in chewing them over and relishing them. In so doing they are savoring a pickle, rather than eating a delicious and satisfying dinner of several courses.
>
> We recognize that our forebears were human. They doubtless made mistakes . . . But the mistakes were minor when compared with the marvelous work which they accomplished. To highlight the mistakes and gloss over the greater good is to draw a caricature. Caricatures are amusing, but they are often ugly and dishonest. A man may have a blemish on his cheek and still have a face of beauty and strength, but if the blemish is emphasized unduly in relation to his other features, the portrait is lacking in integrity.
>
> I do not fear truth. I welcome it. But I wish all of my facts in their proper context, with emphasis on those elements which explain the great growth and power of this organization.[16] (Conference Report, Oct. 1983, 68.)

President Harold B. Lee, in October 1972, said:

> There are some as wolves among us. By that, I mean some who profess membership in this church who are not sparing the flock. And among our own membership, men are arising speaking perverse things. Now *perverse* means diverting from the right or correct, and being obstinate in the wrong, willfully, in order to draw the weak and unwary members of the Church away after them.[17]

President J. Reuben Clark Jr., in the October 1944 conference said "There is creeping into our midst . . . great host of sectarian doctrines."[18] The message is clear for us today. We need to stay in "the love of God" by "contending for the faith." We need to watch out for those false teachers and their snares. Those snares are hidden in Cain's error—spiritual murder for gain, or obedience for inappropriate reasons; in Baalam's error—money for service, or profit for building the kingdom; Sodom and Gomorrah's sin—homosexuality and other sexual perversions; Korah's gainsaying—seeking the praise of men, i.e., business success with shady but legal practices; speaking or writing in vague or half-truths for the honors of the audiences or the intellectual circle; service with boasting of success in service; giving honor to self rather than to God; obedience to God's commandments as a social piety status; worldly learning, money, and sexual lasciviousness through TV, song, and suggestive casual communications.

We must be on guard, holding the "love of God and praying with the Spirit of the Holy Ghost" so as to be found "contending for the faith." I pray that we will be found in harmony with the living oracles and always quick to obey their direction.

Notes

1. Rowston, 554–63.
2. McConkie, 415.
3. Thomas, 1.
4. McConkie, 416.
5. Gaebelein, 382.
6. Kugelman, 78.
7. Glazier, 78.
8. Reicke, 109–110.
9. Smith, 157.
10. Gaebelein, 391.
11. McConkie, 424.
12. Smith 1946, 170.
13. McConkie, 427.
14. Oaks, 1.
15. See Oaks, 5.
16. Conference Report, Oct. 1983, 68.
17. Conference Report, Oct. 1972, 125.
18. Conference Report, Oct. 1944, 117.

Bibliography

Anderson, R. L. *Guide to Acts & Apostles Letters:* "Jude and His Letter." Provo: BYU Press, 1983.

Bo Reicke, *The Anchor Bible*; The Epistles of James, Peter, Jude. Garden City, N.Y., Doubleday, 1964.

Clark, J. Reuben, in Conference Report, Oct. 1944, 114.

Gaebelein, Frank E. *The Expositor's Bible Commentary*. Grand Rapids, Michigan: Zondervan Publishing House, 1976.

Glazier, Michael. *New Testament Commentary*, Vol. 19; Wilmington, Delaware: Abbey Press, 1980.

Hinckley, Gordon B., in Conference Report, Oct. 1983, 68.

Howard, Fred D. *Layman's Bible Book Commentary*, Nashville, Tennessee: Broadman Press, 1982.

Kugelman, Richards. *New Testament Message*: A Biblical-Theological Commentary. Wilmington, Delaware: Abbey Press, 1980.

Lee, Harold B., in Conference Report, Oct. 1972, 125.

McConkie, Bruce R. *Doctrinal New Testament Commentary*, Vol. III, Salt Lake City: Bookcraft, 1973.

Oaks, Dallin H. "Reading Church History," Doctrine and Covenants and Church History Symposium. Brigham Young University, 1985, 1.

Rowston, Douglas J. *The Most Neglected Book in the New Testament,* NTS, 21 (July 1975), 554–63.

Smith, Joseph Fielding, comp. *Teachings of the Prophet Joseph Smith.*, N.P., 1946.

Thomas, Cathy. *Jude: Refuge in God's Love*, unpublished. Brigham Young University, Provo, Utah, 1985.

CHAPTER TEN

Is Any Sick Among You?

Anointing the Sick with Oil in Early Christian and Latter-day Theology and Practice

Walter A. Norton

A modern-day apostle, Elder Neal A. Maxwell, once taught us that the scriptures provide "resounding and great answers to what Amulek designated as 'the great question' namely, is there really a redeeming Christ?" (Alma 34:5–6).[1] He reminded us that the scriptures forcefully testify to "the truth of the coming of Christ" and that "all things which have been given of God from the beginning of the world, unto man, are the typifying of him [Christ]" (2 Nephi 11:4). "Similarly," Elder Maxwell added, "these same scriptures provide us 'with insights we may not yet be able to manage fully,' for 'astonishingly, Alma includes our sicknesses and infirmities, along with our sins, among that which Jesus would also 'take upon him' (Alma 7:11–12). It was part of the perfecting of His mercy by His experiencing 'according to the flesh'"[2] (see Matthew 8:16–17; Isaiah 53:4).

Elder Maxwell further shows that the sacred verses not only verify that Christ "cometh into the world that he may save all men" but also, that Christ "suffereth the pains of all . . . men, women, and children, who belong to the family of Adam" (2 Nephi 9:21). He then concludes: "The soul trembles at those implications. One comes away weeping from such verses, deepened in his adoration of our Redeemer."[3]

Unquestionably Jesus Christ came into the world to bring salvation and relief to both the bodies and the souls of those individuals who would believe on him. One Christian scholar has discovered that, in addition to the Savior's ministry of teaching, "nearly one-fifth of the entire Gospels is devoted to Jesus' healing and the discussions occasioned by it."[4] These findings suggest that there is more than one way in which Christ "hath borne our griefs, and carried our sorrows" (Isaiah 53:4).

Anointing the Sick with Oil in Early Christianity

If healing the sick constituted a major portion of Jesus' ministry, it was also an important part of the ministry of his disciples, according to the Savior's charge and the authority given them. Significantly, Christ himself laid on hands to heal the sick (Mark 6:5, 13; Luke 13:12–13) and sent his apostles out doing the same (Mark 6:7–13). In Mark 6:13, however, we learn something that is revealed in no other place in the four Gospels; that the apostles "anointed *with oil* many that were sick, and healed them" (italics added). In only one other place in the entire New Testament do we find an explicit reference to the ordinance of anointing the sick with oil. That reference is given in the epistle of the apostle James (5:14–16).

Early Patristic Evidence

Although direct references to anointing the sick with oil are few in the New Testament canon, later Christian writings seem to confirm the preservation of the practice. Yet the earliest works do not actually mention the anointing but only healings and concern for the sick. Bishop Polycarp exhorts the "presbyters" (elders) to continue "visiting all the infirm."[5] The Greek apologist Justin Martyr, speaking of the exorcism of demons, makes reference to "our Christian men" who "have healed and do heal."[6] And Origen, in defending the Christians against Celsus, testifies that the Christians "expel evil spirits, and perform many cures," and "take away diseases."[7] These and numerous other early sources attest that until the total loss of the spiritual gifts through the effects of the apostasy, "this healing, centrally experienced, was an indispensable ingredient of Christian life."[8]

The earliest reference to an actual act of anointing does not appear until the third century, by which time apostasy within the Church had taken its toll upon the sacred ordinances, and the anointing with oil appears thereafter in corrupted form. In the *Apostolic Tradition* of St.

Hippolytus (c. 215), we find a formula for blessing the oil which was to be used for the sick, but it implies that the oil is either to be tasted or applied to the body (v. 1–2). The use of holy oil is also mentioned in conjunction with baptism (xxi) and confirmation (xxii), a practice which had become standard in the Christian Church by the third century. Similar passages concerning the blessing of the oil appear in *Constitutions of the Holy Apostles* (VIII.29) and in Serapion's *Euchologion* (V.17) as well as in many later works.[9]

The Sacrament of Extreme Unction

The Anglican Reverend F. W. Puller claims as the earliest patristic reference to James' teaching a passage from Origen's second homily "On Leviticus."[10] Origen, however, speaks of the remission of sins and makes no mention of anointing with oil (4). Puller quotes Origen to show that, though the sacrament of penance had developed by this time in the early church, no sacrament of unction yet existed.[11] He argues strenuously that, as anointing gradually became a sacrament in the Church, it was at first only a sacrament of healing and not of sanctifying grace as the later term *extreme unction* signified. Kelsey reports that this change in the purpose of the anointing "can be traced to about the tenth century when the service of unction for healing was gradually transformed into extreme unction. Thus the one sacrament for healing the bodies of men became a rite of passage for dying, a service to 'save' the individual for the next life and speed him quickly and easily into it."[12]

The Changes of Vatican II

Puller further argues that the idea of seven fixed sacraments, including extreme unction, originated with Peter Lombard's *Sentences* in 1151 and was later declared dogma by the Council of Trent (1545–63).[13] Such was the sacramental doctrine of the Roman Catholic Church until the revolutionary changes made by the Second Vatican Council of 1962–65. Vatican II declared that the rite for the sick would "more fittingly be called 'Anointing for the Sick'" and placed the major emphasis once again upon the healing of the body, removing the emphasis as a rite for the dying."[14] This remarkable turnabout and reemphasis on the true focus of the anointing of the sick with oil as taught by James was in part an attempt by Pope John XXIII (1958–63) to update the church with world scholarship. One area of concern seemed to be the "discovery at Nag-Hammadi in Upper Egypt in 1945 of numerous so-called Gnostic texts . . . [which] raised fresh questions about the religious environment of the New Testament." There was also the 1947 discovery of the famous Dead Sea Scrolls. "These and other discoveries all helped to encourage a biblical scholarship which had used the Bible itself as a source-document of historical evidence, and used other evidence to shed light on its setting and meaning."[15]

Evidence from Jewish Sources

The priesthood ordinance of laying hands upon the sick did not appear for the first time during the mortal ministry of the Savior. We are taught that not only did Adam receive baptism (Moses 6:64–65), but also "he received *all the other ordinances* of the gospel and was given full authority through the priesthood conferred upon him to officiate in God's name in all matters pertaining, under the Great Plan, to the welfare of man"[16] (italics added). It is not surprising then to find in the Jewish traditions some additional evidence for the practice of the laying on of hands. Although the Old Testament contains accounts of healings in some ways comparable to some New Testament accounts (1 Kings 17:19–24; 2 Kings 4:18–37), there is no incident in the Old Testament nor in rabbinic literature of the laying on of hands for healing purposes. The closest thing to it may be in 2 Kings 5:11. However, among the Dead Sea Scrolls in a work called the *Genesis Apocryphon* there exists an account paralleling Genesis 12 in which Abraham heals the Pharaoh by the laying on of hands (XX.16–29).[17] According to one scholar, "The scroll appears to have been actually composed before Jesus' time. Thus the Genesis Apocryphon tells us what we could have assumed, namely, that Jesus was not the first to heal by the laying on of hands, and that this practice was current in some Jewish circles."[18] Fitzmyer adds, "Though the rite is without OT precedents, it is known in older Assyrian and Babylonian texts.[19] Fitzmyer also wonders if this scroll could possibly relate to an esoteric Essene practice[20] since the ascetic Essenes are described by Josephus (*The Jewish War*, II.8, 6) as pious healers and miracle workers.[21] Whether or not the Essenes practiced the laying on of hands is unknown, but these few Jewish sources do at least suggest that the practice existed before the Christian era.

Interpreting James 5:14–16

We should not attempt to comprehend the real meaning of the ordinance taught by James without first recalling that the scriptures testify that "all things" typify the ministry of Christ (Moses 6:59–63; 2 Nephi 11:4).[22] To understand more fully the meaning of the anointing of the sick with oil, some consideration must then be given to symbolic representations since "symbols are the language in which all gospel covenants and ordinances of salvation have been revealed."[23] This ordinance, like other gospel ordinances, in symbolic ways represents and testifies of Christ and his saving mission to mankind. With this in mind, a detailed exegesis of James 5:14–16 is now in order.

Is Any Sick Among You?

In these first words James endeavors first of all to foster within a community of believers a willingness to turn to the authorized representatives of the Lord for relief from their illnesses. The words *among you* indicate that the sick person is a member of the Christian community, or the "church" mentioned in the next phrase. The term *church* (or *assembly*), translated from the Greek *ekklesia*, appears 115 times in the New Testament[24] and provides strong evidence of an organized, viable religious body operating under inspired leadership. The members of the community are the "brethren" (*adelphos*), a generic term meaning both men and women which James uses nineteen times in this epistle.[25]

Let Him Call for the Elders of the Church . . .

James instructs the Church members to call upon the "elders" (*presbuteros*) when they are sick, but Christian scholars have for centuries been at a loss as to who or what the "elders" or "presbyters" might be. The uncertainty rests largely on a misunderstanding of both priesthood function and church government as the Savior instituted these within his church. Within the Roman Catholic Church the Council of Trent (1551) unequivocally declared that the word *presbyters* as used by James refers "either to bishops or to priests."[26] Others claim that the title is used in the Old Testament sense as designating men of age, experience, and great wisdom among the people. Latter-day Saints, however, find ample evidence within the New Testament that an elder was indeed a specific office of authority (see Acts 14:23; Titus 1:5; 1 Peter 5:1; 2 John

1; 3 John 1). There are, in fact, many verses which plainly identify elders and apostles as distinct positions of authority within the Church and suggest as well that an apostle is also an elder.

Some extra-canonical sources help to substantiate the claim that either apostles or bishops can be called elders by virtue of holding the same priesthood. Clement of Rome speaks of a succession of "bishops and deacons," including those whom the apostles had ordained (I Clement 42), but also mentions those "presbyters who have gone before" (I Clement 44), apparently using the titles *presbyter* and *bishop* to refer to the same persons. And Papias, according to Eusebius' record, spoke of receiving gospel doctrines from anyone "who had followed the presbyters" and specifically names the presbyters as "Andrew or Peter or Philip or Thomas or James or John or Matthew, or any other of the Lord's disciples."[27] They were some of the elders who were to watch over the church and anoint the sick when called upon.

And Let Them Pray over Him . . .

James' instructions are clearly descriptive of the manner in which the anointing for the sick are given. The elders are to pray *over* the sick person and not merely *for* him. To pray *over* someone could imply two important facets of that holy blessing. First, James may here envision the intimate scene of the afflicted person lying prostrate upon his bed with the elders standing close and leaning over to make the proper administration. Since proper administration consists of anointing with consecrated oil "upon the crown of the head of the sick person,"[28] this ordinance frequently requires the elders to bend over or to stop in order to reach the individual they are anointing.

A second facet of the anointing which James may imply is the actual laying on of hands. The Greek word *epi*, translated *over* in this verse, has other translations elsewhere according to the context in which it is found. One common translation is *upon* and in at least one place that translation is connected to the act of healing. A certain ruler implored Jesus, "My daughter is even now dead: but come and lay thy hands *upon* [*epi*] her, and she shall live" (Matthew 9:18; italics added). When James speaks of praying *over* the sick, he may be referring to the physical act of laying the hands *upon* the sick as the prayer is spoken. If James does not imply this element of the ordinance, then explicit reference to the laying on of hands is conspicuously absent in these verses.

Anointing Him with Oil in the Name of the Lord . . .

We will comprehend little of the significance of this ordinance if we do not recognize that the anointing must be performed "in the name of the Lord." As one Christian writer notes, "'In the name of the Lord' implies that this is not simply a medicinal remedy. As in Mark 6:13, it symbolizes the healing presence and power of the Lord Jesus Christ."[29] An LDS writer adds, "Thus, strictly speaking, an administration to the sick . . . differs in some important ways from a prayer. It is an ordinance performed by the authority of the priesthood, which is the power to act in God's name."[30] It is even more than an ordinance performed in his name; it is, in fact, an ordinance which can remind us of both his name and of Christ himself.

Anointing in Ancient Israel

In ancient Israel the anointing of persons and objects was a widespread practice. While numerous practical uses of anointing could be listed, the most important use of anointing was for religious purposes. Anointing an object or a person was a form of "setting apart" and consecrating that which was sacred or was to become sacred for God's service.

The term *anointed* in the Hebrew is *mshh*. According to Philip Birnbaum, "Originally the term . . . was applied to any person anointed with the holy oil and consecrated to carry out the purposes of God. . . . When David received the divine promise that the throne would remain in his family forever . . . the title acquired a special reference and signified the representative of the royal line of David . . . the Messiah, the Lord's anointed."[31] Therefore, from *mshh*, or *mashi'ah*, comes "messiah," meaning "anointed," or the "anointed one." When translated into the Greek of the New Testament, the word becomes *Christ*. Consequently, any gospel anointing, simply by word association, and also because it is performed in the name of Christ, may serve symbolically to remind us of his name.

The Oil as the Light of the Spirit

James specifically instructs that the sick are to be anointed "with oil." Scholars unanimously agree that he refers to the pure oil of the olive, "the only oil employed to any extent in biblical times."[32] Various studies on the subject suggest that for the house of Israel olive oil symbolized many things. The legendary account of Enoch equates the olive oil with light, and this same imagery appears in both testaments. The olive oil burning in the tabernacle symbolized the spirit and presence of God in the camp of Israel (Exodus 27:20). And in the symbolic account of the "two anointed ones," the seven lamps shown to the prophet represented the "spirit" of the Lord (Zechariah 4:1–6). Even in the apocalyptic book called "The Testament of Levi" we read that the Lord "will open the gates of paradise; he shall remove the sword that has threatened since Adam, and he will grant to the saints to eat of the tree of life." Thus, "the *spirit of holiness shall be upon them*" (18:10–11; italics added).[33]

In the New Testament Jesus related the parable of the ten virgins in which half the young maidens, because their oil lamps were empty, missed the bridegroom's wedding feast. The oil they were supposed to be carrying in their lamps has been interpreted as "the spiritual strength and abundance which diligence and devotion in God's service alone can insure,"[34] or "spiritual preparedness . . . the kind of oil that is needed to illuminate the way and light up the darkness."[35] The Lord himself has interpreted his own parable and compares the virgins who had oil to those who "have received the truth, and have taken the Holy Spirit for their guide" (D&C 45:56–57). Here again the olive oil represents the presence and influence of the Holy Ghost.

Latter-day Saint scholars certainly recognize the direct symbolic link between the oil and the Holy Spirit. Joseph McConkie explains that "the idea of anointing and the concept of sanctification are consistently associated in the scripture with the reception of the Holy Ghost."[36] He adds that "the outpouring of consecrated oil was a symbol of the outpouring of the Spirit."[37] Therefore, the anointing of the sick with oil signifies placing the Holy Ghost upon the individual. With God's favor, the sick may then be healed through the cleansing, purging, purifying influence of the Holy Ghost.

The Head and the Hands

Not only is the oil symbolic, but so also are the places where the sacred oil is applied and the manner of the anointing, sealing, and blessing. The place is the crown of the head, the head being the governing member of the body and symbolic of power and authority. The manner of administration is the physical laying of the hands upon the head, an actual "touching" procedure called by one writer "the healing gesture par excellence."[38] The hands are "one of the most symbolically expressive parts of the body" and "signify power, strength, providence, or blessings."[39] When the elders place their hands upon the head of the sick, it is as if the sick one is being "touched by the hand of God."[40]

And the Prayer of Faith Shall Save the Sick . . . Pray One for Another, that Ye May Be Healed. The Effectual Fervent Prayer of a Righteous Man Availeth Much.

James strongly urges the important elements of prayer and faith. Actually, his own words define for us the "prayer of faith" of which he speaks. The "prayer of faith" is indeed the "prayer of a righteous man," or woman, or child, whose very righteousness is founded upon great faith in the Lord Jesus Christ and, therefore, whose prayers do produce their intended effect. In the case where one is ill and calls for the elders, his own prayer of faith is necessary and "availeth much," but the ascending prayers of others who love him and are concerned for his well-being also work for his benefit. Of prime importance is the principle of faith. Said President Spencer W. Kimball, "The need for faith is often underestimated. The ill person and the family often seem to depend wholly on the power of the priesthood and the gift of healing that they hope the administering brethren may have, whereas the greater responsibility is with him who is blessed."[41] This same principle was plainly taught by the Savior and his apostles (Matthew 9:20–22; Acts 3:16).

And the Prayer of Faith Shall Save the Sick, and the Lord Shall Raise Him Up . . .

One of the greatest controversies from the age of the apostolic fathers to the present day has centered upon the meaning of the word *save* in these instructions from James. Apparently the controversy began when Jerome produced the Latin Vulgate translation of the New Testament and rendered the word as *salvo* and thus "helped to turn the church's attention away from healing itself, focusing it on healing represented symbolically."[42] Kelsey explains further: "For centuries the Roman Catholic Church officially interpreted this passage to mean the act of saving a person from spiritual death, and supported this meaning with the translation from the Vulgate. It was upon this understanding that the doctrine of extreme unction was based. Instead of the Latin words *curo* or *sano*, which commonly meant to heal or cure medically, only the word *salvo,* to save, was used in the Vulgate to translate 'save' or 'heal' or 'cure' in this passage."[43] This interpretation, after being firmly established by the Council of Trent, held fast in the Roman Catholic Church from the time of Jerome until Vatican II in the 1960s.

The idea that the sick who are anointed with oil are saved by that anointing from spiritual death cannot, however, be supported by the original Greek text. The word translated here as *save* is in the Greek *sosei,* a word which in some contexts can refer to salvation of one's soul (James 1:21; 2:14; 4:12; 5:20), but "the normal meaning of the word [*sozein*] in Greek literature is . . . 'to save from death, keep alive.' When the word is used of persons suffering from disease, it normally means 'to heal, restore to health.'"[44] Even the recent Catholic sources, as a result of changes issued since Vatican II, recognize that this word refers to bodily healing. Charles Gusmer writes that "the verb can have a double meaning—either eternal salvation or restoration of health. The present context would suggest the latter meaning."[45] Another writer also confirms "it is the physical effect that is emphasized."[46]

And the Lord Shall Raise Him Up . . .

A physical restoration is further substantiated by the Greek text which underlies the second phrase of this sentence, "and the Lord shall raise him up." In this case, the Greek word for "to raise" (*egeirein*) can variously mean "to cause to rise," "to rouse from sleep," "to raise from the dead," or "to raise up" (from a seat, from bed, or from the ground). With these meanings, it becomes apparent that the word is used "in connexion with the recovery of those who have been 'down' with disease, lying sick."[47] Puller insists that the translation problem found here again originated with St. Jerome who used the Latin word *allevabit*, rather than the *suscitabit*, a translation previously "used by Pope Innocent I in his letter to Decentius of Eugubium." Puller argues, "If S. Jerome had retained 'suscitabit' in the Vulgate, or if the medieval copyists had refrained from changing S. Jerome's 'allevabit' into 'alleviabit,' a great deal of very doubtful Latin teaching about the effect of unction would probably never have been written."[48]

And if He Have Committed Sins, They Shall be Forgiven Him. Confess Your Faults One to Another . . .

When James teaches that those who are healed also have their sins forgiven, he is not teaching that the elders or ministers of the Church have power to forgive the man's sins. We know "it is not the elder who remits or forgives the sick man's sins, but the Lord."[49] When he speaks of confessing faults, he is not counseling the sick to confess to the elders. Rather, he is reminding us all of the need for confession as we all repent daily. James' emphasis is really upon the fact that unless we are in a state of repentance when we call upon the elders for a blessing, we cannot be forgiven and consequently we cannot be healed. As in the account of the man with palsy (Mark 2:5–11), forgiveness is a prerequisite to the healing miracle. Plainly speaking, "The Spirit will not come to a man unless and until he is prepared by personal righteousness to have the companionship of that member of the Godhead."[50]

Conclusion

The wonderful symbolism attendant upon the anointing of the sick with oil manifests itself in both the healing of the spirit and the healing of the body. Elder McConkie described it this way: "And again we say that all of our Lord's healings . . . are but similitudes and types that point to the even greater reality, that through him the spiritually sick, the spiritually diseased, the sin crippled of the world, may come forth in a newness of life if they have faith in his holy name."[51] It then becomes evident that the very vitality of this symbolism rests squarely on the atoning sacrifice of the Lord Jesus Christ. As the faithful sick call upon the elders of the Lord's Church to anoint their heads with holy oil, they might well utter the words which were spoken by the Nephites under King Benjamin: "O have mercy, and apply the atoning blood of Christ that we may receive forgiveness of our sins, and that our hearts may be purified; for we believe in Jesus Christ, the son of God" (Mosiah 4:2). Having so prayed in faith, their desires to be healed may well be fulfilled, if it be the Lord's will.

Notes
1. Neal A. Maxwell, "The Book of Mormon: Great Answers to 'The Great Question,'" Book of Mormon Symposium Address, Brigham Young University, Provo, Utah, 10 October 1986.

2. Ibid.

3. Ibid.

4. Morton T. Kelsey, *Healing and Christianity* (New York: Harper & Row, 1973), 53–54.

5. *Epistle to the Philippians*, 6.

6. *Second Apology: To the Roman Senate*, 6.

7. *Against Celsus*, I, 46, 67.

8. Ibid., 154. For discussion on additional patristic evidence, see 136–54. See also Charles W. Gusmer, *And You Visited Me: Sacramental Ministry to the Sick and the Dying* (New York: Pueblo Publishing, 1984).

9. See *New Catholic Encyclopedia*, 15 vols. (New York: McGraw-Hill, 1967), 1:570.

10. F. W. Puller, *The Anointing of the Sick in Scripture and Tradition, with some Considerations on the Numbering of the Sacraments* (London: Society for Promoting Christian Knowledge, 1910), 42.

11. Ibid., 42–44.

12. *Healing*, 8.

13. *Anointing the Sick*, 253–55.

14. James A. Coriden, Thomas J. Green, Donald E. Heintschel, eds., *The Code of Canon Law: A Text and Commentary* (New York: Paulist Press, 1985), 702–4. Also, Austin Flannery, ed., *Vatican Council II: The Conciliar and Post Conciliar Documents* (Wilmington, Del.: Scholarly Resources, 1975), 22; and Flannery, Ed., *More Post Conciliar Documents* (Grand Rapids: Wm. B. Eerdmans, 1982), 13–19.

15. Tim Dowley, ed., *Eerdmans' Handbook to the History of Christianity* (1977; reprinted Grand Rapids: Wm. B. Eerdmans Publishing, 1982), 607. See also: Williston Walker et al., *A History of the Christian Church,* 4th ed. (New York: Charles Scribner's Sons, 1985), 698–700. Hugh Nibley offers a similar explanation in "The Early Christian Church in the Light of Some Newly Discovered Papyri from Egypt," BYU Tri-Stake Fireside Address, 3 March 1964 (Provo: Brigham Young University Press), 14.

16. John A. Widtsoe, *A Rational Theology,* 4th ed. (1915, reprinted; Salt Lake City: Deseret Book, 1937), 54–55.

17. Joseph A. Fitzmyer, *The Genesis Apocryphon of Qumran Cave I* (Rome: Pontifical Biblical Institute, 1966), 57–59.

18. D. Flusser, "Healing through the Laying-on of Hands in a Dead Sea Scroll," *Israel Exploration Journal 7* (1957), 108.

19. *Genesis Apocryphon*, 125.

20. Ibid.

21. Many scholars have identified the Essenes with the Qumran community. See Philip Birnbaum, *A Book of Jewish Concepts* (New York: Hebrew Publishing Co., 1964), 52–54.

22. Bruce R. McConkie, *The Promised Messiah: The First Coming of Christ* (Salt Lake City: Deseret Book, 1978), 27–28. See also 387, 571–72.

23. Joseph Fielding McConkie, *Gospel Symbolism*, (Salt Lake City: Bookcraft, 1985), 1.

24. See word listing in George V. Wigram, *The Englishman's Greek Concordance of the New Testament*, 9th ed. (1844; reprinted; London: Samuel Bagster and Sons, 1903), 227–28.

25. Ibid., 13.

26. J. Neuner and J. Dupuis, eds., *The Christian Faith in the Doctrinal Documents of the Catholic Church*, revised ed. (Westminster, Md.: Christian Classic, 1975), 442.

27. *Ecclesiastes History*, III, xxxix, 4. For conservative scholars who defend this view, see Donald Guthrie, *Hebrews to Revelation—New Testament Introduction* (Chicago: Inter-Varsity Press, 1962), 209; and Henry Thiessen, *Introduction to the New Testament* (Grand Rapids: Wm. B. Eerdmans, 1954), 312.

28. Bruce R. McConkie, comp., *Doctrines of Salvation: Sermons and Writings of Joseph Fielding Smith*, 3 vols. (Salt Lake City: Bookcraft, 1956), 3:174–75.

29. *And You Visited Me*, 9.

30. Dennis L. Lythgoe, "Giving Priesthood Blessings," *Ensign*, February 1982), 23.

31. *Jewish Concepts*, 394.

32. *Encyclopedia Judaica*, 16 vols. (New York: Macmillan, 1971), 12:1347–48, 1351.

33. *The Testaments of the Twelve Patriarchs*, 18:10–11. In James H. Charlesworth, ed., *The Old Testament Pseudepigrapha*, 2 vols. (Garden City: Doubleday, 1983), 1:795.

34. James E. Talmage, *Jesus the Christ* (1915; reprinted, Salt Lake City: Deseret Book, 1962), 579.

35. Spencer W. Kimball, *Faith Precedes the Miracle* (Salt Lake City: Deseret Book, 1979), 255.

36. *Gospel Symbolism*, 115.

37. Ibid., 266–67.

38. *And You Visited Me*, 163.

39. *Gospel Symposium*, 261.

40. Ibid., 197.

41. Spencer W. Kimball, "President Kimball Speaks Out on

Administration to the Sick," *New Era*, October 1981, 75.

42. *Healing*, 193–94.

43. Ibid., 115.

44. *Anointing the Sick*, 14.

45. *And You Visited Me*, 9–10.

46. *Anointing the Sick*, 18.

47. Ibid., 18–19.

48. Ibid., 19–20.

49. Joseph Fielding Smith, "Administering to the Sick," *Improvement Era*, August 1955, 607.

50. Bruce R. McConkie, *Mormon Doctrine*, 2nd ed. (Salt Lake City: Bookcraft, 1966), 297.

51. *The Promised Messiah*, 491.

CHAPTER ELEVEN

The Stumbling Blocks of First Corinthians

Monte S. Nyman

The Church members in Corinth were having problems. Word had reached the Apostle Paul of various sins which were causing them to stumble in their progress toward eternal life. The epistle known as First Corinthians was a follow-up of a previous letter giving them admonitions concerning the conditions that existed among them. This previous letter has either been lost from the original New Testament or was never collected to become a part of that canon. Therefore we are left without knowledge of what Paul had previously advised. The letter that has come down to us does contain much worthwhile doctrine and counsel that if followed will also prevent members of the Church from likewise faltering along the path to exaltation in the kingdom of God.

The epistle is lengthy and includes a wide variety of subjects. This paper will be limited to those major problems within the middle chapters of the letter that Paul treats as stumbling blocks to the weak (1 Corinthians 8:9). Furthermore, since Paul addressed these problems, other stumbling blocks have surfaced in the interpretations of this letter undoubtedly because of the loss of plain and precious truths from the original treatise. Thanks to the Prophet Joseph Smith, many of the misunderstandings of the present text have been clarified through his inspired work, now referred to as the Joseph Smith Translation.

The Stumbling block of Immorality

Following a careful accreditation of himself as an apostle of the Lord Jesus Christ (1 Corinthians 4), Paul launched into the most notorious problem in the community of Corinth. "'To live like a Corinthian' was ... a phrase used both in Greek and Latin to express immorality."[1] His counsel is full of doctrine and advice very fitting to our world where similar moral problems abound.

The common problem of fornication had worsened into at least one member having an incestuous relationship with his father's wife. This grievous sin Paul recognized as beyond that indulged in by the Gentiles (1 Corinthians 5:1). He was further perplexed by the church communities' apparent lack of concern and action over the matter (1 Corinthians 5:2). The Joseph Smith Translation renders Paul's decision on the matter as follows:

> For verily, as absent in body, but present in spirit, *I* have judged already *him who hath so done this deed*, as though I were present.
>
> In the name of our Lord Jesus Christ, when ye are gathered together, and *have the* Spirit, with the power of our Lord Jesus Christ,
>
> To deliver such an one unto Satan for the destruction of the flesh. (JST, 1 Corinthians 5:3–5; italics added)

He was declaring that when a church court was held, the church leaders would judge the offender as Paul was then judging if the decision was made by the Spirit. Such gross immorality was an automatic excommunication in that day as well as in our own. This action was necessary for any hope of salvation for the offender (1 Corinthians 5:5). Some sins are so serious that the kindest thing that can be done is to take away Church membership and let the person get a fresh start.

Paul gave some further admonitions to the Church members. If this moral violation was ignored, the entire membership was threatened since "a little leaven leaveneth the whole lump" (1 Corinthians 5:6). Such association cannot be totally avoided. It is a commandment of God to associate with the world but it is not necessary to allow such association in the Church. Of course, those who are excommunicated can repent and regain the more pure association (1 Corinthians 5:10–13).

Other Sexual Sins

Other sins of immorality were also enumerated by Paul. Adultery, child sexual abusers,[2] and homosexuals shall not inherit the kingdom of God (1 Corinthians 6:9–10). Although some of the Corinthian Saints had been guilty of such sins prior to their baptism, they were now forgiven and were no longer free to indulge in such practices (1 Corinthians 6:11). Paul bore testimony that "all these things [immoralities] are not lawful unto me, and all these things are not expedient. All things are not lawful for me, therefore I will not be brought under the power of any" (JST, 1 Corinthians 6:12). Just as Jesus taught that the truth would make people free (John 8:32), so Paul was saying that observing the moral laws of God would keep people free from the bondage of sin. The prevalence of these types of sin in our world shows the universal relevance of Paul's admonitions today.

An argument for chastity was then presented by Paul: "The body is not for fornication, but for the Lord; and the Lord for the body" (1 Corinthians 6:13). In support of his argument, he reasoned that a relationship with a harlot makes the two of one body. Therefore, the whole body is impure. In contrast, the unity of the body with the Spirit makes the whole body pure (1 Corinthians 6:16–17). Every sin committed is against *the body of Christ*; but fornication, declared Paul, is a sin against the body. Why? Because the body is the temple of the Holy Ghost, and when one is immoral, the Spirit withdraws from the body (JST, 1 Corinthians 6:18–19; compare 3:16–17). Since men are bought by the Atonement of Christ, all men are born with the light of Christ. Those who sin lose that inherited gift. Furthermore, the members of the Church have the Holy Ghost conferred upon them as another gift. This gift also withdraws from an impure body.

Celibacy

Another stumbling block related to immorality is the question of celibacy. One justification for this incorrect doctrine comes from 1 Corinthians 7. As this chapter is recorded in the King James Version, it appears that Paul was opposed to marriage. Much theory and speculation have resulted from this corrupted text. Again, thanks to the Prophet Joseph, greater light is shed on Paul's views in the Joseph Smith Translation.

Paul's declaration that "it is good for a man not to touch a woman" (1 Corinthians 7:1) is clarified in the Joseph Smith Translation to be a statement by the Corinthian Saints in a letter previously written to Paul. He responded to the statement in reference to the subject being treated— fornication. Marriage would be a great deterrent to the sin. This is not to be considered the major reason for marriage, as other scriptures would confirm, but the natural consequences of marriage would satisfy innate sexual desire in mankind. As a further precaution against adultery for those who are married, Paul advised the members to be considerate of each other in their sexual desires and aware of Satan's temptations during long abstinence. Paul wisely and carefully labeled these admonitions as his own opinion. In other words, he was speaking by way of reasoning and not by revelation.

Unbelieving Spouses

Paul next gave advice to the woman who was married to a husband who was not a church member. He advised the woman not to leave her husband because she might be a positive influence towards his conversion. However, if the unbelieving husband chose to leave his wife, Paul advised her to let him go because she might not be able to convert him (1 Corinthians 7:13–16). The fourteenth verse may be misconstrued to suggest that a good woman's conduct will somehow save her deviating husband who does not repent—an idea that could cause people to stumble. Joseph Smith was given a revelation clearing up such a possible misinterpretation:

> For the unbelieving husband is sanctified by the wife, and the unbelieving wife is sanctified by the husband; else were your children unclean, but now are they holy.
>
> Now, in the days of the apostles the law of circumcision was had among all the Jews who believed not the gospel of Jesus Christ.
>
> And it came to pass that there arose a great contention among the people concerning the law of circumcision, for the unbelieving husband was desirous that his children should be circumcised and become subject to the law of Moses, which law was fulfilled.
>
> And it came to pass that the children, being brought up in subjection to the law of Moses, gave heed to the traditions of their fathers and believed not the gospel of Christ, wherein they became unholy.
>
> Wherefore, for this cause the apostle wrote unto the church, giving unto them a commandment, not of the Lord, but of himself, that a believer should not be united to an unbeliever; except the law

of Moses should be done away among them.

That their children might remain without circumcision; and that the tradition might be done away, which saith that little children are unholy; for it was had among the Jews;

But little children are holy, being sanctified through the Atonement of Jesus Christ; and this is what the scriptures mean. (D&C 74:1–7)

Paul seems to have said that the salvation of the children is the important consideration. If the woman is able to keep her children in the faith while she is married to an unbeliever, she should remain with him in hopes that her influence might bring about his conversion. However, if the children are going astray because of the influence of their father, it was Paul's opinion that she should leave him for the sake of the children. Before those children were accountable they were saved automatically by the Atonement, but as they became accountable the children's salvation was more important than her husband's who was already an unbeliever. Such advice, although not a revelation, would be applicable in today's world as well.

Missions and Marriage

The next item of instruction by Paul was encouragement to the Corinthians to fulfill their callings and to abide in the Lord regardless of their marital status (1 Corinthians 7:20–25). Paul encouraged them not to change their marital status so they would be able to concentrate their efforts on their callings and do a better job (1 Corinthians 7:26–27). The Joseph Smith Translation makes this clear:

I suppose therefore that this is good for the present distress, *I say*, that *it is* good for a man so to be. (King James Version, 1 Cor. 7:26)	I suppose therefore that this is good for the present distress, *for a man so to remain that he may do greater good*. (JST, 1 Corinthians 7:26; italics added)

However, if they were married, they were not sinning, but Paul said the newlyweds would be given no special considerations, "For I spare you not" (JST, 1 Corinthians 7:28).

Having spoken in general concerning their callings, Paul now becames specific concerning those who are called as missionaries, as the Joseph Smith Translation clarifies:

But this I say, brethren, the time is short: it remaineth, that both they that have wives be as though they had none; And they that weep, as though they wept not; and they that rejoice, as though they rejoiced not; and they that buy, as though they possessed not; And they that use this world, as not abusing it: for the fashion of this world passeth away. But I would have you without carefulness. He that is unmarried careth for the things that belong to the Lord, how he may please the Lord. But he that is married careth for the things that are of the world, how he may please his wife. (King James, Version, 1 Corinthians 7:29–33)

But I speak unto you who are called unto the ministry. For this I say, brethren, the time *that remaineth* is *but* short, *that ye shall be sent forth unto the ministry. Even* they *who* have wives, *shall* be as though they had none; *for ye are called and chosen to do the Lord's work.* And *it shall be with them who* weep, as though they wept not; and *them who* rejoice, as though they rejoiced not, and *them who* buy, as though they possessed not. And *them who* use this world, as not *using* it; for the fashion of this world passeth away. But *I would, brethren, that ye magnify your calling.* I would have you without carefulness. *For* he *who* is unmarried, careth for the things that belong to the Lord, how he may please the Lord; *therefore he prevaileth.* But he *who* is married, careth for the things that are of the world, how he may please his wife; *therefore there is a difference, for he is hindered.* (JST, 1 Corinthians 7:29–33; italics added to show differences)

The mission calling was a full-time responsibility, and those who were married would be expected to devote themselves totally to that labor as if they were not married and thus not be distracted from their work (1 Corinthians 7:35).

Paul conceded one exception to his advice concerning the missionaries' marrying. He who had espoused a virgin, or was engaged, should fulfill the promise of marriage before he left if it were probable that she would be beyond childbearing age before his return (JST, 1 Corinthians 7:36). Paul added that the unmarried stats was still better.

| So then he that giveth *her* in marriage doeth well; but he that giveth *her* not in marriage doeth better. (King James Version, 1 Corinthians 7:38) | So then he that giveth *himself* in marriage doeth well; but he that giveth *himself* not in marriage doeth better. (JST, 1 Corinthians 7:38; italics added to show differences) |

Paul gave a further reminder that the woman is bound to her husband as long as he is alive; following his death she may remarry, but only if done in the manner of the Lord (1 Corinthians 7:39). In his judgment, which he felt was influenced by the Spirit, she would be happier if she waited until after his mission (1 Corinthians 7:40). Thus much enlightenment on Paul's views on marriage is shed through Joseph Smith's inspired work.

The Stumbling Block of Things Offered to Idols

The Corinthian Saints had apparently asked if it was against the newly restored religion to buy and eat things which initially had been killed as sacrifice to other gods or in other religions. In a conference of the elders and apostles previously held in Jerusalem, this question had been considered. The main concerns in Jerusalem seemed to be over whether or not the surplus meat from these festive occasions had been properly bled (see JST, Genesis 9:10), as well as over the fact that it might have been sacrificed to other gods (see Acts 15:20, 29). Whether the question by the Corinthian Saints had been prompted by this decision or whether the decision of the Jerusalem conference was not known to them is not stated. However, Paul's reply gives some further reasoning on the decision of that conference. He gave three bits of counsel regarding the matter. Following a treatise on the danger of knowledge and the value of charity or the love of God (1 Corinthians 8:1–3), Paul said that the "things which are in the world offered in sacrifice" are not affected because of their being offered to a god which really does not exist since "there is none other God but one" (JST, 1 Corinthians 8:4).

Second, to those who have a true knowledge of God, there is no problem. The eating of meat is not against the laws of God, but the danger lies in the possibility that some weak in the faith may assume that those members who eat the idol offerings are doing so as a religious act. This misinterpretation may cause the observer to be misled and worship falsely. Therefore, Paul concluded, it is wisdom that they do not follow any practice which may be a bad example to others (1 Corinthians 8:7–13).

The third instruction of Paul was regarding one's being invited to a feast and being served meat that had possibly been sacrificed to idols. Paul advised them to ask no questions but to go ahead and eat. However, if someone called it to the guests' attention, then Paul counseled them not to eat lest it be a stumbling block to the observer (JST, 1 Corinthians 10:27–33; note v. 27). As the Church today becomes more international, this advice will become more appropriate. Many Church members may wonder about the propriety of eating ritually prepared foods or other special religious-type products. The same three guidelines given by Paul would be applicable in such situations.

The Plurality of Gods

In answering the question of meat offered as sacrifices, Paul also answered another problem raised about the doctrines of the restored church. The Church of Jesus Christ of Latter-day Saints is criticized for believing in a plurality of Gods rather than in only one God. This criticism comes in various forms based on the critics' beliefs. The Christians who believe in the Trinitarian God justify monotheism through the three-in-one concept. As Joseph Smith taught, the teachings of the New Testament are explicit about the three separate members of the Godhead. He referred to Paul's quoting of Psalm 82:6 as further evidence of the plurality of Gods (1 Corinthians 8:5), but also emphasized that there was "but one God—that is pertaining to us."[3] That one God is of course the Lord Jesus Christ, the administrator of this world by divine investiture of authority.[4] The usual interpretation of Paul's comments regarding Psalms is that he was referring to the many pagan gods. Joseph Smith refuted this explanation:

> Mankind verily say that the Scriptures are with them. *Search the Scriptures, for they testify of things that these apostates would gravely pronounce blasphemy.* Paul, if Joseph Smith is a blasphemer, you are. *I say there are Gods many and Lords many, but to us only one, and we are to be in subjection to that one, and no man can limit the bounds or the eternal existence of eternal time.* Hath he beheld the eternal world, and is he authorized to say that there is only one God? He makes himself a fool if he thinks or says so, and there is an end of his career or progress in knowledge. He cannot obtain all knowledge, for he has sealed up the gate to it.[5]

The Bible is very clear on the subject of the Godhead when read under the influence of the Holy Ghost and in light of the Prophet

Joseph's explanation. The philosophies of men as determined in uninspired councils have led the world to confusion.

The Apostleship

Chapter 9 is a defense by Paul of his privileges and responsibilities as an apostle. Obviously, many of the Corinthian Saints had challenged his position (1 Corinthians 9:3). Is this not a stumbling block in our world as well? To those who would discredit some or all of the modern apostles, a review of this chapter should jerk them to their senses.

Paul argued that he was free (from the bondage of the law) through the acceptance of Jesus Christ. He had seen the Lord personally (1 Corinthians 9:1–2). Are not latter-day apostles special witnesses of Christ who are free from the sins of the world? Although the scriptures justified Paul and the other apostles in being sustained monetarily for their work, Paul had not accepted such pay. Nonetheless, he had labored diligently to bring souls to salvation. What was his reward? His reward was the gaining of eternal salvation (1 Corinthians 9:4–19). Paul had become all things to all men in an attempt to save some and at the same time save himself (1 Corinthians 9:20–27). Do not current apostles labor diligently and long, often under trying circumstances, to bring salvation to all who will listen? Through their service will they not assure, or have they not already assured their salvation? O, that all might avoid stumbling over the messages of these gallant servants of the Lord!

The Stumbling Block of Temptation

The apostle next warned his fellow Saints against the evils of temptation. He used the example of the Israelites, who were led by Christ in the wilderness yet yielded to sins such as idolatry, fornication, failure to recognize and worship Christ as their leader through the symbol of the serpent, and murmuring, which allowed Satan to overcome them (1 Corinthians 10:1–11). These same styles of temptation are prevalent in the world today. The same formula given by Paul for avoiding these sins is applicable today. Said he:

> There hath no temptation taken you but such as is common to man: but God is faithful, who will not suffer you to be tempted above that ye are able; but will with the temptation also make a way to escape, that ye may be able to bear it. (1 Corinthians 10:13)

Modern rationalizations or excuses of being tempted beyond endurance are swept away by this scriptural injunction. The Book of Mormon gives a second witness of the validity of this formula (Alma 13:28), and the Doctrine and Covenants adds a third (D&C 64:20). However, man has his agency and must choose to follow the Lord's "way of escape" or the formula is void and he will succumb to the devil's way.

The Stumbling Block of Genders

In our own day, the unisex society has reared its ugly head in a manner apparently similar to that among the Corinthians in Paul's day. Although we have no specifics about the practices and philosophies being taught, the instructions in 1 Corinthians 11 imply that questions regarding the role of men and women had been asked or problems had been drawn to Paul's attention (see 1 Corinthians 11:17–19). Basing the principles upon the customs of that day, Paul reminded the people of the eternal verities of the gospel plan. "The head of every man is Christ; and the head of the woman is the man; and the head of Christ is God" (1 Corinthians 11:3). This is not a dictatorship, or even a democracy, but a theocracy, an order of governing based on revelation and sustaining, or common consent. While the roles of men and women are separate, they are unified through Christ. "Neither is the man without the woman, neither the woman without the man, in the Lord" (1 Corinthians 11:11). The position of the Church in this regard was beautifully stated by President Joseph Fielding Smith:

> I think we all know that the blessings of the priesthood are not confined to men alone. These blessings are also poured out upon our wives and daughters and upon all the faithful women of the Church. These good sisters can prepare themselves, by keeping the commandments and by serving in the Church, for the blessings of the house of the Lord. The Lord offers to his daughters every spiritual gift and blessings that can be obtained by his sons, for neither is the man without the woman, nor the woman without the man in the Lord.[6]

One should learn the role of both the man and the woman and submit oneself to the Lord in those separate roles. This will overcome the unisex society, of which President Spencer W. Kimball warned:

> Some people are ignorant or vicious and apparently attempting to destroy the concept of masculinity and femininity. More and more girls dress, groom, and act like men. More and more men dress, groom, and act like women. The high purposes of life are damaged

and destroyed by the growing unisex theory. God made man in his own image, male and female made he them. With relatively few accidents of nature, we are born male or female. The Lord knew best. Certainly, men and women who would change their sex status will answer to their Maker.[7]

The Stumbling Block of the Sacrament

The law of Moses was a law of ordinances and performances practiced daily to remind the Israelites of Christ (Mosiah 13:30). The sacrament was instituted to remember the greatness and love of our Savior in bringing about the Resurrection and the Atonement. The primary purpose of meeting together, in Paul's day and our own, is to worship the Lord through partaking of the sacrament.

> When ye come together into one place, *is it* not to eat the Lord's supper? (JST, 1 Corinthians 11:20; italics added)

The Lord has given the same commandment today:

> And now, behold, I give unto you a commandment, that when ye are assembled together ye shall instruct and edify each other, that ye may know how to act and direct my church, how to act upon the points of my law and commandments, which I have given.
> And thus ye shall become instructed in the law of my church, and be sanctified by that which ye have received, and ye shall bind yourselves to act in all holiness before me. (D&C 43:8–9)

We bind ourselves through the covenant made in partaking of the sacrament. Through partaking of the bread, we remember the body of Christ and his providing the Resurrection (1 Corinthians 11:24; compare 3 Nephi 18:6–7). Through partaking of the water, we remember the blood of Gethsemane or the Atonement (1 Corinthians 11:25; compare 3 Nephi 18:10–11). To partake of the sacrament requires one to be worthy. Therefore, one must reflect or examine himself before partaking (1 Corinthians 11:27–28). To partake unworthily will cause one to stumble and bring about sickness, either physical or mental, and, Paul said, may even bring death [sleep] (1 Corinthians 11:29–30). Such is the order revealed to the Corinthians by Paul and verified in the Book of Mormon as a second witness (3 Nephi 18: 28–32; Mormon 9:29). The sacrament is thus a stepping-stone or a stumbling block.

Conclusion

The gospel is eternal. Although customs and traditions become linked to their practice in various locations, the truths and principles of salvation are the same. The devil is always opposing the Lord's plan for bringing to pass the immortality and eternal life of man (Moses 1:39). These temptations of Satan were called stumbling blocks by Paul since they obstruct our progress on the path to eternal life. As indicated in the above analysis, these stumbling blocks are almost as eternal as the gospel. There are certain things that Satan always tosses in our way. The sins are the same even if they are dressed in charmingly varied robes of deceit. However, the road signs given us by the Lord's apostles to avoid the turnoffs and chuckholes are also eternal and will lead us through the rough places of the wilderness of Satan to the bosom of Abraham and Christ.

Notes
1. Benjamin Willard Robinson, Ph.D., *The Life of Paul* (Chicago: The University of Chicago Press, 1928), 136.
2. As footnoted in the 1979 publication of the Bible by The Church of Jesus Christ of Latter-day Saints, the Greek work translated *effeminate* in the King James Version is defined as *catamites*. A catamite is a sexually abused young boy. This is the basis for saying Paul warned of child sexual abusers.
3. Joseph Fielding Smith, Comp., *Teachings of the Prophet Joseph Smith* (n.p., 1946), 370–71. This paper will not fully treat the Trinitarian concept but the reader should carefully study this explanation given by Joseph Smith.
4. See "The Father and the Son: Doctrinal Exposition of the First Presidency and the Twelve," quoted in James E. Talmage, *Articles of Faith* (Salt Lake City: The Church of Jesus Christ of Latter-day Saints, 1949), appendix 2, section 11, 465–73.
5. *Teachings*, 371; italics added.
6. Joseph Fielding Smith, *Conference Report*, April 1970, 59; also "Magnifying Our Calling in the Priesthood," *Improvement Era*, June 1970, 66
7. Edward L. Kimball, *The Teachings of Spencer W. Kimball* (Salt Lake City: Bookcraft, 1982), 278.

CHAPTER TWELVE

Interpreting the New Testament

Chauncey C. Riddle

This paper is divided into three parts: Part 1 deals with the place of the New Testament in our lives and why we must know it. Part 2 discusses the three modes of interpreting the New Testament. Part 3 contains special suggestions for interpreting the New Testament.

Part 1: The Place of the New Testament in Our Lives

To understand the place of the New Testament in the life of a Latter-day Saint, we must first inquire as to the place of the scriptures in general. If salvation is the goal for man, then we see that there are three principal helps for man as he seeks to be saved. The first help is God himself. Salvation is not a mortal or human thing. It is supernatural, a lifting of man from human to divine status, and comes to us only in the person of Jesus Christ. It is through the personal power and intervention of Jesus Christ that any man is saved from unrighteousness.

The second help sent by God to draw men unto him that they might be saved is the prophets of God. These are they who are given power from God to teach the true gospel of Jesus Christ and to administer the saving ordinances, which are the covenants thereof. The gospel is necessary because men must understand and desire salvation from unrighteousness before they can be saved. Each person is then saved in and through the covenants each makes with God and the carrying out of the promises made by each person and by God.

A third help for salvation is the holy scriptures. The purpose of the scriptures is to acquaint men with the possibility of salvation, that each might have the opportunity to understand and to desire salvation through Jesus Christ. Those who have that desire are pointed by the scriptures to find a prophet of God, that they, too, might partake of the covenants and thus enter into life, which is salvation. When the scriptures are not adulterated by men, they perform well those two tasks: allowing men to desire righteousness by understanding its possibility in Jesus Christ, and pointing them to find an authorized servant of Jesus Christ who can lawfully and effectively administer the saving ordinances.

Let us note what is necessary for salvation: God is necessary, and since he saves men only through covenants, the covenants are necessary. Prophets of God would not be necessary if God himself were to come down and administer the gospel and the covenants directly to men. But God chooses not to do that most of the time. When God chooses not to come down, then men who desire to be saved must seek a legal administrator sent from God, a prophet. In this case, the prophet, who bears the authority of God to teach the gospel and administer in the ordinances thereof, becomes necessary. The scriptures are not necessary. They are helpful, but men could be saved if there were not one line of scripture written. Men could be saved by the prophet of God without scripture, for the true prophet has all that is necessary.

But the scriptures are helpful. They point our minds to our God and to righteousness. They make us hunger and thirst for the ordinances which make righteousness possible. Each different scripture gives the witness of a different people and/or time, showing that God loves his children and saves men in all ages through the very same gospel and ordinances. The New Testament is the special witness of the prophets who labored in the Old World during the meridian of time. They give us many precious insights into the life and ministry of the Savior and his apostles. But no Latter-day Saint needs those insights to be saved.

We are a missionary people, however. The New Testament is the only record of Jesus Christ and his gospel that much of the world knows. That record therefore is the bridge by which we can put them in touch with the true priesthood authority of God. Because Latter-day Saints are a missionary people, we need to know the New Testament backward and forward, not for our own salvation but that we might be instrumental in bringing the knowledge of how to be saved to others of our brothers and sisters. For us to ignore the New Testament or to know it poorly is not to love either our God or those Christian neighbors whom our God has given us.

Part 2: Three Modes of Interpreting the New Testament

The first mode for understanding the New Testament is private interpretation; the second is scholarly interpretation; and the third is prophetic interpretation.

A. Private Interpretation

Private interpretation of the New Testament is reading some version of it and deciding that it means whatever we think it means. In this method, each person sets himself up as the interpreter and fixes on his own fancy as the standard. There are two principal ways of doing this.

The first kind of private interpretation is whimsical; with it we allow our own creative imagination to tell us that the text means whatever pops into our heads as we read it. Many human beings interpret everything they read in this way.

The second variety of private interpretation is the dogmatic variety, wherein the reader attributes the same meaning to the text which he or she has been told by someone else is the proper interpretation. Without any further thought or inquiry the reader simply accepts what he has been told.

The New Testament has a pointed comment about private interpretation. Peter warns us not to indulge in it: "Knowing this first, that no prophecy of the scripture is of any private interpretation. For the prophecy came not in old time by the will of man: but holy men of God spake as they were moved by the Holy Ghost" (2 Peter 1:20–21). The dogmatic variety of private interpretation is what the scriptures call the "chains of hell" (see D&C 123:7–8). The purpose and end of private interpretation is to confirm and convince the reader of what he already believes. It is principally an occasion for self-justification, a path to be eschewed under all circumstances.

B. Scholarly Interpretation

Scholarly interpretation of the New Testament is applying a rational formula to the translating of a scriptural text into some vernacular and then designating the significance of that text. There are two principal varieties of scholarly interpretation.

First-class scholarship has each of the following criteria as necessary conditions: (a) the most authentic version of the text must be used; (b) the text must be used in the original language (Greek for the New Testament); (c) the scholar must be aware of and account for what every other first-class scholar has said on the topic or passage being interpreted; and (d) the first-class scholar must use a rational formula which he explicitly describes and which any other scholar could discern and use. These rather strict conditions for first-class scholarship cause it to be rare. One mark of the work of first-class scholars is the abundance of footnotes, but many footnotes do not make first-class scholarship. Only a first-class scholar will read all the footnotes, track down the origins, and judge for himself whether or not a writer makes sense. It takes a first-class scholar to identify and deal with a first-class scholar.

Second-class scholarship is interpretation which satisfies any one of the conditions for first-class scholarship but lacks one or more of the other requirements. There is a good deal of second-class scholarship in the world.

The rational formulae which scholars use are of some note, and it serves our purpose to review the principal varieties here.

"*Lower*," or *textual criticism*, is the comparison of texts to determine by both internal and external evidence the text which is most authentic. In the case of the New Testament, this usually is the pursuit of the oldest manuscript, assuming the oldest to be the closest to the source. We have nothing which could be considered an original manuscript for the New Testament, so lower criticism is important to every student of that text.

"*Higher*" *criticism* is the search for authorship of biblical texts by considering internal evidence, such as writing style, vocabulary, historical references, and so forth.

Grammatical criticism, or ordinary textual interpretation, is intense analysis of the words and grammatical forms of the text, in an attempt to establish what would constitute an acceptable modal translation of the text based on what are considered to be the meanings of other nonscriptural texts of the Koine Greek which appears in the New Testament manuscripts.

Source criticism is the attempt to structure the hypothetical original documents which the writers of the Gospels and Acts might have used to compose those works, drawing evidence from the similarities and differences found among the synoptic Gospels in particular.

Form criticism is the attempt to relate the New Testament texts to the literary forms present in the manuscripts of the contemporary Hellenic culture of the writers of the New Testament. Various pericopes or fragments of the text are analyzed as paradigms, tales, legends, myths, and exhortations, interpretation being affected by the perceived literary device employed.

Redaction criticism assumes that there were primary source documents like those which source criticism seeks to reconstruct, and that writers of the New Testament were principally employed in stitching the older fragments together with comments of their own, which is redaction. The work of redaction criticism is to reinterpret the text in light of the perceived biases and emphases of each redactor.

Tradition-history criticism attempts to correlate the biblical text with the historic development of the New Testament church. It is based on two principles: first, that the Christology of the New Testament is not that of Jesus himself but is a product of the legends which grew up in the first century; and second, that it is possible to separate the authentic teachings of Jesus himself from the accretions added by later Christians.

Comparative religion criticism (history of religion criticism) approaches the New Testament by noting what elements it does and does not have in common with the other religions of the ancient Near East. Relationships with Zoroastrianism, Mithraism, and other religions are established, showing that the atoning sacrifice and purification rites were common to many cultures.

Demythologizing is the attempt to relieve the New Testament of its supernatural elements, which, it is said, are no longer tolerable to the enlightened mind, and to discover the authentic, timeless core that lies within those supposed myths. An interesting variation on that theme is the attempt to "remythologize" the text in favor of modern myths, those more acceptable to modern minds.

Hermeneutics, as an intellectual approach, leaves the attempt to say what the text originally meant to others, and concentrates instead on discerning what the text should mean for us in our modern setting. Instead of our judging the text, it is understood that the text judges us who read it. As Jesus established a common understanding with the people to whom he spoke that he might thereby surely deliver his message, so we must seek today that frame of mind in which the teachings of Jesus will be most meaningful to us.

Another scholarly device is that employed by Harnack, Boman, and others in the attempt to characterize the patterns of Hebrew thinking as they contrast with those of the Greek mind. Boman sees the Hebrews as interested in action, whereas the Greeks look for the unchangeable, eternal verities; the Hebrews focus on inner qualities of soul, while the Greeks favor visible particulars in describing persons; Hebrews see action as either complete or incomplete, whereas the Greeks nicely divide time into past, present, and future. Such differences as these, Boman contends, must be taken into account when interpreting the Hebrew New Testament messages in Greek grammatical forms.[1]

An excellent explanation of much that relates to the scholarly interpretation of the New Testament is found in a work edited by I. Howard Marshall, entitled *New Testament Interpretation*.[2] I recommend especially: the article by F. F. Bruce entitled "The History of New Testament Study," one by E. Earl Ellis entitled "How the New Testament Uses the Old," and a third by Anthony Thiselton entitled "The New Hermeneutic."

The end or goal of scholarly interpretation is knowledge. The scholar seeks, with the best rational tools and worldly learning that he can muster, to reach conclusions that are intellectually justifiable. His greatest fear is that he will believe something that is unworthy of rational assent. Often he assumes protective custody of nonscholars in attempting to spare them the horrors of naive belief and private interpretation, thus becoming a brother-keeper. Some scholars, of course, have a real belief that Jesus was divine. They search and reason while believing, hoping to find a better faith, and through their faith have given great gifts to the world. I think here of works such as that of James Strong, who, with others but without the benefit of a computer, produced that invaluable tool for biblical scholarship that we know as *Strong's Exhaustive Concordance of the Bible*.[3] I also recommend the volume by Richard L. Anderson entitled *Understanding Paul*, an interpretive work of first-class scholarship.[4]

Scholarly interpretation is clearly an improvement on private interpretation. Scholarly and rational though it is, much of it is guesswork. But gems can be found in it which are well worth the search. This body of material is much in the category of the biblical Apocrypha concerning which the Lord declared through the Prophet Joseph Smith: "There are many things contained therein that are not true, which are interpolations by the hands of men. . . . Therefore, whoso readeth it, let him understand, for the Spirit manifesteth therefrom; And whoso receiveth not by the Spirit, cannot be benefited" (D&C 91:2–6).

C. Prophetic Interpretation

We now contrast private and scholarly interpretation with prophetic interpretation. Prophetic interpretation is interpretation of a scriptural text under the immediate direction of the Holy Spirit. This is personal revelation, the same kind of personal revelation by which the scripture was originally created. This kind of interpretation is denominated "prophetic" because it is the Holy Spirit which brings the true testimony of Jesus Christ and that testimony of Jesus Christ is the spirit of prophecy. Whoever has the Holy Spirit to guide him or her is for that moment a prophet—not necessarily a prophet to anyone else, but at least a prophet unto himself or herself. Since it takes a prophet to tell a prophet, the Holy Spirit binds the sent prophet to the receiving prophet in the unity of submission to the mind and will of God (cf. D&C 50:13–24).

Thus there are two basic types of prophetic interpretation. The first is the prophecy of receiving from God for one's own personal benefit. As one approaches a scriptural text in prayer and faith, ready to do what is instructed by the Holy Spirit, one indeed may receive specific instruction in connection with text as to how that should be interpreted, then acting accordingly in one's own life situation and predicaments. This is using the text as if it were a Urim and Thummim, a divinely given aid to facilitate the receiving of further revelation from the Lord. Since the Lord has promised that he will give wisdom—that knowledge of how to act in faith—that we might please him, such revelation is a frequent occurrence. Its occurrence is correlated strictly with the degree to which the person seeks and hungers after righteousness through Jesus Christ. We noted above that the purpose in private interpretation is self-justification and that the purpose of scholarly interpretation is the ascertaining of truth, that one might know what to believe. Contrasted with both is the purpose of prophetic interpretation: to be able to act in faith to please God. Action, which includes but goes much beyond mere believing, is the end of prophetic scriptural interpretation. Built into this kind of prophecy is the supposition that this process will take place again and again, and that through much faith and experience in experimenting with those messages delivered by the still, small voice of the Spirit, one will come to know for oneself, unerringly, what is and what is not the voice of God in this world. Thus one becomes sure and established, rooted and tested in the faith of Christ, and through that mature faith comes all other good things from God.

The second kind of prophetic interpretation of the scriptures is the prophecy of receiving from God for the purpose of bearing witness to others concerning God. To safeguard the purity of this kind of revelation, the Lord has put three safeguards on it. First, prophecy may be received and delivered to other human beings only by those who are ordained of God by the laying on of hands by those who have true authority from God, even as was Aaron. Second, the hearer will always be one to whom the preacher or teacher is specifically sent. It will be publicly known to members of the Lord's Church who those preachers and teachers are that are duly sent. Third, each hearer is entitled to personal revelation from God himself confirming any interpretation or prophecy which the one who is sent might deliver to him or her. Thus the prophecy of preaching or teaching for God must be matched by the prophecy of receiving from God by the hearer for the witness of the preacher or teacher to be valid and binding. These three essentials are clearly stated by the Lord as his standard: "And, behold, and lo, this is an ensample unto all those who were ordained unto this priesthood, whose mission is appointed unto them to go forth—And this is the ensample unto them, that they shall speak as they are moved upon by the Holy Ghost. And whatsoever they shall speak when moved upon by the Holy Ghost shall be scripture, shall be the will of the Lord, shall be the mind of the Lord, shall be the word of the Lord, shall be the voice of the Lord, and the power of God unto salvation" (D&C 68:2–4).

Thus, each human being who encounters the holy scriptures has three choices: he may put his own private interpretation on the scripture, he may use the tools and formulae of the scholarly world in interpreting it, or he may seek and find personal revelation that the Lord might interpret it for him. It seems that this is an exhaustive taxonomy; every interpretation can be correctly designated as one of these three.

But what about the value of mixing these three types of interpretation? It is plain that private interpretation is always evil and that it will destroy any good that might otherwise be found by an individual when combining it with either scholarly or prophetic interpretation. Scholarly interpretation is evil if it is private interpretation, that is to say, if it is not done under the inspiration and permission of the Holy Spirit. But scholarship can be noble and spiritually rewarding. The scholarly work of Mormon in creating the Book of Mormon is a perfect model of responsible, spiritual scholarship. But scholarly or not, interpretation of scripture must always be purely prophetic to avoid being evil. The kingdom of our Savior today could use more first-class scholarship by those who enjoy the spirit of prophecy. Of course, what it most needs is more persons reading the scriptures by the spirit of prophecy and then acting faithfully. We have enough scripture; we need to better use what we have. It is promised that then we shall have more.

D. Applications by History

How can an understanding of these three kind of interpretation be seen to operate historically? First, we note that all scripture is produced by prophecy, by the revelations of God to his chosen servants. The intention is that all reading and interpreting of any portion or of all of that scripture should be done by prophecy, either for the benefit of the individual in his own stewardship or for the purpose of instructing others. But when men sin, the gifts of the Holy Spirit are taken from them. If they then interpret scripture, they are forced either to scholarly or to private interpretation.

After prophets ceased in Judah in Old Testament times (c. 400 BC), there arose the schools of rabbinic interpretation. Rabbinic interpretation is scholarly interpretation. It focuses on reading the accepted text in the original Hebrew, knowing what other rabbis have said about it, and elaborating interpretation according to rational formulae. These scholars were known as scribes and Pharisees in the Savior's time. Jesus was a problem to them because he did not have the rabbinic training or outlook: he taught as one having authority, for indeed he was a prophet of God. He spoke only by the spirit of prophecy and instructed his followers to do likewise. In this the Savior threatened the rabbinic tradition of the scribes and Pharisees. They saw themselves as the saviors of the common people, preserving them from the great evil of private interpretation of the holy scriptures, which is generally the scholarly attitude. It was these protectors of the people who called for and gained Jesus' blood, calling him a blasphemer for pretending to revelation from his Father and theirs. So they had their way, and rabbinism has maintained its hold on Judah to this day.

Paul was a rabbinic zealot, persecuting the blasphemers wherever he could. He was cured of his spiritual blindness by a revelation which left him physically blind. But then, knowing revelation, he became a faithful disciple of the Savior, teaching the deadness both of the law of Moses and of the rabbinic tradition of interpretation which refused to see the law as the schoolmaster to prepare Israel for Christ.

During the time of Paul and the other apostles, prophetic interpretation of the scriptures flourished, though not without opposition. But when the apostles were gone, the opposition triumphed and scholarly interpretation replaced revelation, even as it had done in Judaism earlier. Training for the priest became the study of languages and philosophy that scholarly work might be pursued. Thus, the world came to think that one cannot preach unless he is school learned.

The Protestant Reformation provided an interesting twist on the old story. When Luther, Wycliffe, and others translated the Bible into the vernacular languages, they did so as scholars, but they were undoubtedly aided by the Holy Spirit in much of what they did. The result was that prophetic interpretation again began to flourish. Individuals could now read the things of God and interpret them for themselves, and through faithful obedience to God as he gave them revelation, they revolutionized the world for much good. Institutionally, Protestantism has always been weak. Lacking authority for the preaching and teaching gifts, it has foundered on the question of authority. But individuals were not barred or prevented from doing much good. That is perhaps why the practice of Christian religion among genuine Protestants has so often been very good while the theory has been very bad.

The Church of Jesus Christ of Latter-day Saints also reflects the tension among these three modes of interpreting the scriptures. Prophetic interpretation is the core and being of the restored Church. But there are those who insist on their own private interpretation of the revelations. These go off into the desert (spiritually and/or temporally) and form their own private churches and kingdoms. They have their reward.

Others employ scholarly methods to interpret the scriptures, and some of that scholarship is first-rate. Among these scholars there are those who are also submissive to the Holy Spirit, who wait upon the Lord; they have sometimes made important contributions to the kingdom, often anonymously. They know that their blessings come not through their scholarly attainments but from their faith in Jesus Christ. Another group in the Church are scholars of one sort or another who do not brook priesthood authority and the guidance of the Holy Spirit. They come to believe that reason must and will eventually triumph over what they call "blind faith." To them, blind faith is unscholarly faith. They struggle with what the General Authorities of the Church say and cannot fully support those authorities. They are sometimes miffed because persons of lesser intelligence and scholarship are placed in positions of authority over them or are given precedence before them. Their scholarship has become a stumbling block to them. This is one source of the so-called anti-intellectual bias of the Church.

But scholarship and revelation can go hand in hand as long as revelation is the leader, the interpreter, and not vice versa.

Part 3: Suggestions for Interpreting the New Testament

We come now to the third part of this paper, which is to make some concrete suggestions for faithful, prophetic interpretation of the New Testament. It is incumbent upon every faithful member to read the New Testament during the years in which the New Testament is the assigned scripture for Church study, if at all possible. If we read it and how we read it will determine much about our future.

I will make seven specific suggestions as to how one might profitably go about reading the New Testament prophetically. I report these as admonitions to myself, hoping that something I say might find a responsive chord in your spiritual repertoire.

1. I believe that it is important to begin each scripture session with prayer, that we might demonstrate our faith and make ourselves more receptive to the whisperings of the Spirit. Indeed, prayer itself, if done truly, is simple practice at receiving and obeying personal revelation. It is thus a specific preparation for receiving what the Lord would have us do in connection with the text we are about to examine. I call as my witness on this point, Nephi of old: "But behold, I say unto you that ye must pray always, and not faint; that ye must not perform any thing unto the Lord save in the first place ye shall pray unto the Father in the name of Christ, that he will consecrate thy performance unto thee, that thy performance may be for the welfare of thy soul" (2 Nephi 32:9).

2. It has often been noted that we tend to see in a text what we already believe. If what we already believe is true, then we have a great help in interpreting the scriptures. But if we are struggling with new doctrine and have false doctrine as our interpretive frame, we will have a difficult time when the Holy Spirit tells us something contrary to what we already believe. We must clean up the launching pad to avoid misinterpretation.

One excellent way to cleanse our minds of error is to let the Book of Mormon be our standard of doctrine and truth. Of course, the Book of Mormon cannot give us the truth without revelation. But at least we are reading the book with the most correct text in this whole world. A better place to practice interpretation by the Spirit and to establish a true theology and cosmology is difficult to find, and if found, is sometimes not accessible (such as the person of a General Authority). My witness here is the Prophet Joseph Smith: " I told the brethren that the Book of Mormon was the most correct of any book on earth, and the keystone of our religion, and a man would get nearer to God by abiding by its precepts, than by any other book" (introduction to the Book of Mormon).

3.   We need to see all things from the perspective of eternity. There is only one thing which matters in eternity: righteousness. If righteousness is the thing after which we hunger and thirst, then as we read the scriptures prayerfully and faithfully, we will be filled with information about how to obtain righteousness and how to avoid unrighteousness. The Book of Mormon shows us that the larger problem of salvation is to somehow get forgiveness for unrighteousness. The Book of Mormon shows us that the larger problem is getting our personal self re-created into a new being that no longer does anything unrighteous. Studying that process of re-creation through being reborn and growing up into the stature of the fulness of Christ is the key to righteousness and eternity. We have the promise of the Savior: "Blessed are all they who do hunger and thirst after righteousness, for they shall be filled with the Holy Ghost" (3 Nephi 12:6).

4. We can liken the scriptures unto ourselves. When we read the stories of the scriptures, we can imaginatively put ourselves in the place of the characters of the story. How would I think, feel, and act if I suddenly awoke and realized that I am the prodigal son? What should I then feel, think, say, and do? Or do I imagine myself to be the other brother who supposedly never sinned; do I see myself as saved while all about me are prodigal? If so, I probably am in great need of repentance for even allowing myself to suppose that I am *that* son.

When I read of Ananias and Sapphira, do I understand what must have been going through the heart and mind of each when questioned about the consecration? Can I feel the fear of trusting entirely in that unseen Jesus Christ, yet being tugged upon by the Holy Spirit to tell the truth? Can I imagine the anguish each must have felt in deliberately denying the Holy Spirit, grasping at a worldly straw? Can the memory of that imagination help me in the future when my faith wavers and the cares of the world press upon me? I can indeed live a hundred lives in my imagination, and taste the bitterness of sin and the joy of righteousness vicariously. That knowledge then can help me to be strong and reject the bitterness of hell. Through Cain I know murder and perdition. Through Judah I know the pain of adultery. Through David I know the damnation of lust. Through Peter I deny that I know the Christ and have bitter tears. Through Paul I know persecution and stoning. Through John I know what it is to lean upon the Savior's breast and be his beloved disciple. Not that I do these things, but the Holy Spirit causes all these things in me as I prayerfully meditate and ponder the stories which the prophets have carefully preserved for me under instruction from the Holy One. Again, I call Nephi as my witness in this likening: "And I did read many things unto them which were written in the books of Moses; but that I might more fully persuade them to believe in the Lord their Redeemer I did read unto them that which was written by the prophet Isaiah; for I did liken all scriptures unto us, that it might be for our profit and learning" (1 Nephi 19:23).

5. More specifically I can ask myself how I relate to the priesthood authority which my Savior has set over me. Am I Uzza who steadies the ark? Am I Simon who would buy the power of the priesthood if I cannot bring myself to repent to get it? Am I like the rich young man who goes to the authorities for help but then has to go away sorrowing because I love the world more than I love obedience? Can I see how I must not pretend that I am as good as the prophet, as Hiram Page was tempted? Do I see in my bishop and stake president the same authority and power which parted the Red Sea and fed the five thousand?

The brethren who preside over us are human, but the authority they have is not. Can I look both fully in the face and accept them? When those brethren use a scripture to teach us, do I find fault with their interpretation because I fancy myself to be superior, then neglect to do what they tell me, thus compounding the error? Peter tells us that the key to perfecting our love for the Savior is first to learn to love the brethren whom he has sent to preside over us (see 2 Peter 1). If our reading of the scriptures encourages us and enables us to do that, we are profiting from the scriptures indeed.

6. If we love the brethren who preside over us, we then can use our reading of the scriptures to draw us closer to the Lord himself. Have we read the life of the Savior in all the detail preserved for us, then prayed for the confirmation so that we can say with Peter; "Thou art the Christ, the Son of the living God" (Matthew 16:16)? If we read with faith, we will know that our Savior loves us and that he does nothing save it be for the benefit of the world. If we love and serve him, everything which

happens to us he will turn to our good. As our admiration and love for him and our faithfulness to him grow, we will grow in the power and understanding of his word. The scriptures will indeed become a Urim and Thummim to us. We will not be in doubt as to what he would have us believe and do. He himself tells us, "And again, verily I say unto you, my friends, I leave these sayings with you to ponder in your hearts, with this commandment which I give unto you, that ye shall call upon me while I am near—Draw near unto me and I will draw near unto you; seek me diligently and ye shall find me; ask, and ye shall receive; knock, and it shall be opened unto you" (D&C 88:62–63).

7. My final suggestion for interpreting the New Testament and all scripture is that we strive to understand how to apply the great commandment. We are told, "Thou shalt love the Lord thy God with all thy heart, with all thy might, mind, and strength; and in the name of Jesus Christ thou shalt serve him" (D&C 59:5). I take this to mean that there are four basic and distinct ways in which we should love our God. Since everything we do should be an act of love for him, reading the scriptures must be one of those things, and we should use the scriptures to learn how we can love and serve him with all of our heart, might, mind, and strength.

Our heart is the heart of our spirit body and is the factor which determines what we choose among the alternatives furnished by the mind. Most of us have the problem that our hearts are not pure: we want to do what is right, but we also want to sin. So we defeat ourselves, frustrate ourselves by doing some good things but not being able to reap the full benefits because we also tarnish ourselves with sinning. The solution to the problem is to find the one way to become pure in heart, which is found only in the Savior. If we come unto him as little children, believing and obeying, he can purify us. When we read the scriptures, we might well be asking, What does this passage teach me about how I should feel and what I should desire? If I then follow through with what I am instructed by the Spirit to feel and desire, I am beginning to love the Lord with my heart.

Our mind apparently is the brain of our spirit body. It is our mind which knows and understands, which receives instruction and reproof, which contemplates the world and the perspective of eternity. If our mind is right, we will receive many things but admit into our beliefs only those things directly attested by the Holy Spirit, which will show us the truth of all things. Under the direction of that Spirit we will train ourselves to think, to compare, to analyze, to relate, to synthesize, to create, to conjecture, to test, to evaluate. We will strive to furnish our heart with an able and truthful servant and companion. Even as the heart needs to be pure, so does the mind need to be filled with truth and to eschew all error, even until one sees and understands the mysteries both of this world and of eternity. Only the Spirit of Truth, which is Jesus Christ and the Holy Ghost acting as one, can so purify our minds and fill them that we can begin to become wise servants, properly furnished with the perspective of eternity. As we read the scriptures, we should be hungering and thirsting after truth, jealous for every true belief, that we might learn to love the Lord fully, in truth and righteousness, with our mind.

Our strength is our body, our mortal tabernacle. To love our God with all our strength, we must study and train ourselves until we furnish this body with the very best nutrition available, the best hygienic environment we can muster, the most valuable exercise and work which is appropriate. We must treasure our power of reproduction, deeming its purity of more value than physical life itself. We must search out that field of labor where the Lord would have us dwell and be a husbandman to his vineyard, and bring forth upon the earth those physical and spiritual fruits which will please him. Our study of the scripture will help suggest particulars of how we might act as just and wise stewards, how we might keep ourselves unspotted from the world, how we might need to sacrifice our very physical life in the cause of our Master. Thus we learn to love the Lord with all of our strength.

Our might is our sphere of influence in this world: our money, our property, our belongings, our family and friends, our stewardships. We are apprentice gods, and it pleases God to instruct us in all the ways of godliness if we seek righteousness rather than power. As we read his word, we will learn many things about how to be a just and wise steward. Through his Spirit he will show us good examples in the scriptures of the very principles and standards that he himself abides. As we are faithful in complying with that instruction, he is able to make us rulers over many, for we have then learned to love him with our might.

Learning to love God through the scriptures is like learning to braid with four strands. Here and there, line upon line, and precept upon precept, we learn the standards and requirements for loving him with heart, might, mind, and strength. As we obey, we make the strands a reality instead of a possibility. As we obey through time, we twist, turn, weave, and sacrifice until we have formed a tightly woven strand, one that is strong yet flexible, durable yet pliable, ready and able to bear the weight of eternal things. We personally, being reborn and refashioned, have become worthy of the Master of our apprenticeship through loving him and his word.

One example must suffice. We read in John that if we continue in the word of the Savior, we are his disciples indeed; then we shall know the truth and the truth shall make us free. How shall we interpret this according to heart, might, mind, and strength? With our heart we can desire to know him who is the truth, desire enough that we actually repent of our sins and obey his will through his Holy Spirit, hungering and thirsting after righteousness. With our mind we can understand that he is the way, the truth, and the life, and that besides him there is no Savior and no salvation. We see that the world does not know the truth. We must put our whole trust and confidence in him only. With our strength, we can sacrifice to keep his commandments, to get up when we should, to sleep when we should, to eat when we should, to go and come and work and play as we should, to defend or retreat as we should, to till the earth and provide for our own as we should. With our might we can tithe and consecrate, foster good causes and bless, share with our neighbor who is in want, store for a dark future, and invest in that which is eternally worthwhile. For if we love and serve him who is the truth, he will then be able to set us free from every impurity, every smallness, every selfishness, every error, every untoward desire. Then we shall be free indeed.

The sum of the matter is that scripture is of no private interpretation. We must search and strive until we find that Holy Spirit which alone can make the scriptures come alive to us with that life which never ends. May we relish that great treasure, the New Testament, in that way, is my hope for all of us.

Notes

1. Boman, Thorlief; *Hebrew Thought Compared with Greek,* W. W. Norton Co., 1960.
2. Paternoster Press, Exeter, England, 1977.
3. MacDonald Publishing Company, McLean, Virginia.
4. Anderson, Richard Lloyd; *Understanding Paul,* Salt Lake City, Utah: Deseret Book Company, 1983.

CHAPTER THIRTEEN

The Book of Romans: An Orthodox Description of Faith, Works, and Exaltation

Joseph Barnard Romney

It is rather common for Church members to shy away from the epistle to the Romans, as well as from the other Pauline epistles. In part, this reaction may be because those writings seem difficult to understand. Perhaps another reason is that the doctrines they contain do not appear to be exactly orthodox. This second reason is reinforced by the use of certain passages from Paul's epistles by those who say that all one must do to be saved is to verbally accept Christ as one's personal Savior. Since Latter-day Saints understand that conclusion to be erroneous, and since Paul's epistles are used as a basis for that conclusion, Church members may feel suspicious of those epistles. The book of Romans is especially susceptible to this concern because nowadays it is often cited as a source of that doctrine, and historically it was the trigger for Martin Luther's spiritual renovation which led to the emphasis of that doctrine in that Reformation.[1]

The purpose of this paper is to demonstrate that the epistle to the Romans is in accord with what the restored gospel of Jesus Christ teaches about the correct relationship of faith and works as they lead to exaltation. This accord will be demonstrated by briefly describing the orthodox doctrine, then comparing the basic organizational structure of Romans to that doctrine. The result of this comparison is a recognition that Romans is a sound description of this part of the gospel of Jesus

Christ, a description that Latter-day Saints ought to embrace rather than ignore or timidly tolerate.

Other Approaches and This Paper

To begin, some comment will be made on other approaches to Romans which may be helpful in understanding the epistle, but which are not being emphasized in this paper. One approach is to see Romans in its historical setting, particularly in relationship to the background of Judaism out of which Christianity grew and the confrontation of that heritage with that of the Greeks and Romans. Another approach is to analyze the Greek text for insight into word meaning in order to clarify what Paul intended to say. Another approach is to focus on the doctrine of justification by faith or some other teaching presented in the epistle. In this paper, reference will be made to some of these methods, but they will not be emphasized.[2]

This paper is primarily directed toward lay members and teachers of lay members who may feel uncomfortable in using Romans because of the concerns mentioned earlier—difficulty in understanding, and fear over orthodoxy. While the methods mentioned may be helpful in studying Romans, they are not as important as a knowledge and testimony of the basic principles of the gospel. With such a knowledge and testimony, careful study of the epistle as an integrated whole, using the tools included in recent editions of the standard works in concert with the considerations to follow will yield the major messages Paul had for the Roman Saints and which the book of Romans has for us.

Five Considerations in Understanding Romans

In addition to a testimony and knowledge of the gospel, several other considerations should be kept in mind. First, the book is in the form of a letter, so we can expect an initial salutation and closing greetings surrounding the message of the letter. And since the letter was undoubtedly composed with some thought, unlike many letters written today, we can expect some organization in its presentation.

Second, the letter was written to Church members, those who already had an understanding of principles of the gospel. Thus Paul addressed himself "to all that be in Rome, beloved of God, called to be saints" (Romans 1:7 [hereafter only chapter and verse will be used for references to Romans. Other scriptural citations will include the book cited]). As a result, some fundamental gospel principles may be only alluded to or inferred.

Third, the Saints to whom Paul wrote had emerged from two basic traditions. One was the Jewish tradition which included procedures which were sometimes referred to as "the law," meaning aspects of the law of Moses. The Church leadership had earlier concluded that compliance with the procedural aspects of the law of Moses was not a prerequisite for being a Christian (Acts 15:1–31). Still, Saints had to be reminded of that decision. Care had to be taken to distinguish the procedural law of Moses, which did not need to be followed, and the law of the gospel, meaning the universal principles of salvation, which must always be followed. The second tradition was that of the Greeks and Romans which did not anticipate a redeemer at all. Christians from that tradition needed to be convinced that an atonement was necessary and that Jesus of Nazareth was the one who provided that atonement.

Fourth, Paul was well acquainted with the gospel. He had studied it for several years after he was converted on the road to Damascus (Galatians 1:18); he was instructed by Peter (Galatians 1:19), and he received revelation from Jesus Christ (Galatians 1:12), with whom he talked directly (Acts 23:11). He knew of the three degrees of glory (1 Corinthians 15:40–42; 2 Corinthians 12:2). Moreover, he was well acquainted with orthodox Judaism (Acts 26:5) and with the teachings of Greeks and Romans (Acts 17:17–18, 28). In short, Paul understood the traditions he confronted and the fulness of the gospel which he taught.

A fifth consideration is a description of the orthodox doctrine relating to faith, works, and exaltation as we have come to know that doctrine through the restoration of the gospel in these latter days.[3] One principle of that doctrine is that the gospel requirements apply universally to all people, whenever and wherever they live (Acts 10:34; 2 Nephi 26:33; 1 Peter 4:6; D&C 138). So the fundamentals with which we must comply applied equally to the Saints at Rome.

The second principle is that the goal of life is to be as much like our heavenly parents and Jesus Christ as possible, and that the possibility exists of being just like them, that is, of being exalted (3 Nephi 12:48; John 17:21–23; D&C 76:58; Genesis 17:1).

The third principle is that, in order to receive exaltation, one must live a certain way, i.e., one must keep the commandments (Mosiah 4:30; Matthew 7:21; Amos 5:24; D&C 76:51–52).

The fourth principle is that no matter how hard one tries, exaltation is impossible without the Atonement of Jesus Christ and faith in him (John 14:6; Leviticus 17:11; Alma 34:8; D&C 19:16).

Having these considerations in mind, we can approach Paul's epistle to the Romans with confidence. When Paul discussed faith, works, and exaltation, he did so using the orthodox doctrine we have come to know in the restoration of the gospel. But he explained the doctrine in a way that was meaningful to those to whom he wrote.

Outline of the Epistle

In order to provide an overview of the epistle, I offer the following outline. It will be helpful to refer to as you read the rest of this article.

I. Salutation and introduction to the problem
   A. Personal greetings, 1:1–16
   B. Perversions to be resisted, 1:17–32
II. The universality of the doctrines discussed in the letter
   A. The general principle of universality, 2:1–29
   B. The principle applied to Jews, 3:1–31
   C. The principle illustrated in the life of Abraham, 4:1–25
III. The hope for exaltation, also a universal hope
   A. A description of the hope, 5:1–5
   B. The hope realizable through the Atonement of Christ, 5:6–21
IV. The way to accept the Atonement of Christ
   A. Baptism, 6
   B. Relative to Jews and Gentiles in general
     1. The law of Moses pointed toward Christ, through whom joint heirship with him and our Heavenly Father is possible, 7–8
     2. Exaltation results from living up to one's foreordination (predestination), 9
     3. One must have knowledge, particularly of Christ, 10
     4. This offer of the Atonement of Christ was first given to the Jews who rejected it, so it now went to the Gentiles, after which it would return to the Jews, 11
   C. Relative to the Roman Saints in particular
     1. Keep the commandments, 12–15:13
     2. Paul brought them the message, 15:14–33
V. Closing greetings and instructions, 16

A review of this outline discloses that it is similar in its organization to many other gospel sermons or instructions. In Romans, Paul focused on some problems to be resolved, the difficulties, and called upon his readers to do something to overcome the difficulties. Paul himself followed the same organization in defending himself against the Jews in Jerusalem. The problem was their desire to kill him. He responded by explaining what led him to where he was, emphasized the role of Christ, but was stopped before he had time to ask the people to accept his story (Acts 22:1–22). A similar approach was taken by Paul before Festus and King Agrippa, at the end of which his hearers were convinced of his innocence (Acts 26:1–32). King Benjamin likewise discussed some concerns he had for his people, connected his concerns to the Atonement of Christ who would come, and called upon his hearers to live worthy of that atonement (Mosiah 2–4). Then he asked his people to become "children of Christ . . . born of him . . . that ye may have everlasting salvation and eternal life" (Mosiah 5:7, 15), just as Paul wanted his people to be "children of God . . . and joint heirs with Christ" (8:16–17). The defense of Stephen before the Jews (Acts 7:2–53) and the instructions of Alma and Amulek to the Zoramites (Alma 32–34) and Alma to his son Corianton (Alma 39–42) follow a similar pattern. The point is that the general organization of Paul's epistle to the Romans is something with which Latter-day Saints should be familiar and comfortable.

Explanation of the Epistle: Salutation and Introduction

Now let us expand the outline in paragraph form and include some related references in other parts of the standard works. As might be expected in a letter, Paul began with greetings to the Saints of Rome (1:1–16). He identified himself as an apostle of Jesus Christ (1:1–5), and recognized them as followers of Christ, called to be Saints (1:6–7). He longed to be with them so he might more effectively testify to them of the gospel of Jesus Christ (1:8–16). This salutation is similar to that in the letter from Liberty Jail from "Joseph Smith, Jun., prisoner for the Lord Jesus Christ's sake" to "dearly beloved brethren," which contained the beautiful teachings now contained in sections 121–23 of the Doctrine and Covenants (see *History of the Church*, 3:289–90).

Paul then introduced the necessity of faith and the problems it is to resolve. His introduction of faith would be especially effective to Jews, since in it he cited Habakkuk 2:4, "the just shall live by faith" (1:17). Although the universality of these doctrines was more fully treated later, the use of an Old Testament source at the beginning of the epistle indicates Paul's intention to speak of principles that applied before the birth of Christ as well as after.

He next described a variety of sins that had resulted from those who twisted the true knowledge of God into something that seemed to justify a variety of perversions (1:18–32). The central truth that "the Father has a body of flesh and bones" (D&C 130:22) was twisted to emphasize the value of a physical body to the exclusion of the spiritual nature of mankind. Paul said they "worshipped and served the creature more than the Creator" (1:25). Benjamin described the same danger, since "the natural man is an enemy to God" (Mosiah 3:19). Today we commonly see that danger in worship of the human body without reverence for its spiritual significance. Such an unbalanced view leads to homosexuality, fornication, and the other sins Paul so powerfully condemned (1:24–32). Because the apostates from the truth so chose to act, God permitted them to exercise their agency, or as Paul wrote, "for this cause God gave them up unto vile affections" (1:26; see also v. 28). Mormon stated this principle of free agency in talking about the Amlicites who voluntarily turned away from the truth: "and even so doth every man that is cursed bring upon himself his own condemnation" (Alma 3:19).

Universality of the Doctrines

Having introduced himself and the problems he saw, Paul then explained the universality of the doctrines he presented (2:1–29). This is the first of the orthodox principles listed earlier in this paper.

Paul addressed himself to "man, whosoever thou art" (2:1) and punctuated his discussion with statements that God "will render to every man according to his deeds. . . . for there is no respect of persons with God" (2:6, 11). This principle of universality is one that Peter learned before the gospel could effectively go to the Gentiles (Acts 10:34) and for which Paul consistently fought. Paul said Gentiles are accountable for the knowledge they have (2:14–16), a doctrine also taught by Benjamin (Mosiah 3:11). Just as he previously introduced the necessity of faith (1:17), Paul early in his letter directly stated that "not the hearers of the law are just before God, but the doers of the law shall be justified" (2:13). Thus, he clearly understood that faith necessarily includes action, a principle implicit in the last two-thirds of his epistle.

Paul included the Jews among those to whom the teachings he was developing applied (2:17–29). He had already said that everyone must live the law they have, so he applied that directly to the Jews and added another quality that must be present in keeping the commandments. The proper outward behavior must be accompanied by the proper inward attitude. Or as Paul put it, "He is a Jew, which is one inwardly; and circumcision is that of the heart, in the spirit, and not in the letter" (2:29). In our dispensation the Lord expressed it this way: "I, the Lord, require the hearts of the children of men" (D&C 64:22).

In chapter 3, Paul continued to apply to the Jews the universal necessity of having faith in Christ and being doers of the word. They were blessed with having the oracles of God among them (3:1–2), but in spite of this advantage they sinned. But that did not discredit God (3:3–8) since all people sin (3:9–12). The Jews sin in a variety of ways (3:13–18) which are known to be sinful because of what is written in the law of Moses (3:19–20). But even one who lived according to the law of Moses would not be saved without the atonement of Christ (3:20–26). And with the coming of Christ, it was no longer necessary even to follow the ritual of the law of Moses (3:28). This did not discredit the law of Moses, but rather put it into its proper relationship with the Atonement of Christ (3:31). The teachings in this chapter of Romans were also effectively presented by Abinadi to King Noah and his priests when he said, "Salvation doth not come by the law [of Moses] alone. . . . Therefore, if ye teach the law of Moses, also teach that it is a shadow of those things which are to come—teach them that redemption cometh through Christ the Lord" (Mosiah 13:28; 16:14–15). The Savior explained to the Nephites just before his visit to them that "ye shall offer up unto me no more the shedding of blood. . . . for . . . I have laid down my life, and have taken it up again" (3 Nephi 9:19, 22). All this means that, whereas the Jews once had specific practices that were designed to lead them to Christ, with the mortal coming of the Savior, they came under the same general requirements given to all people.

To further demonstrate to the Jews the universal necessity of righteous action coupled with faith in Christ, Paul turned to the life of Abraham. Our account of this part of his letter, in chapter 4 of the epistle, indicates that Abraham was considered righteous by God before he was circumcised (4:9), which allowed him to be considered the father of the faithful, circumcised or not (4:11). Thus Abraham can be considered "the father of us all" (4:16), "if we believe on him that raised up Jesus our Lord from the dead" (4:24). This teaching that Abraham is father of all who follow Christ was succinctly expressed in the Restoration: "For as many as receive this gospel shall be called after thy name, and shall be accounted thy seed, and shall rise up and bless thee, as their father" (Abraham 2:10).

Having established the universal necessity of having faith in Christ and living righteously, Paul turned to the hope for exaltation which is an essential part of receiving exaltation.

The Hope for Exaltation

Those who have faith in Christ and live accordingly can rejoice in the hope of receiving the glory of God (5:1–2), and can also rejoice in tribulation which develops that hope (5:3–5). Moroni wrote of this same hope as "hope through the Atonement of Christ and the power of the resurrection, to be raised unto life eternal" (Moroni 7:41). Paul continued that this hope is available to sinners, which includes us all (5:6–10). It can only be realized through the Atonement of Christ, who as universally as Adam brought death into the world, voluntarily provided the means whereby all may be saved, and many shall "be made righteous" (5:11–21). Among several fine Book of Mormon teachings on this aspect of the Atonement of Christ is the statement of Lehi to his son Jacob that Christ "shall make intercession for all the children of men; and they that believe in him shall be saved" (2 Nephi 2:9). This part of the epistle is an expression of the fourth principle of orthodoxy presented earlier in this paper, i.e., no matter how hard one tries, exaltation is impossible without the Atonement of Jesus Christ.

The Way to Accept the Atonement—Baptism

The third principle of orthodoxy given above is that one must live a certain way in order to receive exaltation. Paul clearly indicated that this is the case before arriving at this point in his epistle, by saying, for example, that we are to be "doers of the law" (2:13). But this part of his letter gives greater emphasis to the necessity of living gospel principles.

In presenting baptism as a prerequisite for exaltation, as he did in chapter 6, Paul was following the teachings (John 3:5; 3 Nephi 11:33–34) and practice of the Savior (JST, Matthew 3:13–17; 2 Nephi 31:4–5; John 3:22, 26; 4:3), and his own practice when he was converted to

Christianity (Acts 9:18) and when others were converted through his preaching (Acts 16:15, 33). He compared baptism to the death and resurrection of Christ (6:1–11) but recognized that being dead to sin requires that one flee from sin, since "to whom ye yield yourselves servants to obey, his servants ye are" (6:16). As Mormon explained to Moroni, even with baptism, "the fulfilling the commandments bringeth remission of sins" (Moroni 8:25). Paul concluded that following Christ into baptism and living properly after it will lead to "eternal life through Jesus Christ our Lord" (6:4, 23). Lehi's son Jacob made the same plea to his people that Paul made to the Roman Saints: "O then, my beloved brethren, repent ye, and enter in the strait gate, and continue in the way which is narrow, until ye shall obtain eternal life" (Jacob 6:11).

Jews and Gentiles Joint Heirs with Christ

Paul implied frequently throughout the epistle that mankind can become like Jesus Christ and our Heavenly Father, the second principle of orthodoxy, but in this section of his letter (chapters 7–8) he more specifically made that point.

Writing directly to the Jews (7:1), Paul said that those who had been under the law of Moses were now free from it (7:1–6). This is not to say that the law was bad, since it had showed what things were sinful (7:7–12).[4] The law thus showed Paul how he sinned (7:7, 14–15), and he struggled with the sin encouraged by his worldly inclinations (7:14, 18, 23) until he grasped the saving power of Christ (7:22, 25). This internal struggle was also described by King Benjamin who preached that "the natural man is an enemy to God . . . unless he . . . becometh a saint through the Atonement of Christ" (Mosiah 3:19). In the same way Alma the Younger described how he "was harrowed up by the memory of my many sins" until he cried, "O Jesus, thou Son of God, have mercy on me, who am in the gall of bitterness" (Alma 36:17–18).

As recorded in chapter 8, Paul explained that those who avail themselves of the saving power of Christ by making spiritual things control their lives (8:1–13) will become "the sons of God" (8:14). He spelled out what this means: "We are the children of God: and if children, then heirs; heirs of God, and joint-heirs with Christ; if so be that we suffer with him, that we may be also glorified together" (8:16–17). This doctrine, which is at the heart of the orthodox restored gospel was obviously understood by Paul and those to whom he wrote, but for reasons which cannot be adequately addressed in this paper, is now lost to Christianity outside The Church of Jesus Christ of Latter-day Saints. Other expressions of this teaching are found throughout the standard works. For example, the Savior called upon his disciples to be perfect (Matthew 5:48; 3 Nephi 12:48) and prayed to our Heavenly Father that his disciples could be "one, even as we are one" (John 17:22). King Benjamin urged his people to take upon themselves the name of Christ so that they could be "born of him and . . . become his sons and his daughters" (Mosiah 5:7). The Lord revealed through Joseph Smith that "he that receiveth me, receiveth my Father; And he that receiveth my Father receiveth my Father's kingdom; therefore all that my Father hath shall be given unto him" (D&C 84:37–38). That is what Paul meant when he encouraged the Saints in Rome to be "joint-heirs with Christ" (8:17). To be a joint heir with Christ is the condition Latter-day Saints refer to as exaltation. Of those who receive this blessing "it is written, they are gods, even the sons of God" (D&C 76:58).

Paul recognized that tribulation will come to those who follow Christ (8:18) and that creation groans in sin (8:22), but those who follow Christ will be saved through their hope of redemption (8:24) and the intercession of the Spirit (8:26), so that those who respond to the love of God will not be separated from Christ (8:38–39). In the same vein, Joseph Smith wrote that "after much tribulation come the blessings" (D&C 58:4), and Moroni said that "ye receive no witness until after the trial of your faith" (Ether 12:6).

Living Up to Foreordination

Just as Paul and his readers understood the possibility of exaltation, they also understood the premortal existence of all people and could discuss it relative to what one must do to prepare for exaltation. Paul referred to this teaching when preaching in Athens (Acts 17:26), and he was undoubtedly aware of references to that truth in the Old Testament (Deuteronomy 32:8; Job 14:5; 38:7). He undoubtedly understood that the concept "many be called, but few chosen" (Matthew 20:16) includes the idea that one must live properly in order to realize the blessings of a calling (D&C 121:34–36). The combination of premortal existence and responding to a call are included in his discussion of election, or as we understand it, foreordination.

Foreordination was first used by Paul to encourage the Saints to endure tribulation. He said "that all things work together for good . . . to them who are the called . . . whom he did foreknow" (8:28–29). Then in chapter 9, we read Paul's encouragement for his Israelite kinsmen (1:4) to live worthy of their foreordination. He explained that merely being born an Israelite does not make one a true Israelite (9:6). Mormon made the same observation about Church members during the time Helaman was chief judge (Helaman 3:33). Paul continued that one must become a child of the promise (9:8), which requires faith in Christ (9:32). So only some of the literal children of Abraham will claim the promise (9:7–13), as prophesied by Hosea (9:25–28) and Isaiah (9:29–30). All of this is under the control of God (9:14–23).

This doctrine of foreordination was explained by Alma to the people of Ammonihah. He said that some were chosen in premortality to receive the priesthood "according to the foreknowledge of God, on account of their exceeding faith and good works" (Alma 13:3). Melchizedek, to whom Abraham gave tithes, was presented by Alma as one so foreordained (Alma 13:14–19). This explanation of faith and works as a necessary combination for progress in premortality, as well as in mortality (Alma 13:10, 12, 18), is the same explanation Paul made to the Roman Saints. It reinforces his general theme of the necessary congruence of faith and works as a prerequisite to exaltation.

Knowledge of Christ

Paul wanted his readers, especially Israel, to be saved (10:1), but he recognized the necessity of knowledge as a prerequisite (10:2). The knowledge needs to be from God, not man (10:3). In the Restoration, the Lord has revealed that "it is impossible for a man to be saved in ignorance" (D&C 131:6). And he decried him who "walketh in his own way, and after the image of his own God" (D&C 1:16). So again, Paul was talking about a principle of the gospel with which Latter-day Saints should be familiar.

Taken in the context of the chapter, which stresses the necessity of knowledge, and the epistle, which couples faith and works, there is truth in the maligned statement that "if thou shalt confess with thy mouth the Lord Jesus, and shalt believe in thine heart that God hath raised him from the dead, thou shalt be saved" (10:9) and "whosoever shall call upon the name of the Lord shall be saved" (10:13). Paul proceeded to say that calling upon the Lord requires knowledge of the gospel (10:18) and even understanding it (10:19), their fault was that they failed to obey (10:21). So Paul's point is that one must both hear the gospel and obey it, not merely vocally confess Christ.

Although Israel generally rejected God and his prophets (11:3), some still had been faithful (11:4) and some were today (11:5), Paul wrote. But those who were saved must turn to the grace of Christ, rather than to the law of Moses alone (11:6). As most of Israel rejected Christ (11:7–8), their fall led to the salvation of the Gentiles (11:11), to whom Paul especially was sent (11:13). So some of the Gentiles would be grafted into the tame olive tree of Israel (11:17), but they need to be cautious that the fate of original Israel does not also befall them (11:18–21). For if the Gentiles also reject Christ, original Israel will again be called (11:23). This is the covenant God made with them (11:24–36). A choice amplification of the analogy of an olive tree can be read in Jacob 5–6, and the story of the scattering and gathering of Israel is a major theme in all the standard works.

Advice Directly to the Roman Saints

Given the fact that some Jews had accepted Christ and the gospel had been taught to Gentiles, Paul could appeal to Saints who were of the blood of Israel as well as to the gentile Saints. He told them to accept Christ and live consistently with the expression of their faith (12:1–2). The next three chapters include instructions on living the gospel. This section of the epistle emphasizes the third principle of orthodoxy, that one must live the gospel.

Little needs to be said about Paul's advice, since it was the kind of sermon Latter-day Saints expect to hear. A summary should suffice. The Saints were told to give according to their particular gift (12:3–8) in all aspects of life (12:9–21). They should be subject to those who exercise civil power on earth (13:1–6), giving tribute to those to whom tribute is due (13:7) and keeping the commandments of God (13:8–14), especially the principle of love (13:9). Believers should not dispute over trivia (14:1–21), but rather should stress faith and that which builds faith (14:22–23). They should help one another, just as Christ helped others (15:1–7), and follow prophetic promises to minister to the Gentiles (15:8–13). Paul himself followed this latter path in bringing the gospel to the Gentiles (15:14–33).

Closing Greetings and Instructions

As would be expected in a letter, Paul closed with some personal greetings to the Saints (16:1–16, 22–24), and with some additional advice to avoid false teachings (16:17–20) and to follow Christ (16:15–27).

As a result of this discussion, it should be possible for us to see the epistle of Paul the Apostle to the Romans as a well-organized presentation of gospel principles that are fully consistent with orthodox teachings on faith, works, and exaltation as revealed throughout the standard works, and especially the Restoration of the gospel. Much more could be said about the epistle, using the approach employed in this paper and those approaches given at the beginning of the paper, but not used very extensively herein. In general, we should feel comfortable in studying and teaching the epistle. Most important, we should try to live more as the Savior lived and now lives, "according to the commandments of the everlasting God, made known to all nations for the obedience of faith" (16:26).

Notes

1. This position was personally presented to me not long ago by James R. Spencer. It is in his book *Beyond Mormonism: An Elder's Story* (Grand Rapids: Zondervan Publishing House, 1984), citing Romans 1:16–17; 3:20–22 on pages 113–14, and his personal subscription to me of Romans 10:1–4. Luther's view was expressed in his own words where he struggled to understand "the justice of God" as discussed in Romans. "Night and day I pondered until I saw the connection between the justice of God and the statement that the just shall live by faith: [1:16] Then I grasped that the justice of God is that righteousness by which through grace and sheer mercy, God justifies us through faith." Quoted in Roland H. Bainton, *The Age of Reformation* (New Jersey: D. Van Nostrand Company, 1956), 97.

2. Sidney B. Sperry, *Paul's Life and Letters* (Salt Lake City: Bookcraft, 1955), 179–200, emphasizes the historical context of this epistle and provides an outline of it, an approach I find especially useful. But Sperry's outline differs in emphasis from the one used in the paper. In the last Sperry Symposium on the New Testament, Rodney Turner stressed understanding the Judaic tradition in "Paul: Apostle of Greece," *The Eleventh Annual Sidney B. Sperry Symposium: the New Testament* (Salt Lake City: Church Educational System, 1983), 113–24. And Richard L. Anderson in the same symposium, emphasized the importance of understanding Greek in "Misleading Translations

of Paul," Ibid., 17–26. In his recent book *Understanding Paul* (Salt Lake City: Deseret Book, 1983), Anderson treats the epistles in the context of Paul's life, the history of the times, source documents in their original language, and latter-day revelation. The CES manual, *The Life and Teachings of Jesus and His Apostles*, 2nd ed., rev. (Salt Lake City: The Church of Jesus Christ of Latter-day Saints, 1979), 314–37, uses several of the methods mentioned. In dividing the epistle using "Man Is Justified by Faith," "Heirs of God, and Joint Heirs with Christ," and "Elected before the Foundations of the World" as chapter headings without a unifying outline, a student may be led to believe that the epistle is not integrated and that the doctrines presented, particularly "justification by faith," are not what are usually considered orthodox. While meritorious in clarifying specific passages, the use of any commentary on selected verses without great care to integrate the commentary in a unified organization also has these deficiencies. Such a deficiency is inherent to the format of Bruce R. McConkie's *Doctrinal New Testament Commentary* (Salt Lake City: Bookcraft, 1970), 2:211–308, which also stresses the consistency of Paul's teachings with the restored gospel, an emphasis of this paper.

3. I believe these principles are not controversial among Latter-day Saints, so only a few references are offered by way of illustration rather than for proof.

4. Here Paul returned to an idea introduced earlier in the epistle (3:20). He did so on several points, which I will not mention each time they arise, in a way that contributes to the coherence of the letter.

CHAPTER FOURTEEN

Joseph Smith and the Apocalypse of John

Rodney Turner

The Apocalypse, or book of Revelation, primarily consists of a series of visions of things yet to come. In addition to the Apostle John, these things were seen and/or spoken of by Nephi, Jesus, and Joseph Smith. As we shall see, the prophetic heart of the Apocalypse is the heavenly book sealed with seven seals given to the Lamb of God (Revelation 5). It is noteworthy that at the close of his earthly ministry, Jesus spoke of those future events described in that heavenly record. The Apocalypse is an elaboration on the Savior's own prophecies—especially as found in Matthew 24. This becomes even more apparent when the additional material provided in Doctrine and Covenants, section 45, is studied in conjunction with Matthew's account.

Were it not for Joseph Smith, the Apocalypse would remain a sealed book. A latter-day seer has confirmed and clarified things beheld by a former-day seer. Modern revelation has provided the key to critical aspects of John's veiled prophecies. Prophecy is fulfilled in time, and yet time is the one thing the Lord seems to guard above all others. Prophecy tells us what will happen, but rarely does it tell us when it will happen. But thanks to the Doctrine and Covenants, the Book of Mormon and Joseph Smith's own commentary, we now know the meaning of at least some of the mysterious symbols in the Apocalypse, and we can establish the general time frame of their fulfillment.

Authorship

Revelation is commonly dated in the time of the anti-Christian emperor Domitian (AD 81–96). While it may have been written earlier, it is doubtful if it was written later than 96. Most scholars deny that the author of the Gospel of John also wrote the book of Revelation. But there is a chiasmic structure to Revelation that, I believe, attests to its essential integrity as the composition of a single author. More important, the Church maintains that in their original forms both were composed by the Apostle John. His authorship of Revelation is implicitly supported by the Book of Mormon (1 Nephi 14:19–27; Ether 4:16–17), and the Doctrine and Covenants (20:35; 77:1–6; 128:6; 135:7).

Christ himself declared that when latter-day Israel is gathered and redeemed according to the ancient covenant, "then shall my revelations which I have caused to be written by my servant John be unfolded in the eyes of all the people" (Ether 4:15–16). I believe that the fulness of John's revelations—together with those of the brother of Jared (on the sealed plates)—will be made known after the New Jerusalem is established and before Christ's world-coming.

The Character of Revelation

Before considering the message of Revelation, it will be well to consider its overall character. First, it is similar in form and style to Jewish apocalyptical writings in general. It contains over five hundred allusions to the Old Testament. Second, while it concerns the last days and Christ's triumphant victory over Satan and his earthly minions, these things are centered in the redemption of Judah by the "Lion of the tribe of Juda, the Root of David" (5:5). Consequently, the only locale specifically identified is the "great city" Jerusalem (16:19). And whereas John describes the holy Jerusalem in elaborate detail (in twenty-four verses), he mentions the New Jerusalem of the house of Joseph in only two widely separated verses (3:12; 21:2).

Third, while Revelation touches upon conditions in John's day as well as the on going period of the "great apostasy," its major emphasis is on those unprecedented events which are to take place in that yet future time of the seventh seal. John's visions pertained almost entirely to futurity. Other than the theophany in chapter one, they begin in the presence of God and the Lamb, and they end in the presence of God and the Lamb.

Finally, the Apocalypse emphasizes the latter-day role of Jesus Christ as a God of justice. The mercy of God is swallowed up in the wrath of God. Jehovah emerges from Jesus. The God of Israel comes to the fore as the Judge, Ruler, and Lawgiver of mankind.

Outline of Revelation

John had been banished to the island of Patmos off the southwest coast of Asia (modern Turkey) "for the testimony of Jesus Christ." While there, he found himself "in the Spirit on the Lord's day" (Revelation 1:9–10).

Revelation can be divided into three major divisions. First is a prologue in which John greeted believers everywhere who would read his book and hearken to it (1:1–4). He then addressed a cover letter to the seven churches in Asia in which he bore witness of their future exaltation and recounted a glorious vision of Christ (see D&C 110:3). The Lord instructed John to write a book containing "the things which thou hast seen, and the things which are, and the things which shall be hereafter" and send it to the seven representative branches in Asia Minor (1:11, 19). Presumably, copies of the book containing all seven messages, as well as John's account of his subsequent visions, were sent to all seven churches. The letters are found in chapters 2 and 3.

The major section is 4:1–22:5 in which John described a series of visions of things in heaven and on earth—primarily set in the future, but also somewhat in the present (from John's perspective) and the premortal past. The most difficult material to interpret is found in chapters 6 through 9 and 13 through 16. These chapters deal with the global struggle between the forces of God and Satan in the time of the seventh seal. The conflict results in Satan's thousand-year banishment, followed by Christ's millennial reign, the final defeat of Satan in the "little season," the last resurrection, the passing away of the earth, and the last judgment. The Apocalypse ends with the Saints of all ages dwelling in immortal splendor in the presence of God and the Lamb on the celestialized earth.

The final section, like the first, is quite brief, consisting of an epilogue affirming the imminent fulfillment of the prophesied events, the certainty of Christ's coming in judgment, and a warning against tampering with the content of the Apocalypse (22:6–21).

The Joseph Smith Translation

While the Prophet Joseph Smith made comparatively few textual changes in his translation or revision of the Apocalypse, some of them are very significant. But as with other parts of the Bible, we do not know whether in every instance he restored the original text or simply clarified it in terms of our day. For example, whereas the King James version of Revelation 1:3 reads "For the time is at hand," the Joseph Smith Translation reads: "For the time of the coming of the Lord draweth nigh." Did John believe the Lord's coming was nigh for his generation? Having God's perspective, it is characteristic of the prophets to telescope time and view future events as imminent (see 1 Nephi 22:15–16; Alma 5:50).

As the prophetic head of this last dispensation, Joseph Smith felt fully justified in rewording earlier scriptures to give them currency. After quoting Malachi 4:5–6 he wrote: "I might have rendered a plainer translation to this, but it is sufficiently plain to suit my purpose as it stands" (D&C 128:18). The most significant textual changes in Revelation are found in 1:1, 3, 5, 7; 2:26–27; 5:16; 6:14; 12:1, 5, 7; and 13:1.

Interpreting Revelation

Revelation, with its vivid imagery—horsemen, angels, trumps, fire, brimstone smoke, beasts, strange creatures, angelic choruses, mystical numbers (3 1/2, 7, 12, 666), and unprecedented signs and cataclysms—is, like Ezekiel and Daniel, subject to a wide range of interpretations. One author has written: "The book of Revelation is one of the least read and the most misunderstood writings of the New Testament. Many Christians do not know what to make of it; a few make of it entirely too much."[1]

Yet Joseph Smith stated: "The book of Revelation is one of the plainest books God ever caused to be written."[2] Nephi would agree. He saw that initially John's writings "were plain and pure, and most precious and easy to the understanding of all men" (1 Nephi 14:23). Apparently the text has become somewhat corrupted. Still, Revelation is more relevant than ever, and will become increasingly so as time goes on.

The Doctrine and Covenants provides the key to some of the more significant and mysterious elements of Revelation. In this respect, sections 29, 45, 77, 88, and 133 are especially useful.

The Book with Seven Seals

Revelation's prophet material originates in a book sealed with seven seals in which only the Lion of Judah and Root of David was worthy to open (Revelation 5:1, 5). What is the meaning of this strange book? "We are to understand that it contains the revealed will, mysteries, and works of God; the hidden things of his economy concerning this earth during the seven thousand years of its continuance, or its temporal existence" (D&C 77:6). Note that the book is centered in God's will and works, not those of mankind.

What are the seven seals? "We are to understand that the first seal contains the things of the first thousand years, and the second also of the second thousand years, and so on until the seventh" (D&C 77:7). In other words, from the fall of Adam—when Earth began its temporal or mortal existence—to the present time, is approximately six thousand years. Joseph Smith accepted this figure quite literally. In an editorial in the *Times and Seasons* entitled "The Government of God" he wrote, "The world has had a fair trial for six thousand years; the Lord will try the seventh thousand Himself."[3]

End of Time of Sixth Seal

We are nearing the end of the sixth millennium since the fall, or the end of the period of the sixth seal. The seventh millennium will see the grand denouement of all prophecy. We are called Latter-day Saints. We live in the "day" before the second coming (D&C 64:24)—the closing moments of the sixth thousand-year day: the "Saturday night" of time. The twenty-first century begins in the year 2001. Will the seventh "day" begin in approximately fourteen years? If biblical chronology is essentially correct, the answer is yes—give or take ten minutes!

On the other hand, if it is seriously flawed, the seventh millennium may not begin for a good many years—perhaps not for generations. But this is most unlikely. Scripture, modern prophecy, and the course of events point to the relative nearness of the Lord's return. Still, the likelihood that the cataclysmic events seen by John will occur in the next twenty years or so is, to say the least, remote. Too many prophecies remain unfulfilled, too much remains to be done by the Church in fulfilling its mission of preparing the way for the Lord's coming.

More important, in my judgment, Revelation 6:12–17 cannot be fulfilled in the time of the sixth seal; it describes *seventh*-seal events. These global and cosmic happenings are directly associated with the world coming of Christ. And that will take place in the time of the seventh, *not* the sixth, seal. The Prophet Joseph Smith explained that the sounding of the trumpets in chapter 8 of Revelation symbolizes "the preparing and finishing of his work, in the *beginning* of the seventh thousand years—the preparing of the way *before* the time of his coming" (D&C 77:12; italics added). This means that final preparations for the Savior's return will be going on *after* the period of the seventh seal has begun. In all likelihood, Christ will not come for some decades after the year 2001.

Opening the Book

The scene described in chapter 5 pertains to the future. The book John saw has not yet been opened; its seals have not yet been broken. Only Christ, the Lamb of God, has the power to do that; he alone is worthy to redeem and judge. And his judgment is not yet. The opening or loosening of the seals and the reading of the book's first six "chapters" signifies a divine review of the works of God and men during the first six thousand years of Earth's temporal existence. This review *follows* the world coming of Christ as part of the great judgment scene.

In the Doctrine and Covenants we learn that Christ's millennial reign begins with Revelation's seven angels of judgment again successively sounding their trumps. As each does so, he reveals "the secret acts of men, and the thoughts and intents of their hearts, and the mighty works of God" in the thousand-year period over which he presides (D&C 88:108–110; see also 2 Nephi 30:17). Since the seventh thousand years will not then be over, this summary review of the past ends with the sixth angel. The archangel Michael, Adam, the Ancient of Day, is the seventh angel (D&C 88:112). The number seven is thought to signify completeness or perfection. It is therefore appropriate that Adam should be the seventh angel since he holds the keys of dispensations. A great council will be held at Adam-ondi-Ahman preparatory to the coming of the Son of Man and his millennial reign. The Ancient of Days will then surrender his priesthood stewardship—"the keys of the universe"—to Christ, while retaining his position as head of the human family.[4]

It is Michael, the seventh angel, who declares the end of the telestial age, of time as we know it—the end of Satan's time of lawless rule.

"There shall be time no longer" (D&C 88:110; Revelation 10:6). Time will become terrestrial; the glorious rule of Earth's rightful king and lawgiver will have begun.

Chronological Interpretation of the Seals

Since the seven seals symbolize the seven thousand-year "days" of earth's "week" of mortal existence, it is widely assumed by LDS scriptorians that the seals represent specific persons and/or conditions seen by John pertaining to each seal. Consequently, the four horsemen are identified with the first four thousand years (Revelation 6:1–8).

The fifth seal covered the first thousand years of the Christian era as represented by the apostolic church with its company of martyr-saints. They are seen in the spirit world ("under the altar," 6:9), from whence they cry out for vengeance on their earthly tormentors. But they are given white robes and told to "rest yet for a little season" (6:9–11). The judgment is not yet.

When the sixth seal (the period from AD 1000 to 2000) was opened, John saw a "great earthquake," the sun became "black as sackcloth," the moon "as blood," stars fell to the earth, heaven was opened like a scroll, mountains and islands were uprooted, and wicked men hid in terror from the "great day of Christ's wrath" (6:12–17).

Prior to that "great day," John (the fifth of the seven angels of judgment, D&C 77:9, 14) and the four angels under his direction are to seal up a previously selected body of 144,000 high priests from the twelve tribes of Israel (Revelation 7:1–8; D&C 77:11). All of the foregoing will occur—if the assumption that each seal relates only to a given thousand-year period is correct—*before* the opening of the seventh seal.

Seals Summarize All Ages

Just as the overall message of the seven letters to the seven churches in Asia is, as Elder McConkie wrote: "For all saints and all congregations everywhere in all ages,"[5] so, I believe, are the first five seals—*as John employs them*—representative in the aggregate of those moral and spiritual conditions which reach their culmination in the seventh millennium. Prophecy can have multiple applications as, for example, Joel 2:28–31 in Acts 2:16–21 and Joseph Smith-History 1:41. Nor is there any reason why symbols cannot apply to different things at different times. The horseman may well represent conditions and events—general and specific—in both former and latter days.

We are in the early phase of the dispensation of the fulness of times. All former dispensations from Adam's day to the present are being gathered and welded together into one perfect whole (D&C 128:18). This is a time of historical recapitulation in which former things pertaining to God and Satan will be reenacted in a decisive fashion. All seven seals are represented in this summary dispensation of all dispensations. Natural calamities, social disorganization, war, famine, pestilence—all these old plagues and more—will parallel the Lord's strange and marvelous work in the decades to come. "As it was in the days of Noah, so shall it be also in the days of the Son of Man" (Luke 17:26).

The Prophet Joseph Smith has provided us with a critical key to understanding the prophetic message of Revelation:

> The things which John saw had *no allusion* to the scenes of the days of Adam, Enoch, Abraham or Jesus, only so far as is *plainly* represented by John, and *clearly* set forth by him. John saw that *only* which was lying in *futurity* and which was shortly to come to pass. See Rev. 1:1–3, which is a key to the whole subject: "The revelation of Jesus Christ [John in the Joseph Smith Translation], which God gave unto Him, to show unto his servants things which must shortly come to pass," . . . also Rev. 4:1. ". . . I will show thee [John] things which must be hereafter."[6]

There is nothing "plainly" or "clearly" written in the Apocalypse to explicitly identify the four horsemen of the first four seals. Consequently all manner of notions of varying merit have been advanced within and without the Church about them. The discredited "White Horse Prophecy" identified the white horse with the Latter-day Saints, the red horse with Great Britain, the black horse with politically enslaved peoples, and the pale horse with the peoples of the United States. These horsemen have also been equated with early Christian history, Christianity's victory over paganism, the Papacy, etc. But only the rider of the pale horse is actually identified by John: he is "death, and Hell followed with him" (Revelation 6:8).

To repeat, prophetically speaking, Revelation is primarily concerned with the time of the seventh seal and the ages beyond it. In his panoramic vision (1 Nephi 11–14), Nephi beheld all that John would see more than five hundred years later (1 Nephi 14:24). However, Nephi was forbidden to record that portion concerning the end of the world and all that was to transpire thereafter. In other words, Nephi did not record things to come in the time of the seventh seal; John was to do that (1 Nephi 14:25). Nephi ended his account in a still future day when war will be worldwide, and the Saints and the scattered covenant peoples of the Lord will be armed with divine power (1 Nephi 14:16–17; see D&C 45:69–70). Remarkably, John's account of things to come begins at virtually the precise point where Nephi's account ends. It is following the redemption of Zion and the manifestation of God's power that the events leading up to and including the Second Coming take place, as summarized under the sixth seal. Nephi and John dovetail perfectly.

Beginning with chapter 4, everything John saw pertained from his viewpoint, to the future. The only exception was that portion of chapter 12 dealing with the origin of Satan and the war in heaven (12:7–9). Chapter 13 (which treats the images of the two beasts) is thematically connected to chapter 12 and to Daniel chapter 7. While it primarily concerns the persecution of God's people in the last days, chapter 13 can also be related to Rome's persecution of the early Christian church.

Interpretation of the Seals

Now let us return to John's vision of the four horsemen. The white horse is a positive, not a negative, symbol. White is consistently used in the Apocalypse, as well as in all scripture, as emblematic of righteousness. John would hardly use a white horse as a negative symbol under the first seal and then have Christ ride a white horse under the seventh seal! The horseman of Revelation 6:2 and 19:11, 19, and 21 is, I believe, one and the same: Jesus Christ.

As the first of the four horsemen, he is endowed with power (the bow). "A crown was *given* unto him: and he went forth conquering, and to conquer" (Rev. 6:2; italics added). His enemies ride the other three horses. Does he conquer them? Yes! In chapter 19, John

> saw heaven opened, and behold a white horse; and he that sat upon him was called Faithful and True, and in righteousness he doth judge and *make war*.
>
> His eyes were as a flame of fire, and on his head were many crowns; . . . And the armies which were in heaven followed him upon white horses, clothed in fine linen, white and clean. . . .
>
> [He is] KING OF KINGS, AND LORD OF LORDS. (Revelation 19:11–16; italics added)

So the first horseman is the last horseman. He will have brought, as Paul wrote, "many sons unto glory" (Hebrews 2:10).

But for six thousand years, Christ's arch-enemy Satan, the likely rider of the red horse, will exercise the agency given him to take peace from the earth and bathe mankind in one bloodbath after another. War's cruel children, famine and pestilence, are represented by the rider of the black horse. Thus with blood and horror Satan continues his primeval rebellion against the Son of God. In doing so, he calls forth the rider of the pale horse: Death, closely followed by Hell. This has been the way of things since Cain killed Abel. The penultimate struggle between good and evil, between Christ and Satan lies before us.

A modern revelation declares:

> With the sword and by bloodshed the inhabitants of the earth shall mourn; and with famine, and plague, and earthquake . . . feel the wrath, and indignation, and chastening hand of an Almighty God, until the consumption decreed hath made a full end of all nations; That the cry of the saints, and of the blood of the saints, shall cease to come up into the ears of the Lord of Sabaoth, from the earth, to be avenged of their enemies. (D&C 87:7)

In contrast to the wicked who suffer Death and Hell, John then saw (under the fifth seal) the righteous in paradise clothed in white robes awaiting their glorious resurrection. They were crying out for vengeance upon their persecutors, but were admonished to be patient; there would yet be martyrs. The Lord would avenge them all at his coming (see D&C 133:50–51).

Note that John combined the then yet-to-be martyrs of the sixth and seventh seals with those faithful martyrs of the apostolic church in the meridian of time who were "slain for the word of God, and for the testimony which they held" (Revelation 6:9–11). Martyrdom started with Abel, climaxed with Jesus, continued with the apostles and ebbed and flowed throughout all sacred history (see Hebrews 11). It is not over. Elder McConkie wrote: "Martyrdom is not a thing of the past only, but of the present and of the future, for Satan has not yet been bound, and the servants of the Lord will not be silenced in this final age of warning and judgment."[7]

Every generation hears the thundering passage of the four horsemen of the Apocalypse. Every generation hears the cries of outraged innocence. Consequently, the horsemen of the first four seals, together with the martyr-saints of the fifth seal, represent—as the Prophet said—those things "lying in futurity and which were shortly to come to pass."[8] There has been an opposition in all things from the beginning. God's work has in some measure gone on side by side with Satan's reign of terror since time began. Only certain events described by John in connection with the sixth and seventh seals are without precedent. And they will happen but once.

Chapter Summaries

Chapter 4 reveals "things which must be hereafter." The scene is heaven. God sits upon his throne surrounded by twenty-four resurrected men (elders) who represent the faithful saints in the seven churches, and of all ages.[9] Resurrected animals—apparently of a celestial order—as represented by four living creatures—are also present.[10] Before the throne is a "sea of glass," symbolic of this earth in its then yet-to-be "sanctified, immortal, and eternal state" (D&C 77:1; see also 130:7–9).

Chapter 5 is a continuation of the foregoing scene. Christ, the Lamb, is about to open the book sealed with seven seals and judge the righteous who have lived in the previous six thousand years. Resurrected saints, angels, elder, and creatures unite in an anthem of praise to him.

As was earlier pointed out, the judgment scene of chapter 6 is fulfilled *after* the glorious coming of the Son of Man and during the formative period of his millennial kingdom (D&C 88:106–110). The scene closes with Michael declaring "there shall be time no longer." Satan's time is up (Revelation 11:12). His kingdom which dominated the governments, laws, and institutions of men is no more. The way is clear for Earth's rightful king and lawgiver to claim his kingdom (D&C 45:58–59). The Lord's prayer will, at last, be answered (Matthew 6:10).

Chapter 7 describes the sealing up of 144,000 high priests—twelve thousand representing each of the twelve tribes of Israel—by John and his four companions (D&C 77:9, 11, 14). These "servants of God," said the Prophet, "are sealed in their foreheads, which signifies sealing the blessings upon their heads, meaning the everlasting covenant, thereby making their calling and election sure."[11] They enjoy a fulness of the Melchizedek Priesthood and will stand upon Mount Zion with Christ when he returns (D&C 133:18).

But prior to that day they will go forth and "bring as many

as will come to the church of the Firstborn" (D&C 77:11). That is, they will extend to others the sealing which they themselves have received. Since the things spoken of in chapter 7 "are to be accomplished in the sixth thousand years, or the opening of the sixth seal" (D&C 77:10), their labors will probably be completed during the half hour of silence preceding the final judgments in the seventh millennium.

Chapter 7, like chapter 5, ends in a future resurrection scene in which those sealed up to the church of the Firstborn (the immortal congregation of the exalted sons and daughters of God) by the 144,000—together with all others of like glory—rejoice in the presence of God and the Lamb. (This scene is reprised in 21:1–7.)

The Seventh Seal

The opening of the seventh seal in chapter 8 is accompanied by "silence in heaven about the space of half an hour" (see D&C 88:95). This half-hour is almost surely the Lord's time, or about twenty-one earth years. It will be broken by the sounding of the trumpets of the seven angels of judgment. In the Doctrine and Covenants we read:

> For all flesh is corrupted before me; and the powers of darkness prevail upon the earth, among the children of men, in the presence of all the hosts of heaven— Which causeth silence to reign, and all eternity is pained, and the angels are waiting the great command to reap down the earth, to gather the tares that they may be burned; and, behold, the enemy is combined.

(D&C 38:11–12; see also 86:7)

The final labors of the Church and the 144,000 will be completed in this period of comparative heavenly calm before the "arm of the Lord" falls upon the nations (D&C 45:47).

Chapters 8 and 9 foretell in vivid imagery the culminating wars and natural disasters preceding the "great day of the Lord." These judgments—largely of man's own making—result in the destruction of a third part of all living things. Even "a third part" of the sun, moon, and stars will be darkened. There are three basic degrees of glory. The recurrent use of the phrase "a third part" may symbolize the ongoing destruction of those of the telestial order comprising the church and kingdom of the devil who constitute Babylon. The "end of the world" is the destruction of the wicked before and at the Lord's coming (Joseph Smith—Matthew 1:4,55).

In chapter 10, Michael—the seventh angel (compare 10:6 with D&C 88:110, 112)—gives John a latter-day mission to gather Israel. This mission is symbolized by the "little book"—a "chapter" in the larger, sealed book held by the Lamb. John is one of the Eliases who, in the aggregate, will restore all things. He holds "the seal of the living God over the twelve tribes of Israel"—meaning, the authority to gather and seal them up before the final judgments begin (D&C 77:9, 11, 14; see also 7:3). Joseph Smith informed the brethren attending the Fourth General Conference of the church in 1831 that John was even then ministering to the ten tribes and preparing them for their return from their long dispersion.[12] John's mission will be completed in the time of the seventh seal when Judah is finally redeemed.

Judah will be the last of the twelve tribes to be gathered into the sheepfold of the Good Shepherd (Luke 13:26–30; Ether 13:12; D&C 133:35). Its redemption is described in broad outline in chapter 11. Appropriately, it is John whom Michael instructs to "measure" (safeguard?) the temple and its altar, and count those who worship therein (see 21:15–17; Ezekiel 40). It is the time of the latter-day siege of Jerusalem. The siege will continue for forty-two months during which time two witnesses (prophets) will exercise Enoch-like priesthood power and preserve the city from being overthrown (D&C 77:15; 2 Nephi 8:19–20; see also JST, Genesis 14:30–31). Jerusalem then will fall, the prophets will be killed, and their bodies will lie in the streets as the city is overrun and the temple desecrated. This marks the second abomination of desolation (the destruction which follows sacrilege) to take place in Jerusalem since Jesus' day (Daniel 12:12; Joseph Smith—Matthew 1:12, 32).

After three and a half days the two prophets are to be resurrected. It is then that the Lord will appear upon the Mount of Olives. An earthquake will cause the mount to cleave in two, forming a large valley into which the surviving Jews will flee for safety (Revelation 11:13; D&C 45:48; Zechariah 14:4–5).

The Lord will manifest himself to this remnant of Judah and show them the marks of his crucifixion. This will convince those survivors that Jesus was, and is indeed, their Messiah (Zechariah 12:10–14; 13:6; D&C 45:51–53).

Heavenly Origin of the Earthly Conflict

John then described the origin of the conflict between Christ and Satan. More emendations were made by Joseph Smith in chapter 12 of Revelation than in any other. These corrections are extremely significant. Without them it would be very difficult to arrive at a correct understanding of the text. The very first verse provides the key: heavenly (first estate) things were the pattern for earthly (second estate) things. The church and kingdom of God existed in heaven (the spirit state) before being established on earth. Eternal things exist spiritually before they exist temporally (D&C 29:32).

The setting of the first eleven verses is man's premortal estate; that of the remaining six verses is this mortal world. Out of the heavenly church (the woman clothed with the sun) came the kingdom of our God and his Christ (her child). This kingdom was foreordained to rule the future nations of the earth with the word of God (the rod of iron). In other words, God's will was to "be done in earth, as it is done in heaven" (Matthew 6:10).

John saw that "a great red dragon" (the devil) and "a third part of the stars" (spirits) rebelled against the kingdom's laws, and "there was war in heaven." This war was fought in the hearts and minds of the Father's spirit children. Lucifer, the first and greatest of all apostates, leveled a barrage of accusations against the Saints. He accused "our brethren . . . before our God day and night" (Revelation 12:10). But to no avail; their testimonies of Christ and his atoning sacrifice enabled them to face death itself. Lucifer could not overthrow Michael, nor the church and kingdom of God.

Instead, he was cast down to this earth where he continues his rebellion by laying siege against God's earthly church and kingdom even as he once besieged the heavenly church (D&C 76:25–29).

Hence the warning: "Woe to the inhabiters of the earth . . . for the devil is come down unto you, having great wrath, because he knoweth that he has but a short time" (Revelation 12:12). A short time indeed! He has less than one celestial week, seven thousand years, to do in this second estate what he could not do in man's first estate: vanquish the woman and her child, overthrow the church and kingdom of God. Failing to do so, his doom will be the bottomless pit of eternal torment.

John saw the devil rage against the Saints in the meridian of time. Because of Satan-inspired persecution *following* the death of the

Apostles, the church (the woman) fled into the spiritual wilderness of the great apostasy for over sixteen hundred years (see D&C 86:3). But it was ordained that the church should come out of that wilderness in the dispensation of the fulness of times. It has begun to do so, but the journey is not over. In dedicating the Kirtland Temple in 1836, the Prophet Joseph Smith prayed

> that the kingdom, which thou hast set up without hands, may become a great mountain and fill the whole earth;
> That thy church may come forth out of the wilderness of darkness, and shine forth fair as the moon, clear as the sun, and terrible as an army with banners;
> And be adorned as a bride for that day when thou shalt unveil the heavens, and cause the mountains to flow down at thy presence. (D&C 109:72–4; see also 5:14; 105:31)

The Church, as such, hears the voice of the Lord, but it is yet to enter into his literal presence. And until it does, it is not wholly out of the wilderness. For the Lord has said: "Behold, that which you hear is as the voice of one crying in the wilderness—in the wilderness, *because you cannot* see *him*" (D&C 88:66; italics added; see also D&C 67:10–13). Only when Zion and the New Jerusalem arise out of the waste places of Missouri, will the church fully emerge from the spiritual wilderness it entered centuries ago (see D&C 113:7–8).

The Devil's Beasts

Chapter 13—with its beast having seven heads, ten horns, and ten crowns, together with a second, two-horned beast whose numerical identity is the enigmatic 666—has been subject to endless speculation. Joseph Smith said: "Never meddle with the visions of beast and subjects you do not understand."[13] That is wise counsel.

The transcript of the Prophet's explanation of chapter 13 is unclear. On the one hand, he is quoted as saying that the beast of verse 1 is only an image. On the other hand, he says:

> The beast John saw was an actual beast, and an actual intelligent being [meaning, the devil] gives him his power, and his seat, and great authority. It was not to represent a beast in heaven: it was an angel in heaven who has power in the last days to do a work. . . . when God allows the old devil to give power to the beast to destroy

the inhabitants of the earth, all will wonder . . . The beasts which John saw [15:7 ?] and speaks of being in heaven, were actually living in heaven, and were actually to have power given to them over the inhabitants of the earth. . . . The independent beast is a beast that dwells in heaven, abstract from the human family.[14]

It seems that the Prophet was speaking of an image at one point (chapter 13) and of a living beast (or beasts) at another (chapters 4–7, 14, 15, 19).

The beast of chapters 13 and 17—with its seven heads and ten horns—is usually identified with Domitian and the Julian emperors of Rome, the city of seven hills. This interpretation may be correct as far as it goes. Certain prophecies and symbols do have multiple applications. Idumea (Edom), Babylon, and, possibly, Rome symbolize the world in all ages. Some government or alliance will play the role of the beast with ten horns in the days of the seventh seal. For we know that a remnant of Judah—and probably others of Israel—will yet be persecuted and temporarily overcome by evil powers (Revelation 13:7; 17:14; Daniel 7:21–26; 1 Nephi 14:13).

John saw the image of a beast rise from the sea with seven heads and ten horns with ten crowns (see also Daniel 7:7, 19–24). This image, as Elder McConkie suggested, probably represents those latter-day nations under Satan's influence.[15] This image may well correspond to the feet and ten toes of Nebuchadnezzar's image (see Daniel 2:33, 42–43).

Portent of Last Plagues

Chapter 14 sets the stage for the actual outpouring of God's wrath beginning at Jerusalem. By that time, I believe, the New Jerusalem will stand in the land of Missouri, the essential gathering of eleven of the tribes of Israel will have been accomplished, and all will be in readiness for the risen Messiah to stand upon the Mount of Olives and deliver Judah. The moment for "the battle of that great day of God Almighty" will have come (16:14).

John saw the Messiah and the 144,000 stand upon Mount Zion in America (see D&C 133:18). He heard a new song being sung by the resurrected celestial host (see Revelation 15:3–4). But only the 144,000—representative of all redeemed Saints—are prepared to sing that song of redemption and everlasting glory.

An angel—one who previously had been instrumental in the

restoration of the gospel and the priesthood—cries out: "Fear God, and give glory to him; for the hour of his judgment is come" (Revelation 14:7). A second angel then announces the imminent fall of Babylon. He is followed by yet a third angel who declares that the wrath of God (everlasting torment) awaits those who worship the beast and have his mark. In contrast, the Saints who were willing to endure death itself are assured that they will rest from their labors and that their righteous works will follow them.

In chapter 15, the time has arrived for the seven angels to be sent forth with their divine judgments. These final plagues "filled up the wrath of God"—the demands of justice. The angels leave the heavenly temple bearing the "vials full of the wrath of God" given them by one of the four beasts. How literally will this be? Will man's depredations against the animal kingdom entitle it to a part in the last plagues?

John looked into futurity and saw the faithful Saints of the celestial earth (the sea of glass) singing the song of Moses and the Lamb—a hymn of praise and adoration of the "King of saints." This may be the "new song" referred to in 14:3.

The Seven Plagues Are Poured Out

Note that the plagues of the seven angels are inflicted upon the world but *once*. Chapters 8, 9, and 15 only presage those judgments actually poured out in chapter 16.

These judgments follow the half hour of silence in the time of the seventh seal. Each angel pours out his vial in sequence. The specific nature of these woes cannot be ascertained with certainty; they are described somewhat differently in different scriptures. (See D&C 29:14–20; 43:21–25; 45:31–33, 41–42; 88:87–91.) Yet they do form a pattern.

In the "times of the Gentiles"—the present period when the Church is proclaiming the gospel to the nations—there will be worldwide war and other forms of social disorganization, along with natural disasters. Thereafter, God will bear his own testimony to the nations when he pours out his wrath upon them "without measure" (D&C 43:20–29; 88:88; 101:11). He will speak through nature: earthquakes, eruptions, tidal waves, solar heat, drought, famine, pestilence, pollutions, and all their misery-breeding companions. These calamities are symbolized by the plagues or woes of the seven angels in the time of the seventh seal.

The fourth angel will magnify the sun's rays, causing mankind to be "scorched with great heat" (see Isaiah 30:26). The Lord told the Prophet Joseph that there would come a time in which no rainbows would be seen: "Whenever you see the bow withdraw, it shall be a token that there shall be famine, pestilence, and great distress among the nations, and that the coming of the Messiah is not far distant."[16] The plagues of the first six angels suggest such conditions.

End of the Kingdom of the Devil

In the days of the sixth angel, extremely impressive satanic miracles will be performed (see Revelation 13:14;19:20). These miracles will encourage the armies of the nations to assemble northward in Israel near the "hill of Megiddo"—Armageddon—from whence they will lay siege to Jerusalem (see Revelation 11:2, 7, 10; 19:19; Zechariah 12:2–9; 14:1–3; Ezekiel 38:16–19; 39:1–2). Ezekiel calls the leader of this force "Gog" and his army "Magog" (Ezekiel 38:14–22; 39:6–12). They constitute the Lord's foe in "the battle of the great day of God Almighty" (Revelation 16:14, 16).

The armies of Gog will be subjected to hailstones weighing a hundred pounds! (see Revelation 16:21; Ezekiel 38:22). This may be the storm that is to destroy the crops of the earth (D&C 29:16; 109:30). And so with seismic upheavals, hail, and searing fire the Messiah will "destroy all the nations that come against Jerusalem" (Zechariah 12:3, 6–9; 14:3; Ezekiel 38:22; 39:2–6; Revelation 19:19). It will be Sodom and Gomorrah on a global scale.

Zechariah prophesied: "Their flesh shall consume away while they stand upon their feet, and their eyes shall consume away in their holes, and their tongue shall consume away in their mouth" (Zechariah 14:12). This horrid scene is confirmed in a modern revelation:

> Wherefore, I the Lord God will send forth flies upon the face of the earth, which shall take hold of the inhabitants thereof, and shall eat their flesh, and shall cause maggots to come in upon them;
>
> And their tongues shall be stayed that they shall not utter against me; and their flesh shall fall from off their bones, and their eyes from their sockets;
>
> And it shall come to pass that the beasts of the forest and fowls of the air shall devour them up. (D&C 29:18–20; see also Ezekiel 39:17–20; Revelation 19:17–21)

Such will be the scene when the high and mighty of the earth cower in the dens and rocks of the mountains saying to them "Fall on us, and hide us from the face of him that sitteth on the throne, and from the wrath of the Lamb: For the great day of his wrath is come; and who shall be able to stand?" (Revelation 6:16–17).

But there is more. "There was a great earthquake, such as was not since men were upon the earth. . . . And the great city [Jerusalem] was divided into three parts, and the cities of the nations fell" (Revelation 16:18–19). So far-ranging and violent will be this global upheaval that the entire planet will be thrown off balance: "The earth shall tremble and reel to and fro as a drunken man; and the sun shall hide his face, and shall refuse to give light; and the moon shall be bathed in blood; and the stars shall become exceedingly angry, and shall cast themselves down as a fig that falleth from off a fig-tree" (D&C 88:87; see also 29:14; 34:9; 45:48–50; Matthew 24:29). The island continents will be reunited and the great mountain ranges will be brought low (see Revelation 16:18–20; Ezekiel 38:19–20; D&C 88:87; 133:21–24).

The great cities of the earth will be reduced to rubble. All political systems will collapse. "The consumption decreed hath made a full end of all nations" (D&C 87:6). "And the seventh angel sounded; and there were great voices in heaven, saying, The kingdoms of this world are become the kingdom of our Lord, and his Christ; and he shall reign forever and ever" (Joseph Smith Translation Revelation 11:15). The rule of men and devils is over.

Still, the Lord's coming in glory is not yet. Ezekiel tells us that the house of Israel will be burying the corpses of the invading Gentiles for seven months and burning their weapons and materiel for seven years (see Ezekiel 39:9–16). Whether Ezekiel employs the number seven literally or figuratively, the point is that there will be an interlude of unrevealed duration between the Lord's appearance to the Jews and his coming in fiery glory to all the world. For when he comes in glory, every corruptible thing of men, animals, fish, and element will be utterly consumed (see D&C 101:23–25; 33:41–44; 2 Peter 3:10–12). All pollutions of whatever kind will be effaced from the earth.

The Great Whore

The enemy of God and the persecutor of Zion is described in chapter 17 as "the great whore . . . With whom the kings of the earth have committed fornication, and the inhabitants of the earth have been made drunk with the wine of her fornication" (Revelation 17:1–2). She symbolizes the very nature and spirit of Satan—the god of this world— who prostitutes the ways of the Lord, twisting and perverting every divine principle even as a whore makes mockery of the most sacred of heavenly relationships (1 Nephi 22:14). She is the world, Babylon, the tares of the earth, the great and abominable church drunk "with the blood of the saints, and with the martyrs of Jesus" (Revelation 17:6; see 2 Nephi 10:16). She dominates the thoughts, actions, and values of those natural men and women who are God's enemies and who are found "among all nations, kindreds, tongues, and people" (1 Nephi 14:11; see also 2 Nephi 10:16; Mosiah 3:19).

Chapter 18 begins with a shout of triumph and ends in a dirge of despair. The great whore is dead. Justice has answered the cry of the martyred Saints at last (see Revelation 6:10–11; 18:6, 20; 19:2). Israel has been gathered; the New Jerusalem is a reality; the prophesied council at Adam-ondi-Ahman has been held;[17] the great and abominable church has been swept into oblivion; Jerusalem has been delivered, and Judah has been redeemed. All that remains is for the Son of Man to come in his glory and cleanse the earth with sanctifying fire. For whatever reason, this ultimate event was not described by John (see Revelation 18:8).

The Millennial Era

Chapter 19 describes the Savior's coming as the victorious Rider of the white horse of chapter 6. Following the marriage of the Lamb to his then sanctified bride, the Church, John beholds the Lamb's victory parade in which the Word of God, the KING OF KINGS, AND LORD OF LORDS, leads the armies of heaven into his millennial kingdom.

In contrast to this joyous scene, the chapter ends with a flashback to Armageddon, where an angel invites the fowls of the air to feast upon the flesh of the vanquished. The beast and his miracle-working false prophet are cast into that lake of fire and brimstone which is the second death (see 2 Nephi 9:16; Jacob 3:11). However, their Babylonish followers will only taste of that death (Revelation 21:8; D&C 63:17). While their fate is not given by John, modern revelation states that the wicked who repent will, after suffering the wrath of God, be resurrected and inherit the telestial kingdom (D&C 76:81–85, 106).

Chapter 20 succinctly outlines affairs following the coming of the Son of Man in his glory. An angel places a seal on Satan to "shut him up" for the duration of Christ's millennial reign—a thousand years (see Revelation 20:1–3; D&C 8:110).[18] The resurrected Saints are judged and crowned by the original Quorum of the Twelve (D&C 29:12–13; 88:107), receive their inheritance, and reign with Christ *over* the millennial earth (Revelation 20:4; D&C 88:107).[19]

Conditions on the renewed, paradisiacal earth will provide a foretaste of the celestial order. Peace and justice will prevail. And death—in terms of a period of separation of the spirit from the body—will be unknown, at least among the Saints.[20] Instead, they will pass from mortality to immortality "in the twinkling of an eye" (D&C 101:29–31; 63:51). The resurrection of the unjust—the telestial order and sons of Perdition—takes place after the "little season" at the end of the earth (see Revelation 20:5–6; D&C 88:100–102; 38:5–6).

The Little Season

Satan's "little season" follows Christ's thousand-year reign. Released from prison, the devil will again marshal the nations—Gog and Magog—against "the beloved city" of the Saints. The final "battle of the great God"—a second "Armageddon"—will be fought. Michael will again come to the defense of the righteous, and their enemies will again be devoured by heavenly fire (see Revelation 20:7–9; D&C 88:111–116). The last battle of the war which began in heaven will have been fought. Thereafter, Satan will join "the beast and the false prophet" in that eternal perdition called the second death.

The Last Judgment

The literal disorganization of this planet—its death—follows the aforementioned resurrection of the unjust (see Revelation 20:11; D&C 29:22–23; 88:101).

The resurrected family of Man—together with Satan and his host—will stand before God in that great and last judgment (see 2 Nephi 9:15; 28:23). However, since the resurrection of both the just and the unjust will have been completed, the last judgment is not altogether judicial in nature. The final destiny of every soul will have already been determined.

All will have been judged by two witnesses: the record of their works on earth, and its companion record in heaven, the book of life (see

D&C 128:7). In its ultimate sense, the book of life contains the names of those who are saved in any degree of glory.[21] For them, there will be no more death; physical and spiritual death will have been absorbed by the second death (see Revelation 20:14; 21:4).

On the other hand, the "*Lamb's* book of life" (Revelation 21:27; italics added) is "the book of the names of the sanctified, even them of the celestial world" (D&C 88:2; Revelation 3:5). They alone obtain exaltation in the presence of the Godhead.

The second death will be the awful fate of Satan, his angels, and all sons of perdition. Their names were long since expunged from the book of life. For, as the prophet Joseph Smith said: "If His children will not repent of their sins He will discard them."[22]

The last judgment is, therefore, something of a reenactment of the council of the human family held in the first estate.[23] The Father and the Son will stand vindicated in all that they did in bringing to pass the immortality and eternal life of man. Even the unrepentant—the "filthy still"—will acknowledge to their everlasting shame that all God's judgments are just (see Mosiah 27:31; Alma 12:15).

A New Heaven and a New Earth

The Apocalypse reaches its climax in chapters 21 and 22. John looked into eternity and saw "a new heaven and a new earth; for the *first* heaven and the *first* earth were *passed away*; and there was no more sea" (Revelation 21:1; see also 20:11; italics added).[24] That new heaven and earth is the everlasting inheritance of the meek.

While the millennial earth will enjoy the presence of the son of God,[25] when the earth "hath filled the measure of its [first] creation, it shall be crowned with glory, even with the presence of God the Father" (D&C 88:19; see also Revelation 21:22; 22:1, 3). In his presence there is "no more death, neither sorrow . . . for the former things are passed away" (Revelation 21:4).

John saw two glorious cities—"brides" of the Lamb—descend to the celestial earth: first the New Jerusalem, and then the "holy Jerusalem" (Revelation 21:2, 9–10; Ether 13:9–11).[26] As in other matters, the first has become the last, and the last first. These cities, like their righteous millennial inhabitants, are immortal.

The centrality of Judah in the Apocalypse is again evident in the fact that only "the holy Jerusalem" is symbolically portrayed. However, each "bride" is glorious; to describe one is to describe the other. John's angelic guide was probably Michael who had previously measured the temple, but not the city (Revelation 11:1–2). But on this occasion he measures the holy city, but not the temple—for it has none (Revelation 21:16–17). The city and, indeed, the whole celestial world is one great temple. This city of God is in startling contrast to fallen Babylon.

The holy Jerusalem (its measurements are multiples of 12) is a perfect cube of fifteen hundred miles in each direction—a microcosm of the entire celestial order of things. It has twelve gates of pearl—each named for one of the twelve tribes—which are guarded by twelve angels. Its walls are about two hundred feet wide and two hundred feet high—144 cubits. It has twelve foundations, each overlaid with a different precious stone, and each named for one of the Twelve Apostles. The city and its streets are of gold "like unto pure glass" (Revelation 21:18, 21).[27] It is representative of that "sea of glass" seen earlier by John—the immortal earth whereon will dwell the celestial house of Israel and the church of the Firstborn (Revelation 4:6; 15:2; D&C 130:7–9).

Unlike the millennial earth—which will be dotted with many hundreds of temples—there are none in that celestial city. "God Almighty and the Lamb are the temple of it" (Revelation 21:22). Sun and moon have been left far behind in their fallen system, being replace by the glory of God and the Lamb (Revelation 21:23–24; 22:5).

John beheld the waters of eternal life flowing through the city. This river is bordered on either side by the tree of life with its twelve varieties of fruit, the leaves of which seem to symbolize those gospel truths which bring spiritual healing to the nations.

The Apocalypse promises those who are faithful that they will see the face of God and have his name written upon their foreheads (see 22:4; 14:1). That is, they will inherit a fulness of celestial glory, being kings and priests unto the Most High (see Revelation 1:6; 3:11; 5:10; 22:5). And whereas their reign over the paradisiacal earth would last but a thousand years, their reign on the celestial earth will last forever (Revelation 22:5). They will become Gods in their own right.[28]

Conclusion

The Apocalypse ends as it began, with the assurance that the things John saw would shortly come to pass and that the Lord will "come quickly." Therefore, unlike typical apocalyptic writings, it is to remain unsealed . . . and unsullied. From the divine perspective, the Lord's coming is near—far less than one celestial day away (see Abraham 3:4; D&C 63:53). Consequently, the central message of the Apocalypse is more relevant by nineteen centuries than when it was first written. Mankind is rushing toward its inescapable confrontation with its Creator, Savior, and Judge. "He which testifieth these things saith, Surely I come quickly. Amen. Even so, come, Lord Jesus" (Revelation 22:20).

Notes
1. James L. Price, *Interpreting the New Testament*, (New York: Holt, Rinehart and Winston, 1961), 518.
2. Joseph Smith, *Teachings of the Prophet Joseph Smith*, comp. Joseph Fielding Smith (Salt Lake City: Deseret Book, 1938), 290. Hereafter designated *TPJS*.
3. *TPJS*, 252.
4. *TPJS*, 157; Daniel 7:9–14; D&C 116.
5. Bruce R. McConkie, *Doctrinal New Testament Commentary*, (Salt Lake City: Bookcraft, 1977), vol. 3, 462. Hereafter designated *DNTC*.
6. *TPJS*, 289–90; italics added.
7. *DNTC* 3:484–85.
8. *TPJS*, 289.
9. Being a vision of futurity, the twenty-four elders seen by John in their resurrected state were in reality still in the spirit world, paradise, awaiting resurrection.
10. See Rev. 15:2; 21:18–21; D&C 77:1–5; 130:9; and *TPJS*, 291–92.
11. *TPJS*, 321.
12. *HC* 1:76. See Rodney Turner, *The Footstool of God*, (Orem, Utah: Grandin, 1983), 189.
13. *TPJS*, 292.
14. *TPJS*, 293–94.
15. *DNTC* 3:520.
16. *TPJS*, 341.
17. See Daniel 7:9–10, 13, 22, 27; D&C 116; *TPJS*, 157.
18. While Satan will be bound by the personal righteousness of the Lord's people (1 Nephi 22:15, 26; D&C 45:55), there will still be wicked men on the millennial earth (see *TPJS*, 268; Zechariah 14:16–19). Satan's agency will be temporarily suspended by the power of God; an angel will bind him for a thousand years (Revelation 20:1–2; D&C 121:4). He will not be able to tempt either the living or the dead.

19. Joseph Smith said that the resurrected Saints "will not probably dwell upon the earth, but will visit it when they please, or when it is necessary to govern it" (*TPJS*, 268).

20. Isaiah wrote: "The child shall die a hundred years old; but the sinner being a hundred years old shall be accursed" (Isaiah 65:20).

21. All who repent will be saved and become—according to the law they abide—relatively righteous in God's sight (see *TPJS*, 356–57).

22. *TPJS*, 189.

23. See *TPJS*, 181, 365.

24. The new heaven and earth spoken of by Isaiah (65:17; 66:22) is the present earth in its renewed, paradisiacal glory (tenth article of faith). Peter's reference (2 Peter 3:13) may parallel Revelation 21:1. In any event, following the "little season" the planet Earth will be disorganized and pass away (Matthew 24:35; D&C 29:23; 43:31–32; 88:25–26). Consequently, the new heaven and earth seen by john was the resurrected, celestial earth on which the Saints will reign forever (see Revelation 22:5; Ether 13:8–9; D&C 29:22–23).

25. Moses 7:63–64; *TPJS,* 84.

26. It is generally assumed that the "new Jerusalem" and "the holy Jerusalem" are one and the same. However, Joseph Smith said "there are two cities spoken of here" (*TPJS*, 86).

27. In his vision of the celestial kingdom, the Prophet Joseph Smith said that its streets "had the *appearance* of being paved with gold" (D&C 137:4; italics added).

28. For an extended discussion of the doctrine of Godhood in the New Testament see Rodney Turner, *Principles of the Gospel in Practice*, (Salt Lake City: Randall Book Co., 1985), 21–37.

CHAPTER FIFTEEN

Securing Divine Protection: Putting on the Armor of God

Clyde J. Williams

In our society we see many examples of efforts being made to protect people from harm and injury. In the game of football, pads, helmets, and braces are worn to try to prevent serious injury. Nuclear arms and a wide range of military weapons and machinery are amassed to try to insure safety from the opposing forces. Anciently soldiers clothed themselves in protective armor. Each piece of this armor was designed to provide specific protection to a portion of the soldier's body.

Paul, in writing to the Saints at Ephesus, used a soldier's armor as a symbol of spiritual protection. Ephesus, a major Roman province located on the west coast of what is present-day Turkey, was a city ripe with the philosophies and moral standards of the world. It should come as no surprise, therefore, that following much counsel and instruction, Paul would close his epistle with a sober warning for the Ephesian Saints to "put on the whole armour of God" (Ephesians 6:11). It was this spiritual armor which would enable those early Saints to "stand against the wiles of the devil" (Ephesians 6:11). The importance of the armor was reemphasized by the Lord when he gave the same message and counsel to the Prophet Joseph Smith in August of 1830 (see D&C 27:15–18).

The Armor Defined

The armor, we must remember, is God's. He provides it, but we must put it on. A careful consideration of the armor will disclose useful insights about its purpose and how to put it on. Concerning this point President Marion G. Romney said: "One can scarcely hope to be fortified 'against the wiles of the devil' by putting 'on the whole armour of God' (see Ephesians 6:11) unless he knows what that armour is.[1]

Loins Girded with Truth

The armor consists first of a girdle about the soldier's loins. The girdle could consist of a wide leather apron designed to protect the warrior. In biblical language the loins denote the location of the organs of procreation where human life is generated. Thus having one's "loins girt about with truth" (Ephesians 6:14) has reference to preserving one's virtue. A knowledge of the truth can prevent the righteous from succumbing to the self-serving arguments of those who would seek to destroy our moral character. In the scriptures the process of girding one's loins implies preparation and forethought (see D&C 38:9). This is certainly the case in the process of building moral stamina. The means by which we can gird our loins with truth would be to study the scriptures continually, listen to the messages of the living prophets, and apply the principles thus learned in our lives (see John 8:31–32).

The Breastplate of Righteousness

The second piece of armor we are instructed to put on is the breastplate of righteousness. In reference to this breastplate President Harold B. Lee stated: "'The breastplate of righteousness' . . . would be placed over the heart which again in biblical language is regarded as the center or the seat of the spiritual or the conscience or the conduct of men. You will remember the Master had said, '[from] out of the abundance of the heart the mouth speaketh" (Matthew 12:34).[2]

The scriptures refer to the desires of our heart (see Alma 41:3; Psalms 37:4). It is our desires which ultimately direct our actions. In putting on the breastplate of righteousness, we must have righteous desires. These righteous desires will come only as we live the commandments and seek to follow the Savior's example.

Feet Shod with the Gospel

The third piece of armor is having our "feet shod with the preparation of the gospel" (Ephesians 6:15). It is our feet which carry us to various destinations in our daily lives. It is our shoes which prevent us from stubbing our toes or cutting our feet on some of the rugged paths we must take. In a spiritual sense our feet will take us along the journey of life as we endeavor to return to the presence of the Lord. By having our spiritual feet prepared with the symbolic shoes of the gospel of peace, we will be prepared to travel life's journey effectively. The jagged stones of sin and obstacles in the path of life will be far less likely to cause us to stumble and lose our way.

The Helmet of Salvation

The helmet of salvation is the fourth part of the armor of God. This helmet, as President Harold B. Lee declared, "is to guide the intellect, the head being the guiding center of our minds which controls our lives, 'for as [a man] thinketh in his heart, so is he' (Proverbs 23:7). No man, said the Master, committed a murder unless he first became angry. No one committed adultery unless he had an evil or immoral thought. Just so, one does not steal unless he covets. So the evil act must be conceived in the mind before the act."[3]

It is the plan of salvation which brings peace of mind. A knowledge of the doctrines of the gospel gives us comfort, understanding, and wisdom. As opposition mounts or unexplained tragedies occur, the helmet of the plan of salvation provides the necessary information to sustain us intellectually.

The Sword of the Spirit

Before dealing with the fifth and final piece of defensive armor, the shield of faith, a discussion of the sword of the Spirit would be helpful. The sword is the only offensive weapon in Paul's symbolic description. We are told in the scriptures that the sword "is the word of God" (Ephesians 6:17). The Lord has often used a sword to symbolize his word. In Revelation 1:16 John saw in vision the Son of God. Coming out of the Savior's mouth was a symbolic representation described as a sharp two-edged sword. This at first glance may seem strange. However, upon careful examination of the scripture, a significant insight can be gained.

In Doctrine and Covenants 12:2 we read, "Behold, I am God; give heed to my word, which is quick and powerful, sharper than a two-edged sword, to the dividing asunder of both joint and marrow; therefore, give heed unto my word." Here we are told that the word of God is comparable to a sharp two-edged sword. Why is the word compared to a *two*-edged sword? A possible explanation can be found by examining additional scriptures. In 1 Nephi 16, Nephi had been chastising his brothers Laman and Lemuel because of their unwillingness to obey their father and the Lord. He had spoken what he called "hard things against the wicked according to the truth" (1 Nephi 16:2). Nephi then explained the effect of the word of truth as it is spoken. "Wherefore, the guilty taketh the truth to be hard, for it *cutteth* them to the very center" (1 Nephi 16:2; italics added; see also Mosiah 13:7; 2 Nephi 1:26). When the word of God is spoken to the wicked, it cuts them to the very center of their souls. Their reaction will almost always be one of two things. They will either strike back in anger, as Laman and Lemuel did, or they will be subdued and embarrassed and desire to withdraw. This, then, could be one edge of the two-edged sword.

In 3 Nephi 11, we find another important reference relating to the meaning of the sword. At the time when the Savior made his appearance among the righteous people of Nephi, they were gathered around the temple in the land Bountiful and they heard a voice from heaven. It was not a harsh or a loud voice. The scripture indicates that "notwithstanding it being a small voice it did *pierce* them that did hear it to the center, insomuch that there was no part of their frame that it did not cause to quake; yea, it did *pierce* them to the very soul, and did cause their hearts to burn" (3 Nephi 11:3; italics added; see also D&C 85:6). Thus we learn that the two-edged sword of the Spirit [the word of God] not only cuts the wicked to the center and causes them to feel guilty, but it also pierces the hearts of the righteous and causes their hearts to burn with conviction. As to the power of this, the only offensive weapon in the armor of God, Alma appropriately said: "The preaching of the word had a great tendency to lead the people to do that which was just, yea, it had had more powerful effect upon the minds of the people than the sword, or anything else" (Alma 31:5). It is the sword of the word of God which will help the righteous teach the gospel and defend its truths. In order to wield the sword, one must study and understand the scriptures (see D&C 84:85).

The Fiery Darts of the Wicked

In order to understand the purpose of the shield of faith, it would be useful to discuss the fiery darts of the wicked. In medieval times, it was common for attacking armies to shoot flaming darts. These would be "arrows or light spears, tipped with pitch and set ablaze."[4] In the Apostle Paul's spiritual analogy the fiery darts represent some of Satan's most deadly temptations. In Ephesians 6:12, Paul indicates that our struggle is not with "flesh and blood," meaning man-made powers. The real need for this spiritual armor is to combat the prince of darkness and his cohorts. They epitomize spiritual wickedness in high places. In verse 12, *epouranios*, the Greek word for *high places*, carries with it the meaning of being in heaven. In this case the word *heaven* has a different connotation than we normally attach to it. This passage refers to Satan and his hosts who are unseen in a spirit state of existence.

Concerning verse 12, President Harold B. Lee once commented:

> Using words that are common to modern warfare, we might say that there are in the world today fifth columnists [spies] who are seeking to infiltrate the defenses of every one of us, and when we lower those defenses, we open avenues to an invasion of our souls. These are carefully chartered on the maps of the opposition the weak spots in every one of us. They are known to the forces of evil, and just the moment we lower the defense of any one of those ports, that becomes the D-Day of our invasion and our souls are in danger.[5]

Clearly Satan desires to find a way to penetrate the armor of the righteous. He knows our weaknesses and will endeavor to get his fiery darts through wherever we have let our guard down. The shield of faith is the first line of defense. It is the shield which will quench or extinguish the fiery darts. Inasmuch as the shield is representative of our faith, the following are five significant ways in which faith is destroyed today. These are, or can be, used as fiery darts by the adversary.

1. Immorality and all of its deviations is more and more becoming a destroyer of faith. One recent survey showed that seventy-eight percent of Americans between the ages of eighteen and twenty-nine saw nothing wrong with a man and a woman having sexual relations before marriage.[6] Video, cable, and satellite innovations have made sexually explicit material available in the privacy of our homes. Satan has

thus found ways to pierce the armor of those who avoided immorality because of possible public exposure.

An example of the effect of this fiery dart was given by Elder Vaughn J. Featherstone:

> I visited a stake in a distant city. I make it a custom to memorize their statistics, which at least gives me some slight understanding of activity levels. In this stake almost every statistic was down dramatically, including attendance at sacrament meeting, priesthood meeting, Relief Society, Primary, Sunday School, and youth activity; and also tithing and temple activity were down. I think I had a sense of righteous indignation, maybe even anger, that we had let Satan take over so much real estate.
>
> I questioned the stake leaders, and together we prayed and pondered for an answer. It came. This stronghold community of the Church had not especially been aware of the subtleties of Satan's strategy. Many in this farming community had purchased satellite receivers, video shops had opened, and naïve parents were letting R- and X-rated movies into their homes through satellite channels, and the youth and even some parents were renting them. Imagine violating the second most sacred place on the earth, the homes of righteous Latter-day Saints.[7]

2. Intellectualism is another fiery dart. There are many who, because of their vast knowledge and learning, have begun to fulfill Nephi's prophecy that "when they are learned they think they are wise, and they hearken not unto the counsel of God, for they set it aside, supposing they know of themselves, wherefore, their wisdom is foolish and it profiteth them not. And they shall perish" (2 Nephi 9:28). Challenges to the Book of Mormon, to Church doctrine, and to the decisions of the leaders all fit in this category. Those who trust only in the intellect say a testimony based on the Spirit is for the simple-minded. Spiritual feelings and emotions cannot be trusted, they would say. In this way Satan can and will penetrate the weak.

3. Our society has been blessed with more conveniences than the world has ever known. However, as useful and pleasant as these possessions may be, they can become a fiery dart. When people become caught up in the pursuit of material possessions, it can destroy all sense of value for spiritual things. Diversions don't have to be sinful to do harm. They just have to distract us from the spiritual things that really matter.

4. Perhaps some of the most visible times when the shield of faith is destroyed or dropped occur in cases of great suffering or trials. Long-term illnesses, unexpected deaths, the tragic loss of loved ones, and many other tribulations often lead to the loss of faith. Although Satan does not generally cause these tragedies, he nevertheless uses them to fire the darts of doubt, despair, and bitterness. The Lord allows these seeming tragedies, and Satan plays upon our inability to explain why they occur. We must not forget that we were sent here to be proved and tested in all things.

5. Apathy is another dart that Satan uses to his advantage. It is easy to become complacent. Satan can carefully lull us away into carnal security. The analogy has been made of cooking a frog in a pan of water. If the water is heated too rapidly, the frog will invariably jump out. However, by bringing the water slowly and carefully to boil, the frog is cooked before he realizes the danger he is in. In a similar way, Satan carefully uses rationalization and apathy to weaken our armor, and then he can easily destroy us with his fiery darts.

The Shield of Faith

In introducing the shield of faith, the King James Version uses the phrase *above all* as if implying supreme importance to this piece of the armor (see Ephesians 6:16). This phrase would more accurately be translated *in addition to all*.[8]

As one commentary indicates, the shield mentioned by Paul was likely a great oblong "which gave shelter to the soldier's whole frame. It consisted of two layers of wood, covered with canvas and then with hide. . . . Arrows or light spears, tipped with pitch and set ablaze, would burn themselves out against the hide-covered shield without harming the man behind it."[9]

To know if the shield is in place we must more fully understand what faith is. The Prophet Joseph Smith said:

> Faith [is] the first principle in revealed religion, and the foundation of all righteousness. . . . Faith . . . is the first great governing principle which has power, dominion, and authority over all things; by it they exist, by it they are upheld, by it they are changed, or by it they remain, agreeable to the will of God. Without it there is no power, and without power there could be no creation nor existence.[10]

Notice, faith is the power of God. It is a more complex doctrine than many have supposed.

Faith Builders

Knowing what builds faith will also help assure us that our shield is in place. Gospel knowledge, obedience, and trials are some of what I would call *faith builders*. Concerning knowledge and its importance in building faith, the Prophet Joseph Smith taught:

> Three things are necessary in order that any rational and intelligent being may exercise faith in God unto life and salvation. First, the idea that he actually exists. Secondly, a correct idea of his character, perfections, and attributes. Thirdly, an actual knowledge that the course of life which he is pursuing is according to his will.[11]

Without a correct knowledge of God and his attributes, it is impossible to exercise faith in him and understand his dealings with our fellow men. As President Marion G. Romney said: "Faith comes from searching, hearing, pondering, and praying about the word of God."[12]

By obedience, our faith can be made perfect (see James 2:22). As we obey the commandments and follow the promptings of the Spirit, we see the benefits of our obedience and our faith will increase.

Tests and trials are often the means of either strengthening or weakening an individual's faith. The scriptures tell us that we "receive no witness until after the trial of [our] faith" (Ether 12:6). The word *trial* could be interpreted to mean the *strengthening* or *testing* of our faith. A willingness to sacrifice becomes a key in allowing tests and trials to build our faith. Concerning this point Elder Bruce R. McConkie made the following statement: "Faith and sacrifice go hand in hand. Those who have faith sacrifice freely for the Lord's work, and their acts of sacrifice increase their faith. 'Let us here observe,' the Prophet continues, 'that a religion that does not require the sacrifice of all things never has power sufficient to produce the faith necessary unto life and salvation' (Lectures on Faith 6:7)."[13]

A classic example of this principle was brought to the attention of certain members of the Church when they were discussing the ill-fated Martin and Willie Handcart Companies. Some were criticizing the leaders for allowing the companies to come so late and so ill prepared. One older man sat and listened until he could stand it no longer. He arose and said:

> I ask you to stop this criticism. You are discussing a matter you know nothing about. Cold historic facts mean nothing here, for they give no proper interpretation of the questions involved. Mistake to

send the Handcart Company out so late in the season? Yes. . . . We suffered beyond anything you can imagine and many died of exposure and starvation, but did you ever hear a survivor of that company utter a word of criticism? Not one of that company ever apostatized or left the Church, because every one of us came through with the absolute knowledge that God lives for we became acquainted with him in our extremities.

I have pulled my handcart when I was so weak and weary from illness and lack of food that I could hardly put one foot ahead of the other. I have looked ahead and seen a patch of sand or a hill slope and I have said, "I can go only that far and there I must give up, for I cannot pull the load through it.' . . . I have gone on to that sand and when I reached it, the cart began pushing me. I have looked back many times to see who was pushing my cart, but my eyes saw no one. I knew then that the angels of God were there.

Was I sorry that I chose to come by handcart? No. Neither then nor any minute of my life since. The price we paid to become acquainted with God was a privilege to pay, and I am thankful that I was privileged to come in the Martin Handcart Company.[14]

It is this type of sacrifice, this kind of test which can strengthen our shield of faith.

Fruits of Faith

Another way to determine if our shield is in place is to examine the fruits of our faith. The following are three of the fruits of faith.

First, signs and miracles are the fruits of faith (see D&C 63:9–10). These signs need not be large, dramatic things. It may be just having our finances work out when on paper it didn't seem they would, or a change in a child who was ill or struggling in some other way. Through faith all things can work for our good.

Second, spiritual or gospel knowledge is not only a builder of faith, but it is also a fruit of faith. It was by faith that Moses chose to suffer affliction with the Israelites rather than to enjoy the pleasures of sin among the Egyptians (Hebrew 11:24–25). It was faith that enabled the three Nephites to obtain the promise that they would not taste of death (Ether 12:17). So great was the faith of Enoch that whatever he said was done, even to the moving of mountains (Moses 7:13). The list could go on and on, but it suffices to say that the greater one's faith, the more power he will possess.

In summary, if we are applying the principles we have called "faith builders" and see the "fruits of faith" in our lives, we can be assured that the shield of faith is in place.

Putting on the Armor

We are engaged in the greatest battle in the history of the world. Satan's hosts are frantic, for they know they have but a short time (see Revelation 12:12). In the words of President Marion G. Romney: "There has never been a time since the world began when Paul's charge, 'put on the armour of God, that ye may be able to stand against the wiles of the devil,' was more imperative than it is today."[15] In order for us to be prepared and come away victorious in the struggle for the souls of men, we must put on the *whole* armor of God. We will be vulnerable in those areas where our armor is deficient. Concerning this point President N. Eldon Tanner wisely counseled:

> Examine your armor. Is there an unguarded or unprotected place? Determine now to add whatever part is missing. No matter how antiquated or lacking in parts your armor may be, always remember that it is within your power to make the necessary adjustments to complete your armor.
>
> Through the great principle of repentance you can turn your life about and begin now clothing yourself with the armor of God through study, prayer, and a determination to serve God and keep his commandments.[16]

Conclusion

We have examined in detail the meaning and importance of each part of the armor of God. Every individual has different weaknesses, and thus different parts of our armor must be strengthened. We must be willing to avoid flirting with Satan's wares and realize that we cannot entertain a single thought that would cause us to weaken our armor in any way. It is the armor which will help us traverse the course to becoming a more Christlike person.

Finally, in the words of Brigham Young: "The men and women, who desire to obtain seats in the Celestial Kingdom, will find that they must battle with the enemy of all righteousness every day."[17] That we may be armed and prepared each day and help others to do so is my prayer.

Notes

1. *Conference Report*, October 1980, 66.

2. *Conference Report*, Munich Germany Area Conference, Aug. 1973, 67.

3. Ibid., 67–68.

4. *The Interpreter's Bible,* 12 vols. (Nashville, Tenn.: Abingdon Press, n.d.), 10:742.

5. *Conference Report*, October 1949, 56.

6. "Morality," *U.S. News and World Report*, December 9, 1986, 52

7. Vaughn J. Featherstone, "The Last Drop in the Chalice," in 1985–86 *BYU Devotional and Fireside Speeches* (Provo: Brigham Young University Press, 1986), 16.

8. Markus Barth, "Ephesians," *The Anchor Bible* (Garden City, N.Y.: Doubleday, 1974.) 34A: 771. It is interesting to note that the phrase *above all* was not used in the revelation given to Joseph Smith in 1830 (see D&C 27:17).

9. *Interpreter's Bible*, 10:742.

10. *Lectures on Faith* (Salt Lake City: Deseret Book, 1985), 1:1, 24.

11. Ibid., 3:2–5.

12. Marion G. Romney, "The Power of Faith," *Instructor,* Oct. 1970, 353.

13. Bruce R. McConkie, *A New Witness for the Articles of Faith* (Salt Lake City: Deseret Book, 1986), 189.

14. See David O. McKay, "Pioneer Women," *Relief Society Magazine*, January 1948, 8.

15. "Historic Conferences End," *Church News*, July 5, 1975, 10.

16. *Conference Report*, April 1979, 65.

17. *Journal of Discourses*, 26 vols. (London: Latter-day Saints' Book Depot, 1867), 11:14.

CHAPTER SIXTEEN

Rhetoric versus Revelation
A Consideration of Acts 17:16–34

Richard P. Anderson

Paul's presence at Areopagus (Acts 17:15–34) provides us with an interesting scenario where we can view on who stated that he "came not with excellency of speech or of wisdom" (1 Corinthians 2:1) to the center of world intelligence and rhetoric (public speaking). Even after the fall of its democracy, and more than 150 years of Roman rule, Athens still remained a center of art and education, having a major influence on western culture.

However, just as modern Babylon searches for answers that satisfy the inquiring wisdom of the world while also allowing for carnal sensualities, so it was with Athens. Many did become believers but the fact remains that in the false security of their own wisdom, the Athenians mocked the resurrection of Jesus Christ which they might have understood had they not rejected revelation in favor of rhetoric.

In his first letter to the Corinthians, Paul stated that the scholars of the world were foolish and their wisdom useless without the simple message of Christ. This message seemed foolish to the Jews because they wanted a sign from heaven as proof, and it seemed foolish to the Gentiles because in their inability to "feel after him," they believed only what agreed with their philosophies (Acts 17 refers to Stoicism and Epicureanism). Equating those called to the ministry with "the

233

foolishness of God," Paul then states that:

> the foolishness of God is wiser than men; and the weakness of God is stronger than men.
>
> For ye see your calling, brethren, how that not many wise men after the flesh, not many mighty, not many noble, are called:
>
> But . . . God hath chosen the weak things of the world to confound the things which are might. (1 Corinthians 1:25–27)

How did the Lord prepare Paul to testify to those assembled on Mars' Hill? How effective was he as a speaker? In speaking to them, to what extent did he use his intelligence and rhetorical skills, and to what extent did he use revelation and the power of the Spirit? By considering the state of Athenian religious and philosophical beliefs at that time, the level of education and rhetorical skills of the people that Paul spoke to, and Paul's preparation and approach in speaking to those at Areopagus, we can find the answers to the above questions and better understand what took place when he spoke at Areopagus.

More important, we can strengthen our testimony of this great apostle and missionary who had a burning knowledge of the Lord, who had seen him, and who had been called by him to be a special witness of his resurrection. In so doing, we can also increase our appreciation for the efforts of our modern-day apostles and prophets to bring us to Christ in a world filled with the wisdom and unfeeling rhetoric of man.

Religion and Philosophy in Athens

Life in Greek civilization embraced the ethical principles of courage, temperance, and justice. Their most important principle was wisdom, a virtue that was achieved by the free exercise of one's rational faculties and the suppression of emotion. To the Greeks, man's original sin was a lack of knowledge. By thinking for themselves in the spirit of free intellectual inquiry, the Greeks strove to formulate and establish a faith based on their reason and logic.[1] This led to the development and fortification of the intellect with its attendant philosophies and religions.

Athens at that time was filled with idols that represented differing gods and religions, including several to the unknown god to which Paul referred (Acts 17:23). Paul stated that the city was "given wholly to idolatry," and according to one contemporary writer, it was easier to find a god in Athens at that time than it was to find the person you were looking for.

We are told in the scriptures that among those present for Paul's sermon at Areopagus were Stoics and Epicureans. We are probably safe in assuming that others were also there who were of differing religious and philosophical beliefs.

Since Stoicism and Epicureanism represent the predominant philosophies at that time, and since they are specifically mentioned by Luke, we will focus our attention on them. Stocism was founded by Zeno, a native of Cyprus who lived at the turn of the third century before Christ.[2] Stoics believed that all matter, including themselves, the world, and all else in existence, was a part of the supreme being and therefore divine. All matter existed as a part of God and differed only in degrees of fineness. All "order and law of the world are his mind and will" and "all events and all acts of will are determined; it is as impossible for anything to happen otherwise than it does as it is for something to come out of nothing."[3]

"As if preparing not only an ethic but a theology for Christianity, they conceived the world, law, life, the soul, and destiny in terms of God, and defined morality as a willing surrender to the divine will."[4] Moral action placed one in harmony with all matter and therefore with God. Immoral action placed one in disharmony with all that existed and therefore with God. If evil were to come to a good man, it would be only temporary, and, if one really understood the whole of things, it would not be considered evil.[5]

A Stoic was to shun luxury and complexity, be content with little, and indifferent to all things except virtue and vice. Pleasure was bad but all things done in what they termed to be virtue would bring joy. A Stoic therefore found joy in horses, hunting, going to parties, and "he will fall in love with beautiful young men."[6]

He suppressed all feelings that might "obstruct the course of question the wisdom of Nature." When he died, it was fate. His spirit consisted of the same matter as God and continued as part of the supreme being. It was illogical to grieve over the death of a loved one. If he grew tired of life, he would have no scruples concerning suicide.[7] Stoicism, though a philosophy, served as a religion to those who followed it.

Epicureans received their philosophy from the teachings of Epicurus. He was born in 341 BC to Athenian parents and wrote more than 300 books in his lifetime. He was considered by some to be an immensely kind man who was devoted to his parents and generous to his brothers and servants; by others he was "villified as a crude and unlettered sybarite (one who loves luxury) that held that "'the beginning and root of every good thing is the pleasure of the belly.'"[8]

Rejecting religion, Epicurus taught that all reason must confine itself to the sensual experience, and this experience is the final test of truth. Man, he felt, was a completely natural product with his life beginning spontaneously. The soul was comprised of a more delicate substance that was diffused throughout the body, and it died with the body's death.

To the Epicurean, virtue was the means to a happy life. Pleasure was good, pain was bad. Sensual pleasures were legitimate, and wisdom found room for them. However:

> When, therefore, we say that pleasure is the chief good we are not speaking of the pleasures of the debauched man, or those that lie in sensual enjoyment . . . but we mean the freedom of the body from pain, and of the soul from disturbance.[9]

For the Epicruean, wisdom was the only liberator and the highest virtue.[10]

The Stoics differed from the Epicureans in at least two important areas of thought. To the Stoics, knowledge arose from reason. To the Epicurean, knowledge arose out of the senses. The Stoics felt that "experience did not always lead to knowledge; for in between sensations and reason lies emotion or passion, which may distort experience into error even as it distorts desire into vice."[11] To the Stoic, reason was the supreme achievement of man; to the Epicurean, it was wisdom.

Secondly, the Stoics believed in an afterlife, and the Epicureans felt that there was no existence after death. The possibility of a resurrection of the body was completely foreign and illogical to both philosophies. The mention of such an

> "unacceptable idea as resurrection" would make it plain to those assembled at Areopagus that Paul's views were not be taken seriously. It was especially out of place to bring it up before the Areopagus: where on "the legendary occasion when that court was founded by the city's tutelary goddess Athene, Apollo had affirmed:
> > When the dust drinks up a man's blood,
> > Once he has died, there is no resurrection."[12]

236

Hence, "when they heard [Paul speak] of the resurrection of the dead, some mocked" (Acts 17:32).

Although religion and philosophy existed together at the time of Paul, the conflict between religion and philosophy went through three stages. Religion initially was attacked prior to Socrates. It was replaced by an attempt to establish a natural ethic, such as we see in the Epicureans. Religion then returned with the Skeptics, who were extremely cynical, and the Stoics.[13] Philosophy remained, and it was not unusual for a person to hold to differing philosophical and religious beliefs at the same time.

An atmosphere of doubt seems to have been the prevalent attitude at the time of Paul. This doubt voiced itself in questions concerning life, civilization, death, and man's ability to answer those questions by his own reason or wisdom. This is evidenced by the declining influence of philosophy, the proliferation of differing religions with their powerless gods, and an increase in acceptance of immorality.

While the philosophies and religions of Athenian society offered ethics for living, and in some case, a hope for an afterlife, they were in stark contrast to the gospel that Paul offered. Had they chosen to feel with their hearts rather than to use only reason and logic, they could have freed themselves from the straitjackets of their society. The powerful influence that society has on one's ability to discern truth was alluded to by President Spencer W. Kimball when he said:

> Simple truths are often rejected in favor of much less demanding philosophies of men, and this [a] cause for the rejection of prophets. . . . The cares of the world, honors of the word, and looking beyond the mark are all determined by a persuasive few who presume to speak for all. Paul had difficulty because . . . among the Greeks, Christianity was seen as foolishness. . . . In multiple scriptures, the Lord has indicated that he will perform his work through those whom the world regards as weak and despised . . . rejection . . . comes because the hearts of the people are hardened, as people are shaped by their society.[14]

For centuries, Athenian society had strived and failed to give its people a religion or philosophy that would provide an ethic of living and answers to questions concerning life and eternity. While in some cases noble ethics were espoused, the society was highly immoral, its members' questions remained unanswered, and, more important, it did not prepare them for the truth that Paul offered.

Greek Rhetoric and Education

In understanding the situation that Paul was in, one must take into account the breadth and depth of Greek education. When Christianity began, Greek education was widely diffused and had a great hold on western society. Greek libraries contained as many as a half-million books. The most frequently studied subjects were rhetoric and philosophy. "The educationist's standard justification for the pre-eminence of these subject was that speech and reason were the most specifically human of all accomplishments."[15]

This emphasis on rhetoric and philosophy had a tremendous effect in developing a people whose attitude stressed the placing of reason and logic over the emotions, dismissing the ability of the heart to discern what reason and logic could not.

One must also remember that this education was not for Greeks alone. Athens was the center of world education. For example, Romans, even though they ruled Greece, completed their formal schooling at Athens. Athens provided the equivalent of postgraduate study. The strength of its system was still evident and in full force in Gaul in the fifth and sixth centuries.[16]

When Paul was invited to speak to the men and women assembled on Mars' Hill, he spoke to educated people who prided themselves on their rhetorical skills. Half the nation was probably literate, and nearly all spoke with skill. Historically, Aristotle first developed a theory of rhetoric, and it eventually became one of the Greek national pastimes, a mainstay of Athenian daily life, and a common activity wherever people were gathered.[17]

In most Greek cities, and especially in Athens, it was very common for one to find debates, speeches, and other displays of forensic skills going on in the public gathering places. It was an intense activity that was a normal part of Greek public life, along with that of the law courts. It guaranteed a secure place to anyone who professed to teach the art of speech. As another author explained: "The love of speech had become to a large proportion of Greeks a second nature. They were a nation of talkers. They were almost the slaves of cultivated expression."[18] When real speeches in the assemblies were not possible, they made up fictitious assemblies and courts to address and argue in.

Artificiality is a key word in discussing Greek rhetoric. If a person spoke extemporaneously, it did not mean he spoke spontaneously.

Rather than being original, speech was imitative. A rhetorician was expected always to speak in the appropriate style, intonation, and dramatic effect.[19] To be able to speak and argue effectively was essential. "To make the best of yourself in a Greek city . . . involved being able to speak, to see strong and weak points in a cases and use them to your own advantage whether speaking in the courts or in the assembly."[20]

Among a people so accustomed to polished rhetoric, it seems unlikely that Paul would have drawn any attention to himself or his subject matter, let alone receive an invitation to speak on Mars' Hill, had he not been a skilled and effective speaker.

Paul's Preparation and Methodology

The Lord prepared a unique man for a unique calling. Paul spoke both Greek and Hebrew. He was both a scholar and a laboring man. Born at Tarsus, "he studied at Jerusalem with Gamaliel, and possibly, but less probably at the university at Tarsus. He quoted Greek literature at Athens and gave evidence that he understood their philosophy."[21]

The use of Greek language was common, even in Palestine:

> We know that Greek was a familiar language in Palestine itself. At a relatively early period we find evidence that classical Greek literature was known in Palestine, and the rabbinic writings of the later period contain a high proportion of Greek loan words.[22]

When Paul addressed a Jerusalem crowd in Hebrew,

> they were pleased; apparently they expected him to speak in Greek and would have understood him if he had done so; in the Diaspora Paul did address Jewish congregations in Greek. It would be very strange if the Jewish literature written in Greek in Alexandria and Antioch were not read and even emulated in Paelstine.[23]

It should not be surprising that it was an educated and skilled rhetorician that the Lord sent to bear witness at Areopagus. Paul's speech has been analyzed in detail by Edward Norden in his *Agnostos Theos*. He demonstrates that it belongs to a standard type of speech for that occasion. it has a typical text with its individual motifs and expressions.

> Each of the four motifs of correcting ignorance, worshipping God, not through material representation but in spirit, calling for

repentance, and referring to resurrection, appears in Poimandres [the Stoic texts], are commonplace in the diatribes and have numerous parallels [with Paul's speech].[24]

E. W. Hunt, in his *Portrait of Paul*, states that because Paul knew his audience contained Stoics and Epicureans, he was able to skillfully use some of their own concepts to forward his position. This was a rhetorical skill first taught by Aristotle.

For example, the concept "God created a world," was a preopposition accepted by the Stoics, who believed that all things came into existence from God. This would not have been accepted by the Epicureans, who believed that the world came into being accidentally. The concept that God does not live in man-made temples, specifically those in Athens, would have been a statement palatable to Epicureans.[25]

More important evidence of Paul's knowledge of Greek intellect was his quoting from two classical authors. "In him we live and move and have our being," is the fourth line of a quatrain in a poem attributed to Epimenides, a Stoic; and, "for we also are his offspring," is part of a line from the Phenomena by Aratus, who also was a Stoic.[26]

Paul knew he was speaking to a people who were used to being convinced of and believing a principle as the result of skillful rhetoric, not revelation; persuasion, not the power of the spirit; and logic, not the feelings of the heart. Areopagus represented the wisdom of the world, but whether Paul purposely or subconsciously used in his speech the knowledge and skills related to his Greek background, we do not know. We do know, however, that he would not rely on those skills to "persuade" those present at Areopagus concerning the truthfulness of his message:

> For do I now persuade men . . . or do I seek to please men? For if I yet pleased men, I should not be the servant of Christ.
>
> But I certify you, brethren, that the gospel which was preached of me is not after man.
>
> For I neither received of man, neither was I taught it, but by the revelation of Jesus Christ. . . . But when it pleased God . . . to reveal his Son in me, that I might preach him among the heathen. . . . I conferred not with flesh and blood. (Galatians 1:10–12, 15, 16)[27]

It is interesting that Paul, the former Jewish scholar and authority, who had looked upon Christianity with such disdain, was now a Christian being disdained in Athens by those who represented a city of scholars and authorities. Like the Greeks, Paul had relied on the external for evidence of divinity. Following his conversion, he knew that the evidence could come only from within.

Like Alma, he knew the extremes. Having been blinded by the light of revelation that now guided him, he understood the darkness of the world's wisdom. As a prophet, he would have had a unique sensitivity toward Alma's teaching of where and how one receives divine rhetoric, wisdom, and intelligence:

> Do you ye not suppose that I know of these things myself? Behold, I testify unto you that I do know that these things whereof I have spoken are true. And how do you suppose that I know of their surety?
> Behold, I say unto you that they are made known unto me by the Holy Spirit of God. . . . And now I do know of myself that they are true; for the Lord God hath made them manifest unto me by his Holy Spirit; and this is the spirit of revelation which is in me. (Alma 5:45–47)

This truth was echoed by another Book of Mormon prophet, Jacob, who said:

> Behold, great and marvelous are the works of the Lord. How unsearchable are the depths of the mysteries of him; and it is impossible that man should find out all his ways. And no man knoweth of his ways save it be revealed unto him; wherefore, brethren, despise not the revelations of God. (Jacob 4:8)

Paul's speech was not meant to have "enticing words of man's wisdom," but be "in demonstration of the Spirit and of power: that [their] faith should not stand in the wisdom of men, but is the power of God" (1 Corinthians 2:4). Paul could logically show the Athenians the error of their unknown gods but as an ordained witness of Christ, his means of persuasion had to be by the power of the Holy Ghost so that that member of the Godhead could bear witness of Christ in the hearts of those who listened.

> Pure religion is a thing of the spirit and not of the intellect alone, and its truths must be carried into the hearts of hearers by the power of the Spirit, otherwise the human soul is not changed, the old man of sin is not crucified, and the seeker after salvation does not become alive in Christ. We find Paul extolling the spiritual powers of the weak and the simple and decrying the foolishness of the worldly wise who seek religious preferment and status on the basis of intellectuality and persuasive power.[28]

Those Greeks who rejected the gospel and the witness of the Holy Ghost appear to have centered their interest in the satisfaction of their intellectual curiosity, not their salvation. They rejected Paul's statements as illogical, mocking him when he spoke of the Resurrection. Some asked to hear more at another time, reflecting cautious interest or polite dismissal, but others felt and accepted the witness of the Spirit and believed (Acts 17:32–34).

The unbelieving Greeks personified what Paul warned the Ephesians to avoid:

> This I say therefore, and testify in the Lord, that ye henceforth walk not as other Gentiles walk, in the vanity of their mind,
>
> Having the understanding darkened, being alienated from the life of God through the ignorance that is in them, because of the blindness of their heart: Who being past feeling have given themselves over unto lasciviousness, to work all uncleanness with greediness. (Ephesians 4:17–19)

With their religions, the Greeks used outward signs (idols) and ritualistic ceremonies for their worship. The altar to the unknown god blatantly demonstrated their inability to know who God actually is, and who and how they should worship. When religion failed, they relied on their intellect by developing philosophies that at times were incorporated into or used as their religion.

Just as the religions and philosophies of Athens failed because they denied or were without revelation, those of today will fail because of this lack also. Joseph Smith taught:

> If one man cannot understand these things but by the Spirit of God, ten thousand men cannot; it is alike out of the reach of the wisdom of the learned, the tongue of the eloquent, the power of the mighty. . . . Whatever we may think of revelation . . . without it we can neither know nor understand anything of God, or the devil.[29]

Paul's writings are replete with the concept of having faith in the Lord Jesus Christ and with the need to gain that assurance the soul receives from a witness that is felt and unseen, not observed, evaluated, or drawn from logical conclusion.

Orson Pratt stated that "the gift and power of the Holy Ghost . . . is the greatest evidence that [a man] can receive concerning . . . God. . . . There is no evidence equal to it."[30] The Greeks had placed so much emphasis on the development of the mind, and so much confidence in mental abilities, that when one came with power, many were "past feeling." Elder Pratt continued by saying:

> The Holy Ghost bears testimony to the man who receives it, and not to somebody else; and if he is pure enough to receive this gift, he has power enough in his heart to regulate his actions according to the law of God, instead of building golden calves.[31]

Conclusion

Paul was a Roman citizen. He was born into the world of Greek thought. He spoke Greek and evidently spoke it eloquently. He was familiar with much that was a part of Greek education. And yet, while all of this provided him with a common ground to approach the people at Areopagus, he spoke as an apostle, as a special witness of Christ, and as one who was sent to teach the principles of salvation to others.

The Greeks were probably able to accept the logic of their relationship to God as Paul presented it. For example, if we are his offspring, he would be close to us and concerned about us, and by creating graven images and conceptions of God, God becomes our offspring and therefore a God with only the power that man can give to him. However, when Paul presented them with a God who possessed the power of resurrection, their logic, reason, and wisdom denied the revelation of the Spirit and made their acceptance of this idea impossible.

Had they listened to the Spirit instead of their own intellect, they would have not only known that Paul was an educated and skilled rhetorician, but by revelation they would have known in thought and feeling that he was an apostle and that the resurrected Jesus Christ had revealed himself to man.

We can learn much from this briefly mentioned incident in Acts. We, too, live in a world that seeks

> not the lord to establish his righteousness, but every man walketh in his own way, and after the image of his own god, whose image is in the likeness of the world, and whose substance is that of an idol, which waxeth old and shall perish. (D&C 1:16)

Because we also live in a society that conditions us to disregard the promptings of the Holy Spirit, the Lord has given his commandments to his chosen

Servants in their weakness, after the manner of their language,
that they might come to understanding.

And inasmuch as they erred it might be made known;

And inasmuch as they sought wisdom they might be
instructed;

And inasmuch as they sinned they might be chastened, that
they might repent;

And inasmuch as they were humble they might be made strong,
and blessed from on high, and receive knowledge from time to time.
(D&C 1:24–28)

The Lord desires every man to "speak in the name of God the Lord,
even the Savior of the world" (D&C 1:20). Such ability presupposes the
presence of revelation and not just its presence, but the recognition and
acknowledgement of it. It is a "feeling" people who recognize, through
the still, small voice, the truthfulness of the gospel as presented by the
Lord's messengers.

It was a "feeling" people who, after listening to King Benjamin's
sermon, "cried with one voice, saying: Yea, we believe all the words
which thou has spoken unto us; and also, we know of their surety and
truth, because of the Spirit of the Lord Omnipotent, which has wrought
a mighty change . . . in our hearts" (Mosiah 5:2).

It was a "feeling" people, known as the Anti-Nephi-Lehies and
numbered in the thousands, who

were brought to the knowledge of the truth, through the preaching
of Ammon and his brethren, according to the spirit of revelation and
of prophecy, and . . . as many of the Lamanites as believed in their
preaching, and were converted unto the Lord, never did fall away.
(Alma 23:6)

It was a "feeling" people, numbering only fifty, who on April 6,
1830, accepted the Lord's revelation through Joseph Smith that the
kingdom of God should be established in these last days. They accepted
the Lord's commandment to receive that prophet's words as if they
came from the Lord's own mouth (see D&C 21:5). They also received
the restoration of revealed scripture, namely, the Book of Mormon, so
that they could know

that there is a God in heaven, who is infinite and eternal, from everlasting to everlasting the same unchangeable God, the framer of
heaven and earth, and all things which are in them;

And that he created man, male and female, after his own image and in his own likeness, created he them;

And gave unto them commandments that they should love and serve him, the only living and true God, and that he should be the only being whom they should worship. (D&C 20:17–19, emphasis added)

Whether it be Paul at Areopagus, or Joseph Smith in New York, prophets are those who "declare the word of God . . . according to the revelation of the truth of the word . . . and according to the spirit of prophecy . . . [and] according to the testimony of Jesus Christ, the Son of God" (Alma 6:8). It is in this way, and only in this way that it can be received. Thin is Paul's prayer answered:

That the God of our Lord Jesus Christ, the Father of glory, may give unto you the spirit of wisdom and revelation in the knowledge of him:

The eyes of your understanding being enlightened; that ye may know what is the hope of his calling . . .

And what is the exceeding greatness of his power to us-ward who believe, according to the working of his mighty power,

Which he wrought in Christ, when he raised him from the dead. (Ephesians 1:17–20)

Notes

1. Fleming, 52.
2. Durant, 650. The name *Stoic* comes from Zeno's establishing his school in the Stoa Pecile, or *Pointed Porch*. Zeno became so influential that he was awarded the "keys to the walls," and a statue of him was created.
3. Ibid., 653.
4. Ibid.
5. Ibid., 654.
6. Boardman et al., 373.
7. Durant, 655. He further states that a Stoic "will seek so complete an *apatheia*, or absence of feeling, that his peace of mind will be secure against all the attacks and vicissitudes of fortune, pity, or love." Zeno himself committed suicide.
8. Boardman et al., 372.
9. Durant, 647.
10. Ibid., 648. "The wise man does not burn with ambition or lust for fame, he does not envy the good fortune of his enemies, nor even

of his friends . . . he seeks the calm . . . happiness in tranquility of body and mind." Epicurus disliked religion because he thought that it "thrived on ignorance, even promoted it, darkened life with a terror of celestial spies, relentless furies, and endless punishments" (p. 646). This view is not unlike that of many atheists and agnostics of religion today.

11. Ibid.
12. Bruce, 313.
13. The Skeptics doubted philosophy as well as dogma. Stoics felt that religion was necessary for the preservation of morals.
14. Kimball, 77. President Kimball also stated that "various excuses have been used over the centuries to dismiss these divine messengers. There has been denial because a prophet came from an obscure place . . . . The swiftest method of rejection of the holy prophets has been to find a pretext, however false or absurd, to dismiss the man so that his message could also be dismissed."
15. Pope, 125. "There was the image of the Homeric hero, who was characterized for his skill in debate at least as much as for his courage in battle. There was practical utility, because before the invention of printing and before the introduction of cheap paper the spoken word played an even greater role in communications than it does now."
16. Edwin Hatch, 32.
17. Ibid., 48. According to Aristotle, rhetoric served the purpose of "maintaining truth and justice against falsehood and wrong, of advancing public discussion where absolute proof is impossible, and of cultivating the habit of seeing both sides of and exposing . . . fallacies, and of self defence." (Aristotle, *Rhetoric*.) Plato had felt that rhetoric was dangerous if not directed to the pursuit of truth and justice. To him, it gave people what they wanted to hear, not what was good for them, "for the power of words led to the exaltation of power itself." (Clark, 40).
18. Hatch, 27.
19. Ibid., 49. The Greek world was one which "had created an artificial type of life, and was too artificial to be able to recognize its own artificiality . . . and [laid more] stress on the expression of ideas than upon ideas themselves. . . . Its rhetoric [therefore] was artificial not spontaneous, imitative not original, appreciative rather than constructive."
20. Clarke, 2.
21. Robinson, 38.
22. Hadas, 35.
23. Ibid.

24. Ibid., 145. He also states: "One or another of several [contemporary] religious teachers Norden cites, who cannot have been influenced by paul, is represented as visiting Athens in the course of a missionary journey, choosing as a text some local monument he has noticed on a walk, and reproving the audience for falsely associating the Deity with material objects and tendance. To say that the author of [Paul's] discourse adapted standard forms is by no means to impugn his earnestness and his sincerity: it would be much more remarkable if a literate man addressing a literate audience did not use the forms associated with his subject."

25. Hunt, 71.

26. Ibid.

27. Brigham Young stated: "Let one go forth who is careful to logically prove all he says . . . and let another travel with him who can say by the power of the Holy Ghost, Thus saith the Lord, though he may tremble under a sense of his weakness, cleaving to the Lord for strength, as such men generally do, you will invariably find that the man who testifies by the power of the Holy Ghost will convince and gather many more of the honest and upright than will the merely logical reasoner" (*Journal of Discourses,* 8:53–54).

28. McConkie, 318.

29. Smith, 205.

30. Pratt, 135.

31. Ibid., 138.

Bibliography

Anderson, Richard Lloyd. *Understanding Paul*. Salt Lake City: Deseret Book, 1982.

Aristotle. *Rhetoric*. Translated by W. Rhys Roberts. New York: Modern Library, 1954.

Baird, A. Craig. *Rhetoric*. New York: Ronald Press Company, 1965.

Baldwin, Charles Sears. *Ancient Rhetoric and Poetic*. Gloucester, Mas.: Macmillan, 1924.

Boardman, John; Griffin, Jasper; Murray, Oswyn. *The Oxford History of the Classical World*. New York: Oxford University Press, 1986.

Bradford, Ernie. *Paul the Traveller*. New York: Macmillan, 1976.

Bruce, F. F. New Testament History. New York: Doubleday, 1980.

Bury, J. B., and Meiggs, Russell. *A History of Greece*. New York: St. Martin's Press, 1975.

Clark, M. L. *Rhetoric at Rome*. New York: Barnes and Noble, 1966.

Durant, Will. *The Life of Greece*. New York: Simon and Schuster, 1939.

Fleming, William. *Arts and Ideas*. New York: Holt, Rinehart, and Winston, 1980.

Hadas, Moses. *Hellenistic Culture*. New York: W. W. Norton, 1959.

Hadas, Moses. *Imperial Rome*. New York: Time-Life books, 1965.

Hamilton, Edith. *The Echo of Greece*. New York: W. W. Norton, 1957.

Hatch, Edwin. *The Influence of Greek Ideas and Usages upon the Christian Church*. London: Williams and Norgate, 1914.

Hunt, E. W. *Portrait of Paul*. London: A. R. Mowbray, 1968.

Hutton, Maurice. *The Greek Point of View*. New York: Kennikat Press, 1926.

Journal of Discourses. 26 vols. London: Latter-day Saints' book Depot, 1867.

Kimball, Spencer W. "Listen to the Prophets." *Ensign*, May 1978, 76–78.

McConkie, Bruce R. *Doctrinal New Testament Commentary*. Vol. 2. Salt Lake City: Bookcraft, 1970.

Pollock, John. *The Apostle: A Life of Paul*. New York: Doubleday, 1969.

Pope, Maurice. *The Ancient Greeks*. London: David and Charles, 1976.

Pratt, Orson. "Personal Reminiscences of the Prophet Joseph Smith; Future Events Foretold." *Masterful Discourses of Orson Pratt*. Salt Lake City: Bookcraft, n.d.

Robinson, Benjamin Willard. *The Life of Paul*. Chicago: University of Chicago Press, 1918.

Sandmel, Samuel. *The Genius of Paul*. New York: Farrar, Straus and Cudahy, 1958.

Sealey, Raphael. *A History of the Greek City States*. Berkeley: University of California Press, 1976.

Smith, Joseph Fielding, comp. *Teachings of the Prophet Joseph Smith*. Salt Lake City: Deseret Book, 1973.